Peabody Memorial Library
Central Bible College
Springfield, Missouri

D1070543

Together

By
KATHERINE TUPPER MARSHALL

37267

PEOPLES BOOK CLUB
Chicago

Pearlman Memorial Library
Central Bible College
Springfield, Missouri

Copyright MCMXLVI, MCMXLVII
by Katherine Tupper Marshall

ALL RIGHTS RESERVED

This is a special edition published exclusively for the
members of the PEOPLES BOOK CLUB, P. O. BOX
6570A, Chicago, Illinois. It was originally published
by Tupper and Love, Inc.

MANUFACTURED IN THE UNITED STATES OF AMERICA

DEDICATED TO THE MEMORY OF

2ND LT. ALLEN TUPPER BROWN

*"For they were friends indeed from
the beginning to the end."*

CONTENTS

Acknowledgment

The Press and the Radio almost invariably supported General Marshall in his efforts to build up the Army, train and equip it. Hardly without exception editorial writers, columnists and broadcasters gave much needed encouragement to the Chief of Staff and clear-visioned explanations and analysis of the enormity of his task and what he was trying to accomplish.

I have used many quotations, in fact, while listening to broadcasters or reading our great columnists, I came to believe that one of the greatest safeguards of our democracy is the guaranteeing by our forefathers of a free and untrammeled press. I would like particularly to acknowledge my indebtedness to the Washington and New York papers which I saw daily and to several of the other great metropolitan newspapers and to the following famous broadcasters and columnists from whom I have quoted: Walter Lippman, Eric Sevareid, Earl Godwin, Quentin Reynolds, Elsa Maxwell, Ernest K. Lindley, Boake Carter, and John Temple Graves.

And, too, I would like to express my gratitude for the knowledge gained in listening to many sides of many questions discussed and analyzed by Hanson Baldwin, Edwin C. Hill, Raymond Swing, Dorothy Thompson, Walter Winchell, Richard Harkness, Morgan Beatty, Eleanor Roosevelt, Cecil Brown, Gabriel Heatter, Major George Fielding Elliot, Drew Pearson, Raymond Clapper (deceased), Fulton Lewis, Jr., George Rothwell Brown, William Hillman, Arthur Hale, Bill Henry, Anne O'Hare McCormick, H. V. Kaltenborn, David Lawrence, Walter Kiernan, Lowell Limpus, Westbrook Pegler, Lowell Mellett, John B. Kennedy and William L. Shirer.

Also I owe a debt of gratitude to the news weeklies, Readers Digest, the radio and news digests, and many excellent papers of some of our smaller cities. From the News-Standard of Uniontown, Pennsylvania, I have quoted an editorial, from the Derrick-Blizzard of Oil City, Pennsylvania, I have quoted a feature story.

K. T. M.

Foreword

During the past three years there have been many requests for a biography of General Marshall. These he has discouraged, with the explanation that a biography to be an accurate evaluation should be written after the subject is no longer of this world. Also, General Marshall has told me that he will never write his own memoirs, his knowledge of people and events being too intimate for publication.

This decision will be understood by all who know him. It arises out of the thoughtfulness for others and selflessness of the man. And yet, obviously, it leaves the historian merely the official reports from which to paint a biographical portrait.

Therefore, when General Marshall was sent to China as the representative of the President on a mission of indefinite length, I felt that I could perform neither a greater service nor pass the long months more interestingly than by putting into an informal narrative the material I had collected since our marriage in 1930.

I have included trivial events along with the more serious ones. This was done for two reasons: first, it is through these seemingly small happenings that a clearer understanding will be gained of George Marshall's character and why a Brigadier General, far down the list of General officers, was chosen by President Roosevelt to be Chief of Staff of the United States Army at a time when our nation was being drawn rapidly into another World War; second, I hoped that these trivial or amusing events might illumine and make more readable this homespun account of our years together.

KATHERINE TUPPER MARSHALL

Chapter I

In the autumn of 1938, General Marshall and I were literally blown into Washington by the hurricane that devastated the Atlantic Coast and all but wiped out Fire Island, New York, where we had our summer cottage.

In June of that year, my husband had been ordered to Washington to head the War Plans Division of the General Staff. At that time we were stationed at Vancouver Barracks in the State of Washington; and, frankly, the order came as a distinct blow to both of us. George had feared he would be taken away from his troops—the fine old 7th Infantry, with its long record of achievements since the Revolutionary War—and be put on the General Staff. We had hoped this would not happen, for the years we had spent in the Northwest had been the happiest since our marriage.

They were indeed interesting years. At the time of our marriage, George Catlett Marshall, then a lieutenant colonel, was Assistant Commandant of the Infantry School at Fort Benning, Georgia, and my arrival at Fort Benning as his wife was my introduction to the Army. As I had never been on an Army Post before, many weird things happened to me. We had been married October 12, 1930, at my home in Baltimore, Maryland. It was the second marriage for both of us, Colonel Marshall having lost his wife, Elizabeth Carter Coles of Lexington, Virginia, three years before, and I my husband, Clifton Stevenson Brown, the same year. I had three children, Molly Pender, Clifton Stevenson, and Allen Tupper Brown. Colonel Marshall had none.

We had met in Columbus, Georgia, on my return from Hawaii two years before. I had spent that winter in Honolulu with my daughter Molly after her father's death. She was fifteen, my sons thirteen and eleven. Molly and I were visiting at the home of her godmother, Mrs. William Randolph Blanchard, in Columbus, when a former collegemate telephoned to ask that I bring Molly with me to dinner. I explained I was not going out, but she said there would be only her husband, herself, and a very interesting officer, Lt. Colonel George C. Marshall, from Fort Benning.

When we arrived the Colonel was standing by the fireplace. My first impression was of a tall, slender man with sandy hair and deep-set eyes. He refused the cocktails when they were served and this attracted my interest, for it was in prohibition times when the main topic of conversation was, "How do you make your gin?"

I said, "You are a rather unusual Army officer, aren't you? I have never known one to refuse a cocktail before."

He asked agreeably how many I knew.

"Not many," I confessed.

This certainly was someone different. At dinner

he related some amusing stories, one of which I recall. We had been discussing Southern hospitality and Colonel Marshall described a relative in Virginia who had a caller one day, a maiden lady by the name of Miss Sue. When Miss Sue was about to go home, a thunderstorm came up and the Virginia hostess insisted upon her spending the night. Miss Sue protested. Finally the Colonel's relative said, "I have no idea of allowing you to go home in this storm. Now go upstairs and take off your things and spend the night." Miss Sue went upstairs, took off her things, and stayed thirty years.

When Molly started to leave with a young escort, Colonel Marshall asked to take me home. Now Columbus is a rather small place and after driving around for an hour I asked, "How long have you been at Fort Benning?"

"Two years."

"Well," I said, "after two years haven't you learned your way around Columbus?"

"Extremely well," he answered, "or I could not have stayed off the block where Mrs. Blanchard lives!"

The next summer I told my sons I had asked Colonel Marshall to visit us at Fire Island as I wanted him to know them. Clifton suspected something at once and said, "If it makes you happier, Mother, it is all right with me." But Allen, then twelve, said, "I don't know about that, we are happy enough as we are." Early the next morning he came to my room. "It is all right, Mother, about your asking Colonel Marshall." That summer George told me Allen had written him a most amusing letter in which he said, "I hope you will come to Fire Island. Don't be nervous, it is OK with me. (Signed) A friend in need is a friend indeed. Allen Brown." And they were friends indeed until the end.

ii.

Our marriage the following October was a rather hurried affair as the Infantry School year had just begun. Colonel Marshall arrived in the morning, we were married that afternoon, and by evening we were on our way to Fort Benning. General Pershing had come from Washington to be George's best man. My sister, Mrs. Allene Tupper Wilkes, was my only attendant, for Molly was at school in Florence, Italy. George's sister and her husband, Mr. and Mrs. John J. Singer, came on from Greensburg, Pennsylvania, and his brother-in-law, Edmund Coles, came from Charlotte, North Carolina. With my two sons, we drove to Emanuel Episcopal Church where the service took place in the chapel. No invitations had been sent out, but I had told close friends I would be glad to have them present if they cared to come.

When we arrived at the church the chapel was full and a large crowd had gathered on the sidewalk. My friends were greatly outnumbered, I fear, by those curious to see General Pershing. At the station after the ceremony the crowd was even larger. This was rather disconcerting to both of us for we had wished to be married quietly. Also we were well chaperoned on the train. It was quite a family affair, with Edmund Coles en route home and my two sons returning to their school, Woodberry Forest, at Orange, Virginia. So our wedding journey started with a party of five in the drawing room.

We arrived at Fort Benning early the next afternoon. The house, an old plantation home, was a bower of flowers. One of the bouquets bore a card with the following poem, written by Major Forrest Harding, afterward

Editor of the Infantry Journal and a Major General of World War II.

TO MRS. MARSHALL

If you rise with the dawn for a cross-country ride;

If you stay up past midnight and dance;

If you swim, and play golf, and shoot quail on the wing,

And read through a book at a glance;

If you're keen about horseshows, like amateur plays

And understand polo and art;

If you sparkle at dinners (which I'm sure that you do)

Then I know you're the Queen of his Heart.

That evening a reception was given to us by General and Mrs. Campbell King, on the lawn of the Commanding General's quarters. I hardly had time to catch my breath from the trip down to Atlanta and the automobile drive from Atlanta to Fort Benning before I was dressing for this reception. While I unpacked, George was telling me of special friends to whom he wished me to show particular attention when they came down the receiving line. There was a group who had served with him in China, young officers and their wives, another group of Infantry School instructors and their wives— one wife in particular, who was the mother of triplets. I must be sure to have a special greeting for her. Also there were his daily riding companions and his older Army friends. When I looked rather aghast at this list he added, "And all of those who have sent flowers here to the house. It will be quite easy," he assured me, "for I will be on your left and General King on your right. As they pass down the receiving line he will give you their names and I will

say, 'China,' or 'flowers,' for example. All you will have
to say is, 'You served with Colonel Marshall in China,
didn't you?' or 'Thank you for your lovely flowers.' It
will be most flattering to them."

I did not say anything but it was with fear and
trembling that I took my place in the receiving line, pray-
ing to make good. I shall never forget that night. The
reception was given on the lawn with a full moon shining
through the huge oak and magnolia trees. Flood lights
illumined the dance floor, while the army bandsmen in
their smart uniforms played soft music. It was like a
beautiful stage setting, the many officers of foreign countries, who were students at the Infantry School, in their
colorful full dress; our officers, spick and span, with their
wives in filmy summer dance frocks; the long slope of the
lawn and the fragrance of flowers everywhere.

I believe I did very well for the first five hundred
or so, but after that the smile began to freeze on my face,
my husband's voice seemed to come to my left ear from
afar off—"China," "Staff," "flowers"—and at the same
time the names of the guests sounded on my right. There
was a whirling jumble in my brain. Suddenly through this
maze penetrated the word "triplets." By that time I did
not know triplets from flowers and I said as graciously as
possible, "Oh thank you so much for your lovely triplets." My husband looked astounded, the mother aghast.

The long line finally ended, the receiving was over.
"How did I do?" I asked George on our way back to our
quarters.

"Very well, but you are a bit slow on the pick-up,"
he said. "Now when I was with General Pershing, I
would say 'Mexico' and he would say at once, 'I remember
meeting you in Mexico.'"

"Well, you must understand I am not running in competition with General Pershing," I laughed as we entered my new home.

The next morning we had breakfast under an arbor covered with grapevines, hanging with fruit. There were fig trees in the garden, a riot of blooms all around us. It seemed like fairyland. I was drinking in the beauty of this setting when my husband said, "This afternoon we give a reception for a class of colonels now at the Infantry School for a short course. About one hundred in all will be invited. Everything is arranged. All you will have to do is to call up this list of ladies—instructors' wives—and say that you are expecting them to assist you in receiving this 'Refresher Class.' After lunch we will ride."

I looked hard at the fig trees. I had not been on a horse since I was eighteen years old and in those days had always ridden sidesaddle. As soon as breakfast was over I sat down by the telephone and made my first call. "Colonel Marshall tells me that you will be good enough to assist me at the tea in honor of the Refreshment Class this afternoon."

"Refresher Class," came from George in a loud whisper.

My hand clapped down over the receiver. "There is no word in the English language such as 'refresher,'" I said.

"It is refresher, not refreshment," he insisted.

With an embarrassed laugh I continued to 'phone: "I am not quite responsible, I mean Refresher Class."

The instructor's wife accepted graciously without the least indication that I had made an absurd error. However, I found by tea time that my "Refreshment Class" was all over the Post.

At lunch George suggested that we ride at four; I would be back in good time to dress for the tea. As we also had an engagement for dinner that evening, I tried to think quickly of some brilliant excuse. "My riding clothes should be pressed. I suggest we start riding tomorrow." I realized afterwards just how brilliant that idea was, for during the next three months I was kept at a slow trot, to get a good seat. Even my teeth were sore at first. Fortunately my house in Baltimore was five stories high—I used to call it the grain elevator—and from many years of going up and down stairs my legs were strong. At least I had a good grip.

After the tea I asked the ladies who had assisted me to remain and I unburdened my heart to them. I told them I knew nothing of Army customs and conventions and asked their help, thereby winning some staunch friends.

I recall one of them said, "At a tea such as this one you always ask the highest-ranking officer's wife to pour coffee, not tea."

"Why is that?" I asked.

"Well, coffee outranks tea," was her amazing reply.

It was not until years later that I found that this custom had good reason: with Americans, coffee is more popular than tea and naturally you put the guest of honor at the end of the table where the crowd gathers. Later, during World War II, when I had to speak before women's clubs and groups of young Army wives, my advice to them was not to cling to their home town customs when they were called upon to uproot and follow their husbands, and not to be critical of strange customs and ideas; that I had found in living all over this country that if you tried you could always find good reasons why these customs had developed.

At the end of our two years at Fort Benning I was a fair Army wife. At least I had learned many things, among them to be on time, to listen rather than express opinions, that lieutenants do not dance with colonels' wives for pleasure, that acquiring a good seat in the saddle takes endurance beyond the power of man to express. Further, I had come to know many of the young Army officers and their wives.

iii.

My husband's four years at Benning, where he had been in close association with hundreds of young officers, were of incalculable value later in choosing his higher commanders. He has always said that he possesses a wicked memory; and this is true—he never forgets a brilliant performance and he never forgets a dullard. Mediocrity seems to make little impression on him, except by way of momentary irritation.

I look back now on those Benning days and many officers come to my mind who have since written their names in history and on the hearts of the people of this country—General Bradley, General Hodges, General Stilwell, General Collins, General Bedell Smith, and a long list of corps and division commanders. They showed great promise then and have fulfilled that promise magnificently.

Often in those two years that I was at Fort Benning older officers or their wives would say to me, "Your husband is revolutionizing the Infantry School. He is a very brilliant man. Some day he will be Chief of Staff."

It was a far cry from lieutenant colonel to Chief of

Staff but I suppose my letters to Baltimore reflected some of this.   I have just read in my scrapbook one letter from a friend, ending, "Remember me to that paragon of virtue you have married."   George saw this and I do not think he has ever liked that friend of mine since.   There is no question that a fresh breath had come to an old Army, and it was being carried to the War College and Fort Leavenworth by the graduates of the Infantry School at Fort Benning.

iv.

From Fort Benning we went to Fort Screven, Georgia, near Savannah.   It was a very small command but George was glad to be back with troops after four years of Army schools.

Yet the Columbus people had been most discouraging.   "You will not like Savannah," they had told me. "The people there do not know the Army people at Screven.   Savannah is a closed corporation, sufficient unto itself."

Rather dilapidated after Benning, Fort Screven is on the coast, separated from Savannah by a ten-mile drive through the marsh lands, edged on either side by wind-blown palm trees and hibiscus plants.

On our first Sunday we drove into Savannah to attend service at a quaint and historic old Episcopal Church.   The Rector seemed pleased that the new C. O. had come from such a distance to attend the service.   He greeted us most cordially and introduced many of his parishioners, several of whom insisted that we have Sunday mid-day dinner with them.

This did not look to us like a closed corporation. We accepted the invitation of Mr. Carl Espy and his wife, and on that day a friendship was born which has lasted through the years. Their home was large and luxurious, situated in the old part of the city and facing one of the quaintest squares in America. We were fascinated by the architecture of Savannah's numerous historical homes.

Shortly after our arrival my husband was asked to speak before the Chamber of Commerce; the Mayor called to deliver the invitation and when Colonel Marshall told him how much he admired the crepe myrtle trees in Savannah, the Mayor sent out a truck load of these plants to beautify the driveway into the Post.

When George was made a full colonel, a year later, and ordered to Fort Moultrie, near Charleston, he carried with him a baton with an inscribed plate "To the Marshall of Savannah." It had been presented the night before our departure at a large civic dinner at which the City officials and many civilian friends had gathered to wish us well.

v.

Fort Moultrie, on Sullivans Island, is three miles from Charleston. It is reached by a toll bridge. Here Colonel Marshall had the 8th Infantry Regiment and all the CCC Camps in South Carolina. This work was familiar, for at Screven he had organized the CCC Camps in Florida and eastern Georgia.

It was at this time that I became aware of a fortunate quality in my husband's make-up. He was completely a part of a post while he was there, but when he had left he never seemed to look back. The new job was all-absorbing. He would start with the freshness and enthusiasm of a young lieutenant on his first assignment. And so it was at Fort Moultrie; no detail was too small for

his attention, no soldier too lowly for his interest. He
moved slowly at first and yet, immediately, things began
to happen. The changes seemed to come of themselves
with none of the irritation of a new broom sweeping clean.
He issued few orders, but those he did issue were necessary
and rigidly enforced. If the post was shabby, with poorly
kept grounds, he began fixing up his own garden and lawn;
and within a few weeks all the lawns and gardens down
the line began to take on a different complexion. There
was never a word said, rarely an order given. And so it
was with the Regiment. He seemed to put as much
thought into the personal welfare of his men as he put into
their military training.

These were lean, depression years. In order that
the men could manage to feed their families on their small
pay, my husband personally supervised the building of
chicken yards, vegetable gardens, and hog pens. He started
a lunch pail system whereby the men could get a good hot
dinner, cooked at the mess, to take home to their families
at a very small cost. We ate this mid-day dinner ourselves until the custom was well established—so that he
might know what the men were getting. It saved their
wives endless toil during that hot summer, a godsend to
the married enlisted personnel.

There was a fine group of noncommissioned officers
in the 8th Infantry, splendid looking soldiers, with records
of long and arduous service; but they had received little
recognition. When the Corps Area Commander came to
inspect the post, George had these old sergeants lined up
on our lawn and introduced them to General Edward
King, mentioning the service of each one.

The organization and operation of the CCC had just
been turned over to the Army by President Roosevelt.

From the first my husband was fascinated by the opportunity he felt it afforded to build up the minds and bodies of the youth of this country and also to lessen the hardship of the depression. I accompanied him on many of his inspection trips to these camps and always attended the opening of a new camp, of which he made quite a gala occasion. For hours we stood that summer under the burning South Carolina sun on little pinewood platforms, hastily erected, so that he might be present at the raising of the flag over a new CCC camp. The boys came from cities, towns and country, mostly from farms. They were rather frail, anemic-looking youths, half-fed, with poor carriage, and nearly always with poor teeth. It was inspiring to see them after six weeks of medical attention, regular hours and good food.

The bootlegger was the evil genius of these camps. Wherever a camp opened he would set up his nefarious business and moonshine would reach the boys in mysterious ways. Town and county officials seemed powerless, so my husband went to the bankers, the leading merchants and businessmen. He advised them that he would move the camp if the liquor traffic was not ended within two weeks. The town, not wishing to lose the trade that the boys' pay checks brought in each month, usually mended matters quickly. Without moonshine the boys began to look and act like different human beings. They developed a great camp spirit, each camp having its own little newspaper. When a national award was offered for the best CCC camp in the country, Major Alex Starke's camp at Sumter, South Carolina, was the winner. Major Starke later became a brigadier general during the Tunisian Campaign in 1942.

vi.

During this summer, a French cruiser on a good-will trip to this country arrived at Boston and the Captain notified the Mayor of Charleston that he would make Charleston his last port of call. The city government of Charleston was at a low ebb financially. Mayor May-bank (later Governor and now Senator Maybank) tele-phoned George of his predicament, and George arranged a dinner for forty at our quarters, followed by a recep-tion and dance at the Officers' Club.

The young officers' wives did all the decorating, made the punch and sandwiches, then hurriedly dressed in their best dance frocks and made merry with the French officers. The Captain was so pleased over the Southern hospitality and the success of his mission—he had been ignored in Boston—that he in turn invited the garrison and many Charlestonians to a reception and dance aboard the cruiser.

That was a beautifully staged affair. The depres-sion had hit Charleston so hard that few people had been gay for a long, long time. The French Captain had thus far had no chance to use the champagne, souvenirs, and delicacies with which he had stocked his ship for this good-will trip. Charleston got the full benefit of his cargo.

During the evening George told the Captain that a CCC Camp near Georgetown, South Carolina, was soon to be opened, across a narrow strip of water from the spot where Lafayette had made his first landing in America. He said he would like to name it Camp Lafayette and invited the Captain to raise the flag in the presence of his officers and crew. I looked a little astounded. The contrast be-tween the reception on this brilliantly lit ship, decorated from stem to stern with flags, and a CCC Camp seemed almost absurd. George, however, continued quietly to explain the CCC project, how the President had conceived it to meet a tragic financial condition in this country and what it was doing to alleviate the depression and put the poverty-stricken young men on their feet. The Captain was so interested that he talked late into the night. Long after his other guests had gone he was still asking questions and George was still explaining with astonishing enthusiasm.

The Captain accepted the invitation at once and wired to the French Consul at Philadelphia to come to Charleston for this great honor to be shown France. Here was something he could report to his country as a tangible result of his mission.

On our way home I asked George what in the world he was going to do to make it a fitting occasion.

"I have it all worked out," he said. "I shall ask the Mayor of Georgetown and his wife, who live in the house where Lafayette spent his first night on American soil, to receive the Captain and his party at their home and escort them to the camp. Mayor Maybank will drive down with us. They will be given a regular CCC Camp dinner under the live oaks on the camp site, then we will have the speeches and the flag raising. We will take the band from Fort Moultrie and after the ceremony is over the CCC boys will act as hosts and show the French sailors around the camp. It should be interesting for them and for us also."

"When did you plan all this?" I asked.

"Well," he said, "I only thought of it on the ship. The idea came to me that it was something a little different that I might do."

If the Captain's affair aboard the cruiser was a great success, the opening of Camp Lafayette was a howling one. It was a beautiful day. The crew was driven over in Army trucks with the band in the lead; Mayor Maybank, the French Consul, the Captain, and the officers rode in private cars, loaned for the occasion. The wife of the Mayor of Georgetown, who herself was young and pretty, had asked five lovely looking girls to assist her in receiving the French officers. As we drove up to the old Colonial house they came out on the porch and stood in a group at the head of the steps. Fresh, young and smiling, they formed an entrancing tableau.

You know a Frenchman, and you can imagine these —after many weeks on a ship. The luncheon was delicious, served on the side lawn with a group of Negro spiritual singers to make music while we ate. The French officers were shown over the lovely old house and grounds, after which they left for the Camp site.

When the cars drove in the camp the band struck up the Marseillaise. George had given a holiday to the surrounding CCC Camps and as far as you could see lines of young American boys and French sailors stood at attention. It was a thrilling sight.

A platform had been built in the center with the new camp building in the background. Much saluting and ceremony accompanied the raising of the French flag by the Consul and the American flag by the Captain. Then the band struck up the Stars and Stripes and Camp Lafayette came into being.

The dedication had been solemn, impressive; but when the formalities were over everyone, young and old, entered into the spirit of the occasion. There was no depression at Camp Lafayette that day; for one afternoon at least all were joyously happy.

Three months later Colonel Marshall received a copy of L'Illustration with several pages devoted to the ceremony at Camp Lafayette. Mayor Maybank had been awarded the decoration of the Legion of Honor.

vii.

Our quarters at Fort Moultrie were not a home, but a hotel. The house had been built by the Coast Artillery in its palmy days, but now the place was in bad repair. It had 42 French doors leading out on the lower and top verandas, which extended around three sides of the house. I had a truck load of my antique furniture brought down from Baltimore—thinking that at last we were settled for at least two years. Colonel Marshall had his regiment, he was back with troops—all was well with the world.

There had been no allotment for repairs during that fiscal year, so George immediately applied for WPA funds to recondition the Post and, to everyone's surprise, received a large allotment. Before starting the painting of buildings and necessary repair work, he asked the wives of officers and enlisted men what work they wanted done on their quarters and what colors they wished used on the interior work, thereby making some very happy housewives.

I got to work with a seamstress and made up 325 yards of curtaining for the French doors of our quarters, and by the end of the summer Fort Moultrie had begun to look like a different place altogether.

But, alas! The very week that the last curtains were being hung, orders came for Colonel Marshall to go to Chicago as senior instructor for the Illinois National Guard.

He wrote to General MacArthur, then Chief of Staff, that he was making the first request for special consideration that he had ever made while in the Army. After four years as an instructor at Fort Benning, he felt it would be fatal to his future if he was taken away from troops and placed on detached service instructing again. He asked that he might remain with his Regiment. . . .

We left for Chicago within a week. The family, my daughter and two sons, waited in Baltimore until we could find a place to live.

viii.

Those first months in Chicago I shall never forget. George had a grey, drawn look which I had never seen before, and have seldom seen since. By Christmas, however, his enthusiasm had returned—the training of the Guard was going well, he was planning spring maneuvers, the men were interested, the officers had caught the spark and were loyal in their support. They were a fine group of men of whom Illinois could be proud.

Chicago seemed particularly hard hit by the depression. Illinois had not passed its Relief Bill; there was suffering and unrest everywhere. Many hotels and apartment houses were in the hands of receivers; many of the larger homes were closed. Business seemed at a standstill. The distraught people had little knowledge of, or interest in their National Guard—they were far too depressed by personal losses and too bogged down by fear.

The Century of Progress Exposition had given the city a temporary lift, and under the aggressive leadership of General Charles G. Dawes it was decided to carry the exposition into a second summer. General Dawes had known George in France and Washington and arranged for him to meet the leading business men and to speak before various civic organizations.

Returning one night after such a speech, he told me: "I tried out something tonight. After my talk I asked three questions of the audience. How many of those present knew how many National Guard Armories there were in the city and where they were located? No one could give a complete answer. What were the names of the men in command of the regiments? Two answers. How many soldiers were there in these regiments? No answer. Then I said, 'Gentlemen, is it reasonable that you should know nothing of the organizations that you support as taxpayers to protect your business, your city, and your families, in these turbulent times? I ask you, is that reasonable?'" This, he felt, had awakened their interest.

We had found an apartment on the North Side, near the Drake Hotel. By agreeing that no painting or repairs should be done, it was let to us at half its original rent. The family moved in.

The Fair reopened, many visitors arrived and the hotels were full once again. Chicago began to lift up her head.

I have never known a city as kind to Army people as Chicago. Immediately after our arrival we received numerous invitations. I am not much of a "joiner," but I received cards to join the Friends of Art, Friends of China, Friends of France, and finally Friends of Opera. When the last one came I told my husband that what I would really like to have were a few friends of my own.

ix.

There was a little periodical, published monthly, called "The Illinois Guardsman," and supported by the individual subscriptions of the men.   Due to difficulty in financing the magazine, my husband was asked to take over its management in addition to his regular duties. He not only edited it but wrote most of the articles himself. He would go through stock plates to get attractive covers, and search the art galleries and the records of the Chicago Historical Society to find paintings of local historical interest.   These he would use for the cover and make them the subject of his lead articles.   He encouraged the men to contribute and introduced a Personal Column that grew to unexpected proportions.   By the spring of that year "The Illinois Guardsman" was doing well, and some of its articles were being reprinted in other magazines. Colonel Marshall was as enthusiastic and energetic an editor as if he had been responsible for TIME Magazine.   Also the knowledge gained from this editorial training proved to be of inestimable value to him later in Washington.

x.

Our second winter in Chicago was quite different from the first.   I recall going to a reception at which a somewhat fulsome lady rushed up to me and said, "Where is your husband?   I want to meet him for I hear Colonel Marshall is the cream of the Army."   I felt like saying, "Maybe so, but the cream was a bit sour a year ago."   But, of course, I held my tongue.

Secretary of War Dern came to Chicago during this winter and after a dinner given by General and Mrs. Frank

McCoy, who had taken the apartment across from ours, I had an interesting talk with him. He said he had heard from many sources of the brilliance of my husband's work. One man in Washington had told him that George Marshall was the kind of fellow who, if he had a pile of wood to cut, would have his wood cut more quickly and piled higher than anyone else's. This was all very pleasant to hear, but the fact remained that he was still a colonel on detached service and time was fleeting—toward the year for his retirement. . . .

The following spring we moved to a cottage—White Gate Farm Cottage—near Dunham Woods Country Club, forty miles outside of the city. Here we could breathe good country air, George could ride, and life in many ways was more pleasant for all of us. My daughter and I went up into Canada for a few weeks in August and on our return George was waiting for us at the cottage. As he was usually at his office in Chicago at this hour, I should have suspected something, should have known there was something he wanted to tell me; but I only thought how wonderful of him to be here to welcome us home.

As I entered the house the telephone rang and I answered it. "Oh! Mrs. Marshall, you have returned," said a woman's voice. "I just called to congratulate *General* Marshall." I do not know to this day who called, for I let go of the receiver and sank into a chair. The strength had gone from my knees. I could not speak. I sat there just looking at George. I think that lady unwittingly had deprived him of one of his biggest moments.

With the announcement of George's promotion had come orders for him to take command of a brigade of the 3rd Division at Vancouver Barracks, in the State of Washington, where the 7th Infantry was stationed. General Malin Craig was now Chief of Staff. The waiting was over—General Marshall was back with troops.

xi.

Shortly before we were to leave, George called me to the door and there right in front of the cottage stood a beautiful new Packard car—to replace our little Ford. So he had one thrill out of his generalcy, for a Packard in those times of depression was indeed a marvelous thrill. I was quite overcome with joy.

This is a trait that has remained with him from his boyhood days—he loves to give surprises, but he does not like to receive surprises himself. Each birthday some unusual thing is sprung on me, I never know what, but something that has required thought and ingenuity to make the day wonderful.

We drove out to Vancouver, George, Molly and I. Our Irish setter, "Pontiac," was expressed out by train. General Marshall was our guide, and he knew Indian Wars and frontier history by heart. I recall he stopped at an isolated spot in New Mexico and said, "That meteor crater should be somewhere near here." When I asked, "What meteor crater?" he replied, "One I read about some years ago in the National Geographic." He took out his map, retraced our way for about two miles and turned off on an almost untraveled road. After a half-hour's ride I began to feel nervous. We were getting farther and farther into no-man's land, and the hour was growing late. Then, suddenly, we came out on the edge of a huge, gaping hole in the earth, three-quarters of a mile in diameter. A caretaker came out from a shack and greeted us joyfully: "I ain't seen many visitors!"

To my amazement General Marshall said, "Where are the men who are trying to locate the core of the meteor? What success are they having?"

"None, since I been here. There ain't nobody here but me."

"That's strange," said General Marshall. "Several years ago they had gone down several hundred feet."

We left, with the old man shaking his head and saying, "I never heard nothing about that."

Molly and I heard a great deal "about that" by the time we reached our next stop.

As we drove through one state after another, each with its tremendous resources, it restored in me a feeling of confidence. Nothing could destroy the greatness of this country of ours; sooner or later the depression would be over and all would again be well.

George had telegraphed ahead that he wished to enter the Post quietly, with no ceremonies, but when we reached the entrance of Vancouver Barracks the band and a Guard of Honor was waiting at the gate. The Colonel in command proved to be an old friend George had not seen since his lieutenant days in the Philippines, thirty-four years before, and he had arranged a most elaborate reception.

When we arrived in front of our quarters "Pontiac" was on hand, held on a leash by an orderly. The troops were standing at the "present." George got out of the car to acknowledge the salute as the band played the customary ruffles and "The General." But when "Ponty" saw his master he gave one leap, broke the leash and landed square on George's chest, all but knocking him down. Then he ran like mad in and out of the formation, jumping up on the soldiers, throwing his whole body first against one and then another. He completely disrupted the ceremony. The Colonel was a very military man and there was murder in his eye. His face was a study—anyone could see he would gladly have thrown "Ponty" into the Columbia River. He did not realize that such a welcome from his dog meant more to George Marshall than any formal reception that could have been given him.

xii.

Thus began two of the happiest years of our life. General Martin, then Governor of Oregon, was an old friend of my husband's and he and Mrs. Martin saw that we met their many friends in Portland; and such friends as they have proved to be!—a year never passes that we do not see some of them in Washington, while George still goes, whenever possible, to fish with Mr. Erskine Wood at his camp on the lovely Metolius River.

Portland was settled by Scots and New Englanders. Before San Francisco was established, they came around over the Oregon Trail, a friendly people, not seekers of gold but of good earth, with their ploughshares in their wagons. Their gardens surpass in beauty any I have seen, their clubs are excellent and their hospitality informally lavish. Their knowledge of food is truly epicurean. We spent many happy weekends with friends in their cottages on the coast and in the mountains, whose grandeur I shall always remember. Who could forget the huge redwoods growing down to the water's edge of the vast Pacific!

The 7th Infantry was a fine command, and the Post delightfully located overlooking the Columbia River.

Not long after we arrived, George and I were sitting in the library one evening listening to the radio tell of the progress of the Russian flight over the North Pole. The plane, then somewhere over northern Canada, was expected to land the following morning at Oakland, California, where the Russian Ambassador and his party were waiting to receive the flyers. We retired for the night, greatly thrilled at this marvelous accomplishment.

At eight the next morning there was a knock at my door and the orderly said, "Mrs. Marshall, the Russian plane is circling the Vancouver airfield. It is landing here. General Marshall has gone to meet it and says to have breakfast for the flyers."

Twenty minutes later three polar bears walked, or more exactly, staggered into the house. They wore huge parkas of fur, only their faces showing and these were so streaked with oil and dirt, so haggard and covered with beards, that the men hardly looked human. My guest room was ready for a friend whom I expected that day and the pilot, Valeri Chekaloff, and the navigator, Alexander Beliakoff, were put in there. Another room was quickly made ready for the co-pilot, Georgi Baidukoff. They immediately got into their baths, but none of them knew how to work the modern bath-room fixtures and none of them spoke English. However, with the help of a Russian-born doctor on the Post and a CCC boy of Russian parentage we discovered that they were calling for cognac. I had sent up orange juice, bacon, eggs and coffee, which they ate while still in the bathtub.

Our orderly came down with his eyes bulging and said, "General, there are $100 bills blowing all over the rooms and I don't want to be responsible."

Evidently, before leaving Russia, each flyer had

been given a large roll of American bills and had just thrown them on the dressers. The wind from the open window had caught the bills and hundreds of dollars were found on the lawn.

This was the first non-stop flight from Europe to America by way of the North Pole. The flyers had run out of gas and had been forced to turn back and make a landing before reaching Oakland. This lack of gas, a fog and a heavy storm had driven them to our little airfield.

By nine o'clock the circus began. The bridge from Portland, eight miles away, was packed with cars three abreast; the Post was now a seething mass of humanity. There were about 75 reporters, radio men and photographers in the house. Also the Mayor of Vancouver with the members of the Chamber of Commerce had arrived. Fortunately my husband had gotten things organized. Guards had been posted around the plane, to keep off the souvenir hunters, at the gates of the Post, to control the crowds, and at the front and back doors of the house, to keep out the curious. A soldier was on guard at the foot of the steps leading up to the second floor and one in front of each of the flyer's bedrooms. George had turned over the library and two 'phone lines to the reporters, and the front porch to the motion picture people. Stationed at the other two 'phones were Army officers who were relieved every hour. The radio people were on the roof and in the cellar. They asked if they could bore a hole in the floor and I told them, yes—in anything they wished, except my new couch.

All that morning Moscow, London, New York, San Francisco, Washington, and other large cities were calling. All this excitement seems strange now, but at that time this flight across the pole was considered little short of a miracle.

We received word the Russian Ambassador, Mr. Troyanovsky, on his way up from San Francisco with a party of six, would arrive for luncheon and requested that the flyers make no statement until he talked to them.

When I went back into the library I found the reporters like a pack of wolves. They were hungry for food and hungry for news. They had known the plane was having trouble and had expected a forced landing on another field. Most of them had been up all night and none of them had gotten to Vancouver until after the flyers were asleep and none had had any breakfast. I had a cooked ham, loaves of bread, and a big GI pot of coffee sent up from the mess and let them make their own meal. While I attended to the luncheon for the Ambassador, I also gave the correspondents such items of news as I could gather. This gave them something to feed into their papers.

The plane had landed on Sunday and the flyers had no luggage of any kind. George telephoned to Mr. Myer, owner of one of the large department stores of Portland, at his home and asked if he would open the store and let an Army truck pick up 20 suits and 20 pairs of shoes and socks; also shirts, ties, underwear, and pieces of hand luggage, and two tailors and their machines. He turned the sewing room into a haberdashery and the orderly's room next to it into a barber shop where he installed the Post barber. By this time the crowds were well-nigh impenetrable and the trucks had a hard time getting across the bridge into Portland even with an escort of traffic police on motorcycles.

When the flyers awoke about three-thirty all was set. They appeared downstairs immaculate in dark business suits, well fitted out in every detail. Although delighted by the double-breasted cut of the coats, they would have none of the shorts. They clung to the pale blue woolen underwear which they had worn on the flight. For all of this equipment Mr. Myer sent to the Post, he would accept no payment; his only request was that he might borrow one of the flyer's flying suits and equipment to display for two weeks in his show window.

Before Ambassador Troyanovsky and his party arrived, a large box of red roses was delivered by a Vancouver florist to the pilot, Valeri Chekaloff. The flowers had come from his fiancee who had cabled to the florist from Moscow. At that time this seemed to me the most remarkable thing of all, and I felt particularly sad a year or two later when I heard that Chekaloff had been killed while on a flight.

The Ambassador and the flyers stayed with us until Monday afternoon. At noon a reception on the Post gave all the garrison an opportunity of seeing them; in the afternoon they were entertained at a luncheon followed by a parade in Portland. When they left for Washington they were greeted as conquering heroes all across the country.

xiii.

At Vancouver, as in Fort Screven and Fort Moultrie, General Marshall was fascinated by the potentialities of the CCC Camps. Under his command, these camps were all over the Northwest, the boys coming from some twenty states. We spent many days together in that magnificent country on inspection trips. Without a driver, but always with a cooking outfit in the back of the car, we would be down in the valleys, a riot of color with wild flowers blooming everywhere, like a carpet covering the earth with glory, and the next hour we would be high up in snow-covered mountains with great canyons at our sides; then down again through the lava beds, where Nature had twisted the earth into a likeness of the inferno.

George paid special attention to the educational program of these camps. He strove to have the best instructors it was possible to get. Over them he placed an exceptionally capable civilian instructor, a Mr. Mace. What would become of these boys when they left the camps? He wanted to prepare them as far as possible to take responsible jobs back home. Indeed, where were their homes? There were 10,000 youths from all parts of the country—north, south, east and west.

I recall one camp sign which read "18 Miles to Tillimuck, Oregon" and under this was written by some homesick lad, "3,200 to Providence, Rhode Island."

During our first summer at Vancouver George started a competition whereby the ten outstanding boys from the various camps were to be given a trip to Portland. He arranged for them to have luncheon with the Portland Chamber of Commerce at its regular meeting. After the luncheon each was to tell of his background, experiences in camp and hopes for the future. The business men of Portland were rather surprised when my husband suggested this program. They knew, of course, of the CCC Camps throughout the region, but did not quite appreciate the relation of these camps and boys to the affairs of Portland. However the boys strove hard for this honor; it proved a keen competition.

When the day arrived the first boy who spoke made a profound impression. The men sat up and began to take notice; and by the time these youths had finished talking there was scarcely a dry eye in the room. The men were greatly touched that 10,000 jobless, almost hopeless youths had come into their country and had found health, courage, and real manhood in what the people of Portland had considered merely work camps.

Everything possible was done to help the morale of the camps. If a boy had driven a truck for so many miles—fifty thousand, I believe—without accident, he received a personal letter of congratulation, reciting his record and signed by General Marshall. This was to assist the boy when he went forth looking for a job.

If a boy's teeth were in bad condition, woe befell the CCC dentist who extracted when he could have filled! General Marshall had a study made of the parts of the country from which came the best, and the worst, preserved teeth. This was written up and published in the OREGON JOURNAL and then in several dental magazines, and finally in TIME. The medical officer whose name was mentioned in the article gained considerable notice. I had to smile when his name appeared in TIME for my husband had had some difficulty in getting this officer interested. George pointed out that this was a chance in a lifetime—never again would the dental officer have such large groups, representing practically every state, from which to make such a survey. Indeed, General Marshall was so insistent that I think the man thought he was a bit touched on the subject, but he no longer thought so when he found himself, an obscure young dentist in a CCC Camp, the subject of national attention. Our friend, Mr. Mace, had written the article.

xiv.

It was about this time that I first noticed a prisoner who worked with a detachment in our garden. He was quiet, appeared intelligent, and seemed to be an excellent gardener. He was serving a sentence for desertion and soon would receive a dishonorable discharge from the Army as his time was about up.

I spoke to my husband about him and asked if anything could be done. He looked into the man's record. The prisoner, Private Jones, had turned himself in, but had deserted before—once from the Army and once, I believe, from the Navy. It looked hopeless so I said no more about it.

A month later General Marshall went to Fort Lewis on maneuvers. I was still interested in this man Jones, who never spoke to the other prisoners,—a lone wolf, whose intelligence was obviously above the average. You are not supposed to talk to prisoners, but one day when he was helping me with the sweet pea bed, away from the other men, I asked him a few questions. He had graduated from a teacher's college, taught in a country school, and worked as a clerk in a city bank. He was unmarried but had a father and sisters living in the East. Upon his mother's death, he had left home and joined the Army. I asked if he would like to be reinstated and given another chance. He straightened up and looked at me squarely. "Yes, Ma'm," he said, "I would—very much."

That night I wired to General Marshall, "Not because I ask it but because I think you are losing a good man, will you reinstate Jones? He gets his dishonorable discharge Monday."

I received no answer, but Monday morning the

maid told me there was a soldier at the kitchen door who would like to speak to me. I went to the kitchen and there was Jones. "I am back in the Army," he said. "I was reinstated this morning. I would like to say, the General will not regret it—never."

On my husband's return he asked one of the Captains if he would mind taking Jones into his company. The officer looked embarrassed and said his men had a fine record and he knew they would not welcome a deserter in their ranks. "Besides," he added, "General, that fellow will never soldier." Understanding the Captain's attitude George told me he was at a loss to know what to do with Jones, now that he had him back in the Army. He decided to take him in our home as his orderly.

Jones was with us for four years and rose to the grade of Sergeant. Each spring when winter began to break he would say, "Mrs. Marshall, I think the birds will soon begin to sing." And I would reply, "Jones, don't say one word to me about birds or you will end up in the gutter." He would smile, look longingly out of the window and say, "I love to wander." So, when George's orders came assigning him to the General Staff in Washington, we let Jones go with our baggage and furniture around by way of Panama while we came East by train. George stopped in Washington and my daughter and I went to Fire Island for the summer. Jones had asked to spend his furlough with us on the Island. He joined us later.

That was a terrifically hot summer everywhere and Washington was almost unbearable. My husband was working from early morn to late at night as distinct rumblings could be heard over Europe and the thunder was growing louder and more ominous as the summer advanced. George's letters were hurried notes written on scraps of paper whenever he could snatch a few minutes between conferences. He was to find us a house in Washington by the fall, but Sunday afternoons were the only free time he had to look around. It seemed as though we would be homeless.

When I realized how things were going, I started to pack for Washington. Jones was helping me when suddenly the front door was blown open by a terrific wind which blew a boy into the house. He had a note from an eccentric friend who lived in a cottage near mine. It said, "We have just heard over the radio that a hurricane is coming up the coast. We are taking the first boat over to Long Island." My sister who lived in the house next to mine was with me. I handed her the note and laughingly said, "Look at this! She is certainly getting queer!"

In an hour the hurricane struck. Fire Island was in the vortex of the storm. It raged for an hour, followed by a period of calm, and then returned with renewed fury. In that first hour the high sand dunes along the sea front of our slender island were washed out by terrifying black walls of water. The houses along the waterfront were sucked into the ocean like matchboxes and the wreckage went streaming out to sea. The ocean came rushing down through the island in a mad torrent to join the waters of Great South Bay.

Fortunately my cottage, built on a high dune somewhat inland from the shore line, was protected by concrete walls built to hold flower beds. When the wind abated somewhat, Jones, at the risk of his life, struggled through the rushing torrent, holding to debris, crawling when he could not stand, and succeeded in reaching the Fire Engine House. He returned with the crew and the chemical engine. They lifted us down from the second story and made for the bay front. There we were taken in by a friend whose cottage had been built of concrete. When the hurricane returned we were safe.

My sister, my daughter and I slept in one bed and Jones lay on a cot outside our door. We were bitterly cold and wet, but Jones had even thought of warm clothes and had stuffed three sweaters under his coat. The storm raged all night; none of us slept.

When dawn broke, the sun came out smiling as if greatly pleased to see us once more. We could not get up our own sidewalk because of the debris, so took the next walk. As I came near my house I hardly dared look, but when I did, I saw my green roof shining in the sunlight. My love of flowers had saved the house, for the concrete walls had held. And, too, my sister's house, though flooded, was not washed away.

Exhausted, we did little to get things straight—just made coffee and went to bed. I was awakened by Jones' knock on the door, "Mrs. Marshall, I think the General is coming. I hear a plane."

I turned my face to the wall, "Go away, Sergeant, no one will ever get to us."

A little while later I heard a noise and turned my head. In the doorway stood a weird apparition. It looked like a deep-sea diver. Through a helmet that covered the entire face and head, two eyes peered through thick lenses. The whole body was covered with some kind of deep-sea outfit. I lay there and stared. Presently I heard my husband's voice. "Can't you speak? Say something!"

"Is it you?" I gasped. "You! Why you are the most beautiful thing I ever saw in my life!"

The apparition turned. "Sergeant," it said, "order another hurricane."

When General Marshall had gone to his office that morning the first thing he saw upon opening his paper was the headline: "Hurricane Devastates Atlantic Coast—Fire Island Wiped Out." He drove to Bolling Field, got in a small open plane and was over the Island in an hour and a half. As they flew low over the coast he heard the pilot whisper, "My God!" Salt Air, the village two miles above us, was completely wiped out, the sea having swept it as clean as a broom could sweep a dusty floor. The beach was a mass of twisted rubble, washed back on the incoming tide. There was no airfield on the Island so the plane circled and finally made a landing on the beach, though the tide was rapidly coming in.

And so, as I have said, I was blown into Washington in the autumn of 1938. Upon my arrival I wrote the Captain at Vancouver: "Jones may not be a soldier, but he saved the lives of three women during the hurricane on Fire Island and he is a hero in these parts."

Chapter II

On arriving in Washington I was greatly pleased by the home General Marshall had leased for us. It was a small home, 2118 Wyoming Avenue, just two doors from Connecticut Avenue. His office was in the Old Post Office Building. There were trees in our yard, we were near Rock Creek Park, and for a city home it was sunny and uncrowded by tall buildings.

That summer had been a difficult one for my husband. The heat had been excessive and his work as head of the War Plans Division most exacting and depressing. To give some idea of the nature of this work I quote from his first Biennial Report on the state of the armed forces a year later:

"On July 1, 1939, the active Army of the United States consisted of approximately 174,000 enlisted men scattered over 130 posts, camps, and stations. Within the United States we had no field army. There existed the mere framework of about 3½ square divisions approximately 50 per cent complete as to personnel and scattered among a number of Army posts. There was such a shortage in motor transportation that divisional training was impracticable. There were virtually no Corps troops, almost no Army troops or GHQ special troop units. The Air Corps consisted of but 62 tactical squadrons. The funds which were authorized for training were less than 5 per cent of the annual War Department appropriations. As an army we were ineffective. Our equipment, modern at the conclusion of the World War, was in a large measure obsolescent. In fact, during the post-war period, continuous paring of appropriations had reduced the Army virtually to the status of that of a third-rate power."

In October General Marshall was appointed Deputy Chief of Staff. He was so occupied with the critical condition of our defense that there was little time for him to get proper exercise, so we devised a plan: He would walk the two miles to his office each morning and I would start from the house in the afternoon when he 'phoned he was leaving and we would meet about half way, usually at Dupont Circle. Walking back to our home we would talk of trivial and amusing things, usually my experiences of the day. At that time I knew as little of the demands of official life in Washington as I had of Army traditions and customs when I arrived at Fort Benning.

Of course I had heard stories of hostesses who, through ignorance of established customs, had made blunders embarrassing to them and amusing to the rest of official Washington, but also I had heard of mistakes which had more unhappy results. As these lesser affairs were my responsibility, I made up my mind to arm myself with all the knowledge available. To help me in this, George had the War Department send me a protocol list. I see it here in my scrapbook and it may be of interest:

ORDER OF PRECEDENCE*

President of the United States
Vice President of the United States
Living Ex-President of the United States
Ambassadors
Chief Justice of the Supreme Court
Speaker of the House of Representatives
Secretary of State
Ministers Plenipotentiary of Foreign
    Countries
Associate Members of the Supreme
    Court
Secretary of the Treasury
Secretary of War
Attorney General
Postmaster General
Secretary of the Navy
Secretary of the Interior

Secretary of Agriculture
Secretary of Commerce
Secretary of Labor
Governors of States
Senators
Chief of the Budget
General of the Armies
Admiral of the Navy
Acting Heads of Executive
    Departments
Representatives of the
    Congress
Charge d'Affaires of Foreign
    Countries
Chief of Staff
Lieutenant General
Secretary to the President

Protocol was not so perplexing for it was a cut-and-dried code, but there were many unwritten rules and customs, even more hide-bound. In official life your first duty was to leave your cards at the White House. The wives of Cabinet members each had her day At Home, and you were expected to call at least once during the season—on those days only and the call must be no longer than fifteen minutes. This was also true of the wives of the Ambassadors and Justices of the Supreme Court. Any invitation from the White House was a command, always accepted, the reply being delivered by hand, not mailed. It was considered more courteous to answer Embassy, Cabinet, and Supreme Court invitations in the same manner.

* Avoid having Chief Justice with Speaker or an Ambassador or an Associate Justice with a Minister at same dinner.

Of course, at any social or official affair other than a reception you waited for the first on the protocol list to leave first, and this was the most boring and exhausting part of the Social Code, especially for us. My husband was one of the busiest men in the Government and by evening he was really too tired to go out, yet in order not to give offense he had to accept certain invitations and stay until extremely late, for there was nothing more lowly in Washington than a Brigadier General. Everyone, all the Senators, all the members of Congress, and their wives preceded the Army, and a Brigadier General was outranked by a Major General, a Lieutenant General, and a General, and my husband was a junior brigadier at that. So it is quite easy to see where the Marshalls came in—and went out!

If we could have retired into our shell, life would have been far easier, but as Deputy Chief of Staff George's job placed him on the official list. We were on it but not much of it; and yet certain demands had to be met. At least that was true of our first winter in Washington. Later on, as the octopus of war reached out and seized the whole of Europe in its tentacles, the greatest consideration was shown to my husband, who had become by then the Chief of Staff. Of necessity he made his own code and retired from the social life of Washington without giving offense. When he did accept invitations, he left extremely early without apologies, just disappeared, so to speak; or he would be called to the telephone and when he left to answer the call, that was my signal—I would slip out. Nothing was said of this until one evening, after a long-drawn-out Embassy dinner, one of the Cabinet members whispered in my ear, "I hear the 'phone calling your husband."

I laughingly asked, "What do you mean?" and had hardly finished the sentence when the call came for General Marshall. The Cabinet member still laughs about the incident.

In speaking of the strict observance of protocol, which literally governed our social life, it was interesting to me to hear politicians criticize and ridicule the Army and Navy for observing rank—as required by regulations. In fact the persons most insistent upon their social prerogatives were these same politicos themselves.

ii.

That winter while George was concerned with great affairs I had my hands full with the smaller ones. By Christmas I had made all my official calls and had received hundreds of Army callers at home. The Deputy Chief of Staff meant nothing to Washington, but to the Army a great deal, and the Army had its code—a very rigid one. There were endless invitations to be answered, engagements to be kept straight, and entertaining in a small way. Jones and a colored cook were our entire staff, and both performed wonderfully.

Sunday afternoon was George's only time off, and Sunday afternoon was the favorite time for the Army to call. After two months of receiving capacity houses, we needed recreation and fresh air, so each Sunday we would make for the park with a picnic lunch. Coming back late, invariably we would find at the front door a snow-drift of cards. I had heard Army wives on Posts count how many calls they had gotten off their list on Sundays when they knew the officers would be out, so this was not as unsociable as it sounds. The code was kept, they had made their gesture and we had enjoyed a few hours of peace in the park.

One of our first joint calls that fall had been on the Chief of Staff, General Malin Craig, and his wife, who lived across the Memorial Bridge at Fort Myer, Virginia. We were greeted most warmly, General Craig putting his arm around my husband's shoulders and saying, "Thank God, George, you have come to hold up my trembling hands." The men retired to talk business and as they disappeared up the stairway Mrs. Craig turned to me and said, "I shall never forgive Washington, they have crucified my husband." I did not then understand what she meant but later understood only too well. Mr. Harry Woodring was Secretary of War at that time, Mr. Louis Johnson was Assistant Secretary. They were at complete odds with each other. Repeatedly it was announced—probably at Mr. Johnson's instance—that Mr. Woodring would resign shortly and that Mr. Johnson would be appointed Secretary of War. Then Mr. Woodring would announce that he had no idea of resigning. General Craig was sitting on the fence between these two gentlemen. If he followed the Secretary's instructions he would be in bad odor with the Assistant Secretary, who was quite powerful. If he followed the lead of Mr. Johnson, Mr. Woodring would have called him to account. It was an impossible and tragic situation. This continued for months, and when my husband was appointed Chief of Staff he inherited this feud along with an approaching world conflagration.

By that fall my husband's plans for the largest peace-time expansion the Army had ever known had gone to the President. George was constantly before the House and Senate. As I look through my scrapbook I see such newspaper headlines as: "General Marshall Asks Congress to Strengthen Antiaircraft Defense," "High Army Official Stresses Army's Needs," "George C. Marshall Asks 9,-000,000 for Plane Protection in U. S."

I quote again from his Report to the Secretary of War:

"In February, 1939, while Deputy Chief of Staff, my statement to the Senate Military Affairs Committee included this summary of the situation, that it was of vital importance that we have modern equipment for the Regular Army and National Guard; that we modernize our artillery; that we replace our 34-year-old rifles with more modern weapons; that we have the antitank and antiaircraft materiel in the actual hands of the troops; that we have the necessary reserves of ammunition; and that these matters be emphatically regarded as fundamental to the entire proposition of national defense.

"During the post-war period the encouraging moves in national-defense preparations had been the augmentation of the Air Corps to an authorized 5,500-plane program, including an increase on July 1, 1939, of the strength of the Army from 174,000 to 210,000 men, and an appropriation of $116,000,000 for materiel and seacoast defenses. The increase in manpower was entirely devoted to the garrison in Panama and to the increase of the Air Corps."

iii.

On April 27, 1939, President Roosevelt announced: "Brigadier General George C. Marshall is to succeed General Malin Craig, on his retirement August 31, as Chief of Staff of the U. S. Army."

This was on a Monday, but the news was not to be released until later—in order to give George a chance to leave for the West Coast on an inspection trip before the announcement. For one thing he wished to avoid the interviews and congratulatory type of publicity when the news broke in Washington.

I had acquired an acute case of poison ivy sitting on an old cemetery wall watching a point-to-point race in Green Spring Valley, and was in agony Monday morning when he came to tell me good-bye. He said, "I hate so to leave you like this. You look pathetic all bound up and lying there so I am going to tell you some news. When the President sent for me last week it was to tell me that he had chosen me as his Chief of Staff. The papers will probably have it in a day or two, and now I must be off."

A few days later I was moved to Walter Reed Hospital and was greeted there by a box of lovely roses from General Gasser's wife. The card read: "Aren't you ashamed of yourself? While your husband is covered with glory, you are covered with poison ivy." For the next three weeks I was bound hand and foot with wet compresses. The nurse would bring me the papers and cut out the various announcements, editorials, and comments on my husband's appointment. They were more than reassuring: "Marshall President's Personal Choice," "A Soldier and a Gentleman," "Ideal Choice" (Hugh Johnson), "Army to be Led by Officer Who Can Really Run a War," and so forth and so on. As the pile grew I asked for a scrapbook and when I could use my hands amused myself by pasting the clippings. This was the beginning of my scrapbook which has grown to many volumes; and now that General Marshall is in China, I console myself by going over its pages, and he does not seem so far away from me.

The inspection of the West Coast defenses took several weeks and by the time my husband got back I was well enough to leave the hospital. I had returned 600 of my Army calls between Christmas and April, but was in no shape to finish them and I made up my mind then that never again — code or no code — would I exhaust what strength I possessed climbing up and down steps and getting addresses only to find the officers had been ordered elsewhere.

iv.

George had hardly reached Washington on his return from the West Coast when President Roosevelt sent for him to come to the White House.

At this time, all those in authority were watching developments in South America with growing alarm. The Panama Canal was a decided danger spot—George had gone before the Military Affairs Committee in January asking for better antiaircraft and plane protection, naming Panama as a crucial point. Brazil was a particular source of concern. Its population in some parts included many Germans of second and third generations, and its army had been largely equipped with German materiel. Also the State Department had gotten wind of the fact that General Goes Monteiro, Chief of Staff of the Brazilian Army, had been invited by Field Marshal Herman Goering, at the direction of Chancellor Hitler, to visit Germany. He would be received "with open arms" and given the honor of leading a division of German troops in an impressive parade, to be staged in honor of the Brazilian Army.

The situation was a delicate one. It was hardly an opportune time for a Brazilian soldier to place himself at the head of a column of German troops. So it was immediately announced by the President that General Marshall, the newly designated Chief of Staff, would make a good-will trip to Brazil.   The upshot was that Chancellor Hitler was informed that General Goes would not go to Germany at this time; instead he was to stay at home to welcome a distinguished American soldier who was coming to Brazil.

As to Hitler's reaction to this, nothing was known officially; but almost immediately Mussolini announced that his daughter, Madam Ciano, would leave for Brazil on a good-will visit.   Madam Ciano's ability for intrigue and her political power were well known, but her charm seemed to be inadequate so far as Brazil was concerned, for in the good-will competition she was decidedly the loser.

In a letter written by William Burdett, Counsellor of the American Embassy at Rio de Janeiro, he says:

"General Marshall sailed yesterday, June 7th, after the most gratifying example of military friendship that I have seen in many years abroad.   He made such a good impression that they simply turned everything over to him and the enthusiasm of the reception, the full cooperation of the Brazilian Army, and the excellent political results of his mission were most fortunate.   General Goes will make a return visit to the U. S. A. to further strengthen the good-will that General Marshall has built up here."

This was a report on my husband's first diplomatic mission.   For a more personal and colorful account I turn to a letter written me by Sgt. Jones, who as an orderly accompanied him on this trip:

"July 27, 1939
"Dear Mrs. Marshall:
"Thank you for your card.   You were quite right when

you expressed the opinion that I would be glad to get home, but that does not detract from our trip. It was grand and the best I have ever taken.

"We went aboard ship in New York and General Marshall was assigned to the Admiral's Cabin, and I to the Chief Petty Officer's Quarters. General Marshall had a large reception room, bedroom, and bath. . . I liked San Juan, Puerto Rico, and thought Trinidad, even though English, was the dirtiest, smelliest place I ever saw. At Rio, General Marshall received a big reception at the gangplank. They had a band of about 100 pieces waiting. I had charge of the baggage from the ship to the hotel and you would have laughed. I had a list of each person's baggage and the total number of pieces. When it was placed on deck I could account for all but one piece. All those Brazilian soldiers on the detail were trying to pick it up and take it to their trucks but I would say *no, no, senor*, about all the Spanish I could think of and they would jibber around but after about an hour I found the piece and we rushed to the hotel just in time because General Marshall had to dress about five times that day and held a reception at 6 in his suite.

"I guess I saw everything there was to see. The other fellow and me finally met two English-speaking girls and had a nice time. We went to all the points of interest worth while as far as sightseeing was concerned and I guess to all the night clubs almost too. But they were not very expensive and we decided since the trip was both business and pleasure we might as well have a nice time. I met Lt. Col. Sackville, on the American Military Mission. I used to work for him over ten years ago.

"General Marshall received all honors everywhere he went. Major Compton said he had never seen its equal. He told me as the tour progressed General Marshall's graciousness traveled ahead of him. He said thousands of school children paraded and the day was a holiday most everywhere with the whole population turned out. I was ashore at Recife and almost everyone seemed to be in the parade. I wondered at the time where all the American flags came from. All the kiddies had one in their hands. General Marshall had a motor-cycle escort everywhere he went and they had a regiment lined on both sides of the street when the party drove down to the ship. The representative of the New York Times told me the reception to General Marshall both in interest and enthusiasm was greater than to President Hoover.

"I bought you, Miss Molly and Nellie a knickknack which I will send with John. A sailor is making you a door mat and will send it on.

"We have a Colonel here tonight and General Marshall is out to dinner.

"Good night,

"Respectfully,

"Sgt. Jones."

Afterwards I learned that the Brazilian Military Band, knowing only one of our military airs, "Anchors Aweigh," struck up that tune when General Marshall stepped off the ship and whenever he appeared in public thereafter. He had a hard time keeping his face straight while he stood erect as they played the refrain of "Sink the Army, Sink the Army," so familiar to football audiences.

In preparing for this trip, Jones, by mistake, packed a pair of trousers to my husband's dinner clothes that were left-overs from his Lieutenant days. These trousers lacked several inches of meeting around his now more robust figure. This was not discovered until he came from his bath to dress for the first official dinner in Brazil. He had allowed himself only fifteen minutes' grace so there was no time to get another pair of trousers. With a deal of pulling and hauling and sucking in of breath, the waist was gotten together and secured by the length of a long safety pin.   The entire evening he was not only in physical discomfort, but in mental agony as to what might happen.   It was impossible for him to bend, so he sat like a ramrod for hours.   The next morning the papers spoke of General Marshall's erect carriage and military bearing.   Little did they know that the dignity of the Brazilian Mission hung on the strength of a safety pin.

At Curityba the Governor—or Interventor, as I believe he is called—had arranged a parade of the school children for General Marshall.   Some five thousand participated.   The uniform of the girls consisted of white middy blouses, blue pleated skirts and sandals with bobbysocks.   The boys wore a more military-looking dress, and all presented an immaculate and persuasive picture.   Each school was preceded by a small Drum Corps and all the children marched with pride and precision.

This feature of the trip appealed very strongly to General Marshall as he is as deeply interested in children, I believe, as he is in grown-ups.

In the middle of the parade there appeared about 200 little boys from six to twelve years old, dressed in blue overalls with pink piping, and carrying various farm tools. One little boy was pushing a hand-cultivator in front of him.   This group made quite an impression on my husband and on inquiry he discovered these children were members of a small agricultural school for foundlings, in which the Governor was much interested.   Consequently, after the parade, though it was very late and a formal dinner was about due, the Governor took George a few miles outside the city to inspect this school.   The pupils had just arrived in trucks from the parade and were filing in for their dinner.   All the surroundings were neat and orderly and the boys themselves seemed happy and very well cared for.

That night at the dinner, which was an elaborate affair and lasted from eight until midnight, George was turning over in his mind what he might do to repay the bountiful hospitality he was receiving on every hand. Returning hospitality by giving dinners, does not greatly appeal to him, yet that is the usually accepted method in diplomatic procedure. Thinking over the events of the afternoon, he decided that a small gift to the foundlings would be much more appreciated than an elaborate dinner to dignitaries. As he had to leave by plane at eleven o'clock he directed a member of his staff to start out early in the morning, as soon as the shops opened, and purchase a box of candy for each of the little agricultural students, and to take the candy out and present it to them that morning. This was done, and it not only made a profound impression on the little boys but, as a result of press reports, it seemed to make an even greater impression all over Brazil. Consequently children were turned out en masse everywhere General Marshall went, and as their parents of course turned out to see their children, unusually large crowds resulted. At several places as many as twenty thousand children marched or lined the streets to receive General Marshall. When he returned to Rio where his program was completed, he was urged to visit the schools in the city. This he did.

In looking back on the reactions to his mission to Brazil, George felt that more good had resulted from the small presents to the children than from any other single factor. This story always amused Lord Halifax and whenever we dined with him he would press George to tell the other guests how he won out on his Brazilian Mission with a "tin of taffy."

During my husband's visit to Porte Alegre, which

was the great German stronghold in Brazil, a rather amusing incident occurred in connection with the mother of Oswaldo Aranha, Minister of Foreign Relations in Brazil. Senhora Aranha was much interested in a charitable effort for foundlings and was chairman of a group which, to raise funds, operated a tearoom located on the principal square of the city. She asked General Marshall to have tea with her there—in order to draw a crowd. The result was a little too successful, as the table where they were sitting was almost mobbed by autograph seekers. The confusion became so great that George asked Senhora Aranha, a lady in her seventies, if it did not make her nervous. She replied, "Not at all, I am the mother of 21 children!"

v.

Before my husband left for Brazil it had been arranged that I would stay in Washington to do the honors for the family at the reception to the King and Queen of England at the British Embassy, June 8th. Thereafter I would go to Fire Island where my husband would join me on his return. I had never witnessed a social upheaval in Washington before but this event certainly produced one. When the invitations were issued to 1,400 "carefully chosen guests" as the newspapers put it, the heavens fell. I have never known such bitterness, such recriminations, nor such an extraordinary display of ill-breeding. Lady Lindsay, the American-born wife of the British Ambassador, was beset on all sides. Unwittingly she had offended the press in her first arrangements, and woe betide the hostess who does that.

The invitations were most impressive. They bore

37267

an embossed gold crown with the initials G. R. E. above an entwined monogram. They read:

"The British Ambassador has received Their Britannic Majesties' command to invite (name) to a Garden Party at the Embassy on Thursday the eighth of June, 1939."

Large yellow labels were enclosed for your car with the words, "British Embassy—Not Transferable," in black letters. Also enclosed were instructions as to what entrance should be used.

The guests gathered in the gardens adjoining the Embassy a half-hour before the King and Queen were to make their appearance. When the hour came, the King appeared first, escorted by the Ambassador, Sir Ronald Lindsay, and followed by his Staff. The Queen followed with Lady Lindsay and her Ladies-in-Waiting. As she came out on the portico I have never seen anyone more exquisite. She was very slender at that time and looked very young. Her gown of white embroidered muslin was made with a full skirt which just cleared the ground. She wore a large hat of white embroidery and carried a parasol of the same material. If she had stepped from the pages of a Fairy Book she could not have been lovelier.

A low murmur of admiration was heard through the crowd as she came down the steps. The King and Queen were not introduced to the guests but separated and each wandered in different directions through the grounds, admiring the flowers and smiling and bowing to the people as they passed. The King looked much younger than his pictures. The Queen had the bluest eyes and the sweetest of smiles imaginable. She won the hearts of every one present. George VI had done well by him-

Pearlman Memorial Library
Central Bible College
Springfield, Missouri

self and the British Empire when he chose his Elizabeth, for she appeared and proved to be every inch a Queen.

vi.

As soon as my husband could get away from Washington, on his return from Brazil, he joined me at Fire Island for a short rest. When he arrived all the members of the family were there, my sons having come on for the reunion. It was wonderful to be together in our own home once more after several years of separation. The air was like champagne, the bathing superb. We would spend long, lazy days lying on the beach, or George and the boys would go deep-sea fishing. One morning as we were walking along the beach, watching the children flying their kites on the dunes above us, I began to laugh. "What are you laughing at?" George asked.

"They remind me of Army wives," I said.

"What? The kites?"

"No," I answered, "the tails. They have no say as to where they go, but they are always there, trailing along in the rear."

"How high do you think a kite would fly without its tail," he mused. "If the tail is too heavy it falls to the ground, if too light it flies a devious course, but if well balanced the kite soars high. There is nothing more important to a kite than the good appendage that steadies it." I repeat this for the encouragement of all wives. Perhaps it is true in all walks of life.

As twilight came on I would pack our lunch baskets and we would go far up the stretch of white sand, build a fire and, under a glorious moon, cook our supper. Then we would sit around the fire and tell tales until the chill of the night air drove us home.

One evening, after a beach supper, George suggested that we do a play. It was to be a melodrama, each one improvising his own lines. Clifton was to be the villian, Allen the hero. After Clifton had done his worst to Molly, the unsuspecting heroine, he turned his venom on me. Just then Allen rushed out from the dunes crying, "Stop, vile creature! Unhand my poor old gray-headed mother." I can hear George laughing now. My hair was just beginning to turn a little gray and this reference amused him greatly. Later, during the war, when Allen was in Italy I sent his Christmas package, "From your old Gray-Headed Mother of Fort Myer, Virginia." This was true by then, for those three years had turned my hair almost white.

What a summer that was! In spite of the growing tension and increasing responsibilities, George would fly up for weekends whenever possible. LIFE magazine sent a photographer, Tom McAvoy, to take pictures of the new Chief of Staff and his family on Fire Island. For three days, at meals, while swimming, wherever we turned there was the click of a camera. This was the family's first taste of publicity, which afterwards became at times most trying.

One weekend George brought with him an old friend, a rather portly Major General, who very much fancied his swimming prowess and, particularly, his ability to float. His first day on the beach, in spite of warnings, and before we knew it, he had floated far out and was going still farther. Fire Island has a wicked surf; the great swells often carry along with them what is known as a "Sea Puss" and if caught in one you are swept out to sea. The boys had been raised on the beach and were

not only water ducks but powerful swimmers. George
called to them and in a few seconds they were diving
through the breakers and were soon on either side of
George's friend. He got in safely and seemed to have no
idea of the risk he had taken.

That evening my husband took the boys aside and
told them he was greatly concerned about the General and
that they were never to allow him to go in alone. No
matter what they were doing, if our guest started in the
water they were to drop everything and swim along with
him.

When our guest was leaving he came to me and
said, "Mrs. Marshall, I have had the most wonderful weekend. I have never known young men as attentive to an
older one as your sons have been to me. I have been
greatly complimented by their desire to be with me. Even
when they were with a group of young people on the
beach, if I went in for a swim they would leave their
friends and join me. It has been most flattering." When
I told the boys this they looked at each other and said,
"Well, we are glad he enjoyed himself; it is more than
we did."

vii.

As the summer advanced, affairs in Washington
became so demanding that George's weekends on the Island ceased. General Goes Monteiro paid his return good-
will visit and I prepared to close the cottage. I did not
dream that this would be our last summer on Fire Island.
For twenty-two years we had spent our summers there. I
felt as one of the old natives used to say, "If you once get
the sand of Fire Island in your shoes, you never get it out."

I returned to Washington late in August; and on

September first, the day that General Marshall was sworn in as Chief of Staff, the blow fell—Germany invaded Poland.

On September 8, 1939, the President issued his "Limited Emergency Proclamation" in which he authorized an expansion of the active army from 210,000 to 227,000 men, and an increase of the National Guard to 235,000 men. The War Department was also authorized to correct certain deficiencies, including the purchase of approximately twelve million dollars' worth of motor transportation.

viii.

Uniontown, Pennsylvania, George's birthplace, had "Marshall Day" in his honor on September 9, 1939. His sister, Marie Singer, met us at the airport. She had come from her home in Greensburg for his homecoming. There were ten thousand people on the field as our plane flew in, many of whom were the workers in the coal mines, for it was the day of their yearly picnic. My husband held an impromptu reception and then drove into town with the Committee appointed to meet him. There was a formal reception held at the hotel, during which I had the pleasure of meeting George's old sweetheart, who, after a Kermis in which George had been featured at the age of ten, had told him that "he made her sick!" This, he said, had taken away his nerve with women for many years.

It was a memorable and touching reception that they gave to the Chief of Staff. A beautiful tribute was paid to George's mother by the patriarchal speaker, who said, "General Marshall's mother was a woman of rare intelligence, refinement, and culture. No young man privileged to spend an evening in the library of the Marshall home but left it a better man than when he entered it. From such a home and its atmosphere General George Catlett Marshall, known to us as 'Flicker,' left to enter Virginia Military Institute."

An article in the Uniontown paper of that day, headed "Welcome Home, General Marshall," contains my favorite tribute to him:

> "For almost 40 years, General Marshall, you have been preparing for the position you now hold, for the great burdens for which you are now responsible, and to you, as Chief of Staff of the United States Army, our special welcome is for 'Flicker,' the snub-nosed, freckle-faced red-head who was a natural-born leader of boydom in the 90's, who coasted on Gilmore's Hill, staged shows in Thompson's Stable, and kept things generally astir. Today we hope that you can lay aside your honors and your burdens and make friends with your youth. Flicker Marshall has been gone for such a long, long time. Don't look too closely for the vine-clad home of your boyhood with its towering trees, nor too long for the faces of your friends, the boys and girls whose fingers Miss Thompson used to crack when they weren't immaculate, the young men and women who went to Professor Hopkin's school with you, but do go down to look at the honey-locust in Miss Minnie's yard, just as beautiful, spreading just as majestically as ever. It centers the lawn where the daisies and the flowering shrubs bloom in spring, near where the vine-covered wash-house used to stand. Perhaps in its whispering leaves and gracious shade you will find 'Flicker' and the boys who aren't here to receive you, and your visit home will be well worth while."

ix.

Late in September the family moved into the Chief of Staff's house at Fort Myer, Virginia. General George

Patton, then a Colonel, was in command of the Post. I had never met him nor his wife before, but in the years that followed a lasting friendship grew up. They were both people of many parts, he a fine soldier, excellent horseman, dare-devil yachtsman. Both wrote exceedingly well. It is seldom that you meet a couple in the Army, or out of it for that matter, who were blessed with so many gifts. They loved life and made the most of all it had to offer.

In going over the house, General Patton asked me not to hesitate to make any changes I wished, nor to tell him what I wanted done. Mrs. Craig was with us when I said, "I would like those two cannons on the front steps removed, the first thing. This is to be our home, not an arsenal, and I feel that my brains may be blown out every time I enter." Colonel Patton seemed greatly amused and when Mrs. Craig left he said, "Mrs. Craig searched for two years to get those cannons. That was a body-blow that you delivered."

The Chief of Staff's house, "Quarters Number 1," was a large, comfortable red-brick building, of no special period. Each occupant had added what was needed for his family and thus it had grown into a conglomerate style of architecture. On the first floor there was a library, drawing room, sun porch and lovely large oval dining room. On the wall in the hall was a brass plaque bearing the names of all the Chiefs of Staff who had occupied these quarters. Upstairs on the second floor a sun porch ran the length of the building. This had been constructed at the instance of General MacArthur—for his mother, I think, and a small elevator also had been put in for her use.

The sun porch proved to be where George and I practically lived for the next five years. A peaceful, attractive room, it looked out through huge oak trees and down upon the gardens. Its windows commanded a clear view of the Capitol. I think this room had much to do with my husband's good health in the difficult years ahead, for it was flooded with sunlight. We had our breakfast served here each morning, and here after lunch George rested for fifteen minutes on his old chaise-longue before returning to his office. After his daily ride in the later afternoon, we had our coffee by the large windows, and it was here we spent our evenings—never downstairs, unless we had guests.

During this and the following years—until the war was over—we got up at 6:30, had breakfast at 7:00 and General Marshall was at his desk in the War Department usually at 7:30. During the winter mornings the pale shape of the moon could still be seen in the sky and I laughingly said, "You know, we eat our breakfast by moonlight and our dinner by the light of the sun."

x.

My husband was away on inspection trips a great deal that winter. He flew about 60,000 miles a year before we entered the war and, thereafter, his air mileage was greatly increased. When he returned home he would work feverishly to correct the faults he found and strengthen the weak spots. He would find his desk piled high with official matters, which he would clear by nine each morning in order to meet his endless conferences. His secretary told me that one person staying five minutes overtime would disrupt his whole schedule for the day.

There was little time for anything but work. He was before the Congress constantly, asking for appropriations or special authorizations. As soon as he had caught up with the Washington work, he would be off again on inspection trips.

During this expansion of the Army so many thousands of new ideas and inventions were sent to the War Department that it was difficult to separate the wheat from the chaff. These did not come to General Marshall until they had been passed on by experts of the Department; but it was his responsibility to make the final decision. He was on the alert constantly not to miss anything that would further the efficiency of the Army. His immediate Staff had access to his office at all times but there was nothing that annoyed him more than to have one of them open the door, look in, and seeing he was busy, back out. To prevent this he had a notice put on his office door, "Once you open this door, WALK IN, no matter what is going on inside." Often he would not look up until he had finished what he was doing and then he would ask, "What is it?"

One day Colonel Bedell Smith, then Secretary of the General Staff—now Ambassador to Russia—opened the door, but seeing several generals talking with General Marshall, started to back out when George said, rather irritably, "Come in, Smith. Didn't you see that sign?" He paused in his conference and turned to Colonel Smith, "Now, what is it?" Colonel Smith explained that there was a man in his office whom he would like General Marshall to see. This man had come to Washington weeks before, with the drawings of a small, sturdy car which he wished to offer to the Government for a test. He had been sent from one person to another. No one was interested, and the inventor, angry and discouraged, had appealed to the Secretary of the General Staff as a last resort.

After talking to him for some time and going over his drawings, Colonel Smith was convinced that he had something well worth while. "General, I wish you would see this man. He is right outside." George asked a few questions, then said, "Did you go over the plans thoroughly?"

"Yes, Sir."

"What was your reaction?"

"That he has a find."

"Well, that is enough for me. Order one."

"But, General," Colonel Smith protested, "one car is not sufficient for a test, we should have at least fifteen."

"Can you find the money, Smith?"

"Yes," said Colonel Smith. "They will cost about $12,000."

"Very well," replied General Marshall. "Do it."

This was the birth of the famous Jeep now familiar to all the world. The discussion had lasted about three minutes. The most interesting phase of the matter was the disinclination of the Armored Forces, then in its infancy, and other arms to test the completed models. Yet three weeks later they recommended an initial order for 39,000!

Later on I had very much the same type of experience. If General Marshall was convinced, his decisions were instantaneous. I had been to a Board Meeting of the Red Cross and after the business was over, Mrs. Dwight Davis told me she and Mrs. August Belmont were greatly depressed. It seems they had planned a Red Cross kit, to be filled with small necessary articles not furnished by the Army, which would be given to each soldier as he went aboard ship on his way overseas. They had a tentative contract for 2,000 of these packets, which had to be closed at once if they were to be ready in time. A letter had been received that morning from the War Department saying it did not want the kits. Mrs. Davis showed me a sample and after looking the articles over I said, "Of course I am no authority, but this seems to me an excellent idea. May I take this sample home?"

That evening when George came in he was so tired that I did not wish to worry him with business matters, so I waited until the next morning. When he came to breakfast I had the contents of the kit spread out on the chaise longue. "What is this?" he asked. I explained, adding: "You see each article would be used up before the ship landed so it would not add to a soldier's burden, only make his passage more comfortable. Also, it would give him a less lonely feeling as he went aboard to receive a present from the Red Cross."

"Who saw this, and who turned it down?" he asked.

"I don't know. The War Department just said they did not want it."

He looked at the contents, examining each article, and then picked up the container. "Here is the trouble. The idea is excellent but the case is too bulky. Couldn't the Red Cross workers sew small canvas bags with a drawstring that the soldier could slip over his wrist?" Then picking up a pocket edition of one of our well-known novels, which was one of the articles included, he said, "I particularly like this idea. The men could pass them around and have reading matter all the way across. I will phone Mrs. Davis this morning."

At eleven o'clock Mrs. Davis telephoned to me. She was elated. "We have sent out orders for all our Chapters to start their workers immediately on making the bags,"

she told me. That paper-backed pocket edition of our
novels was to grow into millions. Many a soldier in the
front lines was to be helped by the G. I. library, and the
weary hours of suspense made less unbearable.

xi.

On February 23, 1940, General Marshall stated to
the House Appropriations Committee that "if Europe
blazed in the late spring or summer we must put our house
in order before the sparks reached the Western Hemisphere." Poland had been conquered but the situation in
Western Europe was to all appearances stabilized. There
was much foolish talk of a "phony war." It was also felt
by many that the elaborate field fortifications—the Magi-
not Line—constructed in France and Belgium furnished
ample security to those nations. Requests for further in-
creases in the armed forces of the United States were regarded in many quarters as mere war-mongering. As late
as March 1940 the War Department estimate for a small
number of replacements of airplanes for the ensuing fiscal
year was cut by the House of Representatives to 57 planes.
The estimate of $12,000,000 for the development of a
defensive force in Alaska was refused, leaving that critical
area with only some wooden barracks at Sitka constructed
about forty years before.

General Marshall felt it was essential that the higher
commanders and staffs be given opportunities for training
in technique, tactics, and teamwork and that the troops be
accustomed to operating in large groups. In the late spring,
appropriations were passed for the first genuine Corps and
Army maneuvers in the history of this country.

As the Army grew and soldiers began to flood

Washington, I spent most of my days working toward keeping them off the streets and out of the parks at night. At this time there was no adequate place for them to go. Many slept in the station or stopped at hotels of questionable character. During the summer I had received a letter from a Sergeant complaining of conditions at the Soldiers, Sailors & Marines Club for enlisted men. On my return to Washington I looked into this organization. A left-over from the last war, it was run by the officers' wives of the three Services. I found conditions deplorable. The house, a very fine one, was dirty and in bad repair. It had been turned into an old soldiers' home instead of a club for the young soldiers coming to Washington on furlough or passing through the city.

We called a board meeting and passed a regulation providing that no soldier could stay over three weeks at a time, which gave us a chance to clear the place. We started immediately to raise funds. A $15,000 legacy had been left to the club to be used in case of an emergency. We leased the adjoining house and hired plumbers and painters. The running of the club was done by officers' wives so our overhead expenses were light, but the work became extremely heavy as our clientele increased.

We gave a horse show at Fort Myer to buy new beds and furniture. I recall that one lady, prominent in Washington society, who became quite active in much publicized war work later on, was asked to assist us but refused, frankly declaring she did not think this work was "glamorous." This may illustrate how little people were prepared at that time to face what was to come.

General Patton helped us with the horse show and we made quite a large sum of money. A rummage sale, lasting for three days, also helped and by spring we started remodeling the stables in the back of the building, thereby providing space for forty more beds. Before the war was over, the Soldiers, Sailors & Marines Club was accommodating 25,000 soldiers every month, feeding and housing thousands weekly. I recall one note left by a rather rough-looking sailor. It read, "I do not know who to thank for this, but I do know that the Bible says 'If you do it unto the least of these, you do it unto Me.'"

xii.

Whenever I could find time I would drive through the Virginia countryside to look for a place near Washington where we could spend weekends when summer came. I knew Fire Island was now out of the question and so that spring we bought "Dodona Manor" in Leesburg, Virginia. Although only 35 miles from Washington, the place had been ours for months before General Marshall had a chance to see it. He was greatly amused when he read in one of the Washington columns: "To show how autocratic Generalissimo Marshall is, he has bought a country place in Virginia without consulting his wife and which she has never seen."

xiii.

The Army and Navy Reception was the last of the official affairs given at the White House each season, and by far the most colorful. This year it was the last large reception of President Roosevelt's second term, and the first for George as Chief of Staff. General Craig had insisted on his wearing a special dress uniform which he had designed for himself while holding the office. The broad sash with gold fringe was too yellow, I thought, and I had labored to tone it down with dye to a soft old-gold shade.

On February 2nd, the day of the reception, the uniform was laid out—all ready for my husband when he came in. I was in my room, also dressing, when the door was flung open and George stood there in full regalia. "Look at me!" he said. "I feel like a musical comedy star. I am not going tonight dressed up like this, nor any other night." In vain I pleaded that General Craig would be offended, but to no avail, and when we arrived at the reception he was dressed in a plain dark blue dress uniform. I did not realize it then, but his uniform, contrasting with the splendor of that evening, heralded a changing world.

Never again in my lifetime, nor perhaps in the history of our country, will there be such a gorgeous display. The scene that greeted us in the Grand Ballroom was indescribably colorful. Flowers were banked around the entire room half-way up the walls. Tall palm trees formed a background. The uniforms of the various Military Attaches, especially of the Balkan States, were ornate in the extreme—high polished boots set off by gold tassels and spurs, capes of heavily encrusted embroidery swung over one shoulder and elaborate gold aiguillettes on the other, broad sashes of every shade and color bound their waists, while gold, red, blue or yellow striped the sides of the trousers.

I whispered to my husband, "You look like a farm boy among all this glittering throng." He came back with, "Well, you glitter enough for both us!" This made me laugh, for I had chosen a silver lame dress drawn back with a kind of bustle effect which fell in quite a long train. On the shoulders were turquoise clips set with brilliants.

I have saved this dress and it is now packed away in the attic at Leesburg. Some day my grandchildren may adorn themselves in it and, with mincing steps, portray their grandmother at that gathering.

In the morning newspapers the only man's uniform mentioned was that of General Marshall. They spoke of his unassuming and military appearance in a plain Army dress uniform of dark blue.

At dinner that evening, the President sat across from his wife in the center of a U-shaped table. Sitting on my left was a rather quiet man who told me it was his first affair in the White House and that he had never seen such magnificence anywhere. I noticed during the second course that the guests across the table had their eyes fixed on him in an astonished gaze and I heard the woman on his left say, "You can't do that." I looked down and saw a fluff of pale green chiffon in the man's lap. The lady afterwards told me that she had felt her skirt first being pulled and then it was given a decided yank. This was when she had protested. It seems the poor man had dropped his napkin and not wishing to attract attention had leaned down without looking and grabbed what he thought was his napkin and placed it across his knee. As it happened to be the lady's dress his embarrassment was pathetic to see. He disappeared immediately after the dinner.

xiv.

That spring I took great interest in the grounds around the Chief of Staff's house at Fort Myer and superintended most of the planting. It was a real joy, for the little flagstone terrace which we built back of the house under two old apple trees gave us a place to eat out of doors. Before the war was over, the great and near-great of many countries had eaten luncheon under those gnarled old trees.

While superintending this work one day I was rather disconcerted by the blare of a megaphone. A Washington sightseeing bus had stopped in front of the house and the guide was saying: "This is the house of the Chief of Staff of the U. S. Army, General Marshall." All heads were craning out of the bus windows, when he added "For which he pays no rent." Ever after when I was on the lawn and saw a sightseeing bus coming up the hill I would hide behind a bush.

My son, Allen, was married that summer to Margaret Goodman Shedden of Westchester, New York. He was my youngest child and first to be married in the family. We took two days off to be present at his wedding in Westchester; but with this exception we did not leave Washington that summer. As George's days grew more and more hectic, I would try to think up something we could do when he got home to relieve the strain of his ever-increasing burdens. Usually he would ride for an hour before breakfast, then in the evening we would go for a walk or, after an early dinner, go to the Post movie. At home by nine o'clock we would retire immediately for the night. But as the heat grew more intense, riding became an endurance test rather than relaxation and so, fortunately, at this time I discovered canoeing on the Potomac River.

I would have our basket packed late in the afternoon and when George arrived at the house, we would drive over to the foot of 35th Street, hire a canoe and paddle up the Potomac as far as Chain Bridge. Then we would let the canoe drift back while I served the picnic dinner, with a lantern hanging at the stern after dark. The river was beautiful in its upper reaches once the houses of Georgetown had been left behind. The high cliffs, hung with wild grape and edged with weeping willows, might have been almost anywhere remote from a great city. There was always a cool breeze, and so we would get back by nine or ten o'clock greatly refreshed. This canoeing proved a Godsend for the next two summers. After that we were so interested in the grounds and garden at Leesburg that we spent our few free hours down there.

We took the Secretary of War and Mrs. Stimson on one of our evenings on the river. We hired two canoes and the Secretary, who loved to exercise, paddled my canoe all the way up to Chain Bridge. He was 73 then. Under the bridge we lashed the canoes together and drifted back down stream. I had brought my usual picnic supper of fried chicken, hot biscuits and green salad, topped off with ice cream, brandied peaches, and coffee. Mrs. Stimson said as we arrived at the boathouse, "This is the nicest evening I have ever had in Washington."

By this time the newspapers had learned of our canoeing trips and in a Sunday colored supplement appeared a most extraordinary drawing—two figures representing George and me lying back in a canoe, a picture hat on my head and a cup, presumably of coffee, in George's hand. Under it was written: "General Marshall and his Sweetie."

XV.

During May and June of 1940 the German avalanche had completely upset the equilibrium of the European Continent, France was eliminated as a World Power and the British Army had lost most of its heavy equipment. To many, the invasion of Great Britain appeared imminent. The threat to the security of the United States became suddenly apparent to our people. On May 16th in a Special Message to Congress President Roosevelt recommended the appropriation of approximately one billion dollars—of which $732,000,000 was for equipment. The Message also recommended increasing the Army by 28,-000 men—13,000 for the Air Corps. Two weeks later on May 31st, in a second Defense Message to Congress, the President recommended another appropriation of about one billion dollars and this, together with an additional appropriation added to the bill by the Senate Appropriations Committee, brought the Army to an authorized strength of 375,000.

An interesting story explains these messages and large appropriations. In considering the previous appropriations act the Congress had eliminated 24 million for which General Marshall had secured the approval of the Budget Bureau and the President. Later when Hitler made his surprising invasion of Denmark and Norway, George seized this moment to renew his request for the 24 million. There was a long delay and finally, when Mr. Roosevelt docked at Miami on returning from a cruise on the ill-fated cruiser Houston, the War Department was notified that approval for only 18 of the 24 million had been given. Further, there was a request for my husband to see the Secretary of the Treasury, Mr. Morgenthau, on the subject. He then learned that the 18 million item was still open to question—not the 6 million already cut which had been intended principally for the radar detecting stations against air raids on the West Coast. The trouble was this: the Government was approaching the 50 billion dollar debit limit stipulated by law.

During the conference with Mr. Morgenthau, George passed over the 24 million and turned his guns on the tragic state of our defenses due to lack of materiel. Mr. Morgenthau was impressed, then aroused, and asked George to give him a detailed statement the following morning. This was done. Mr. Morgenthau, now completely convinced of the dangers of our position, sought an interview with the President for himself and General Marshall. The result was not the mere restoration of the 24 million dollar item but the acceptance of the 732 million dollar proposal, for which George drafted a large part of the message to Congress.

Meanwhile the German Army swept over France; the world seemed to be rocking on its axis; and at last many manufacturers who previously would not bid on Government contracts for fear of labor uncertainties and of jeopardizing the interests of their stockholders, were in a more patriotic frame of mind and ready to take chances on literally any contract. Hence the second message to Congress, about two weeks later, asking for 709 million dollars for the Army. At first the President was greatly perturbed that his Army Chief of Staff and Mr. Morgenthau should bring up a proposal for a second message after so short a time, but he was quickly convinced that there was no choice in the matter, clearly it must be done, and George got to work on the draft of this second message.

About this time my husband explained to the President the necessity for calling out the National Guard. Although sadly lacking in modern equipment and at less than 40 per cent of its full strength, the Guard represented one of the few organized defense assets. However, this step alone would have been a futile procedure without making available necessary equipment and the authorization for inducting the National Guard into the Federal Service and integrating its personnel with the Regular Army in order to train them for the defense of the country. Interminable delays followed. On August 5th General Marshall testified before the Appropriations Committee:

"Shelter is a serious problem at the present moment. I thought the Congress would settle the question of authority to order out the National Guard and the matter of compulsory training by the first of August. On that basis, the Guard was to be brought into the Federal service during September and the first induction of men under the Selective Service Act during October. What has happened is that the weeks have been passing and we have no authority to enter into contracts to provide the additional shelter required.

"We have been trying to find some manner, some means for getting started. We want to proceed in an orderly and business-like manner. We know exactly what we want to do and exactly where we want to do it, but we have neither the authority nor the funds, and time is fleeting. So far as construction is concerned the winter is upon us, because it requires from 3 to 4 months to provide proper shelter. We had hoped at first to gain time by providing a progressive mobilization of the National Guard during the summer. We planned to put troops in tent camps, while better shelter was being prepared in the climates that demand special protection against the winter. However, weeks have come and have gone and we have been unable to make a start. The present uncertainties make a business-like procedure almost impossible. We must make a start toward getting water lines laid; a start on the sewage-disposal systems; a start on the temporary roads and certainly the walks to keep our people out of the mud; and we must get under way the construction of temporary hospital facilities. These are fundamental necessities and take time to develop."

Authorization for the National Guard to be called into Federal Service was finally given August 27th, 1940. The First Guard units were inducted on September 16th, the same day that the Selective Service Act was signed by the President. Money for Selective Service construction became available September 24th. The passage of the Selective Service Act in effect authorized the Army of the United States to be increased to 1,400,000 men, of which 500,000 were to be in the Regular Army, 270,000 in the National Guard, 630,000 selectees. At this time the headlines read: "Marshall Urges U. S. to Prepare," "New Boss—New Army," "Our Flying Chief."

It was pointed out by National Aeronautics "that our Chief of Staff has travelled by air in the discharge of official duties more miles than the Military Chief of any other country. He is now in the Hawaiian Islands before speeding back to testify before a Congressional Committee."

In June the words of Winston Churchill echoed around the world:

> "We shall not flag. We shall not fail. We shall fight in France and on the seas and oceans. We shall fight with growing strength in the air. If invaded, we shall fight on beaches, landing grounds, in fields, in streets and on the hills. We shall never surrender."

One headline reads: "Twenty-three Years Ago Today Unprepared United States Went to War. Are We Safe Now?"

xvi.

The strain of that winter on my husband and his Staff, the long days and evenings of feverish planning, the unrest and uncertainty that were felt by everyone, began to tell.   George felt something should be done to relieve the tension.   We had been at Fort Myer for nearly a year and had had no time to think of receiving the Army. Few of the officers had ever been in the Chief of Staff's house, many did not even know him by sight.   When spring came we decided to give a garden party on May 1st. There were twelve hundred invitations mailed, we prepared for fifteen hundred people, two thousand came.

Knowing Washington receptions, my husband had trucks of provisions stand by to take care of the situation in the event of shortages.

We had often remarked about the tendency of people to congregate in one room and particularly to stand in doorways at official affairs while they talk to friends, utterly unconscious of newly arriving guests.   To relieve this situation, George devised a plan: Mrs. Stimson was to receive with me and we were to stand in the drawing-room and receive the guests as they came in; George would be on the side lawn.

As the guests arrived it was amusing to see their faces when they realized General Marshall was not there. They would say, "Oh! Is General Marshall Away?"   I would answer, "No, he is waiting to see you out on the lawn."   They would look relieved, and those two thousand people passed through the house steadily with no signs of congestion anywhere.

The same refreshments were served out of doors as in the dining-room.   Outside there were tables and gay-colored chairs so that guests could form groups and sit comfortably, while the band played on the terrace below. At five-thirty when the sun-set gun went off, Mrs. Stimson and I joined General Marshall just before the flag was lowered and the band played the Star-Spangled Banner. This was a solemn moment to that gay crowd. There was a long pause before the guests moved; they stood silently as the flag was folded. It was a dramatic moment, for each one present knew that war was growing daily nearer.

When we first moved to Fort Myer I noticed that as soon as we had planted shrubs and young trees, a group of little boys would crawl through the hedge and play havoc with the tender new plants. They would shake the bushes, rocking them backward and forward, and try to climb the small trees. As soon as a gardener appeared they would scurry back through the hedge in a gale of laughter and run headlong down the road. This practice grew so annoying that I strolled out on the lawn one day just as their heads came through the hedge. "Come on through, boys," I called. "I want to ask you to do something for me." They crawled through and stood facing me sheepishly. "You know my husband, General Marshall, has guards to protect him, but I have no one. I have been fixing up my lawn and I would like someone to guard it for me. Will you four boys be my personal guards and look out for this place? If you see anyone even walking through who you think should not be here, come right to the house, ring the bell, and report it. Anything you say goes, and if you four can't handle it, the men at the house will. Just call for help."

"We'll manage it all right," said the leader. "Lady, you don't have to worry."

"Well," I said, "I would like to shake hands and know the names of my guards."

They told me their first names and gave me limp, tough little hands and then went on down the hill with their heads together. I could hear snatches of their con-

versation as the argument grew heated, "I'm the Captain."
"You ain't, I am." "No, Joe is." "Well, anyhow I'm
the Sergeant." "You ain't the 1st Sergeant, because I am,"
and so on.

That evening I told my husband of my strategy
and he was much amused. "Well," he said, "we will see
how it works out and if it proves sound I will have Sergeant Powder get four policeman suits for your guards."

By the time Christmas came they were perfectly
at home on our lawn. They policed it beautifully and no
other child could walk on the grass nor touch a shrub.
Each day after school they reported for duty to the "Captain." On Christmas Day I asked them to come in and
when I gave them the policeman suits from General Marshall as a reward for their services they were inexpressibly
delighted. The suits had helmets, jackets, trousers, a play-
pistol in a holster and a rather formidable-looking "Billy"
that hung from a wrist strap. I was terrified for fear
they would brain each other and we would have murder
on our souls, for the swinging of those Billys seemed to
fascinate them.

On the day of our reception in May, the four appeared on the front porch. Nothing the guards could
say or do would keep them out, they had to see Mrs. Marshall. When I came down they said they wanted to police
the lawn for the party and see that no one took anything.
They called to a ragged little fellow in a torn green sweater
and said they had brought him along as their "G-Man."
"But," I protested, "he has no uniform. He can't come
like that. That sweater will never do."

"Oh!" they explained, "we got that green sweater
on purpose so he could crawl through the grass and report
to us without anyone seeing him."

Their faces were so eager, explaining this brilliant idea of theirs, that I said, "Well, go ahead. You police the lawn but keep the G-Man hidden in the bushes."

I was not on the lawn when the guests began to arrive, but George said that the four little policemen and the G-Man, whom he pointed out peering from around a large boxwood bush, were the main attraction of the afternoon. They really were of great assistance too, for when I did come out I found them as busy as bees, picking up cups, moving chairs, and bringing ice cream. Whenever they went for ice cream they would stop long enough to see that the police force was well taken care of. How much they ate during the afternoon no one will ever know. I trembled to think of the results. The next morning the papers headed their account with, "Police Guard at Fort Myer Carries Off the Honors at the Reception Given by the Chief of Staff and Mrs. Marshall," followed by an amusing description of the guards' activities.

xvii.

During that summer and fall, as the plans for our defense took form and George's appearances before the Senate and House began to bear fruit, he would go out every other Sunday afternoon to Walter Reed Hospital to see General Pershing. Often I would go with him and some Sundays we would lunch together in the General's sitting-room. George would go over the whole situation with him and bring him up to date. General Pershing was very feeble at this time but still dapper and immaculate in his dress. I have here a letter from him written September 19th:

"My dear Mrs. Marshall:

"I appreciate more than I can say your thought of me. It was a distinct pleasure and like old times to have you and your distinguished husband lunch with me

"With affectionate regards to you both,

"John J. Pershing."

It was also in this month that my daughter's engagement was announced to Captain James J. Winn, of the Field Artillery. He was then stationed in Panama. Molly left for New York to get her trousseau, but I was unable to go with her for my war activities were daily growing heavier and my duties at home increasingly arduous. The mail took several hours each morning, the telephone rang constantly. At night after the staff was off, I would take the night calls, never awakening my husband unless absolutely necessary. Many times it was the newspapers which had gotten wind of some new development and wanted to make sure their information was correct. If possible I would assist them, but often I would have to say, "You will have to call the office in the morning, I cannot awaken General Marshall now." I could feel and greatly regretted an increasing indignation on the part of the Press; but, surely, it was of first importance that General Marshall should keep physically fit for the great task ahead. One night when the 'phone rang at 3:00 A. M., I said, "General Marshall is asleep. Can you give me the message?" I could sense the indignation over the wire. There was quite a pause, then the voice said, "Yes, I'll give you the message. This is the Times-Herald, and when the General wakes up you can tell him the War Department is on fire."

I went into George's room, and in five minutes he

was dressed. I 'phoned Sergeant Powder, the chauffeur, to come at once but George would not wait for the official car. Despite a heavy mist, he jumped in our car and arrived at the War Department as the hose was being dragged into the building. The War Department was then on Constitution Avenue and he told me later that as he drove across the Memorial Bridge he could see the whole sky lit up and the top of the Munitions Building aflame. The blaze turned out to be mainly from the awnings, and no great damage was done.

Another night a long-distance call came from Cincinnati. I asked if I could take the message but the operator said no, that it was very important for the caller to speak personally to the Chief of Staff. I awakened George and he came into my room to take the call. I heard him say, "What's that?" and then, "You don't mean to say you called me at this hour of the night to tell me how to stop tanks! Why don't you practice on yourself?" As he left the room he was grumbling something about a drunken fool.

My fight to see George get some recreation and privacy at this time had begun in good earnest. He said on several occasions, "I think I prize my privacy more than anything else." This is one of the reasons he has never had a personal aide.

In October we planned a trip to Charlotte, North Carolina, to see the VMI football game. The invitation had been accepted, his brother-in-law had made arrangements for George's reception, and he was to have that weekend off. Then the Secretary and Mrs. Stimson announced a reception for the General Staff that Saturday and, of course, George felt he must attend. He had just been through the long, hot summer with its inspection trips, defense plans, the National Guard induction, and the Selective Service Act, with no leave even for a day, so I was determined he should go to Charlotte. I took it upon myself to see Secretary Stimson and explained that George must have a respite, that he was sleeping poorly and that I was greatly concerned. Mr. Stimson agreed with me, but asked how he could persuade George to go to a football game.

"By a direct order," I said. "That is the only way."

The Secretary's eyes twinkled, and the next morning the following order was handed to George in his office:

> "The President of the United States directs that General George C. Marshall during the period between Friday, October 11th, and Monday, October 14th, shall visit the city of Charlotte, North Carolina, for the purpose of making a report upon the comparative skill and valor of the football teams of Davidson and Virginia Military Institute.
>
> "During said period he shall be under the exclusive control and direction of Mrs. Marshall and shall be protected against all interruptions, particularly by members of the War Department and of the Congress.
>
> "During said period the War Department shall be relegated to the tender mercies of the Secretary of War, the Assistant Secretary of War, and the Deputy Chief of Staff, General Bryden.
>
> (Signed) "HENRY L. STIMSON."

George saw that game.

xviii.

That fall the whole world seemed to be courting the favor of the United States. There were many delegations from the countries in South America and from Finland, England, China, Australia, Canada. Also there was an endless chain of midday luncheons at our quarters. After lunch George would go upstairs and I would lead the guests into the library and hold them with small-talk for the next fifteen minutes. As George passed me on his way upstairs he would murmur, do not discuss this or that. Frequently I was hard pressed to avoid the subjects foremost in our guests' minds. In this way he could get a short rest on the chaise longue on the sun porch, often dropping off to sleep for a few minutes. He would talk business coming to and going from the house and thereby save time for other interviews and conferences. Also, the delegations had been entertained in the Chief of Staff's home, which pleased them.

Molly's wedding was to take place on Christmas Day of that year and I was busy trying to get the house ready for the wedding and house guests. In addition there were several luncheons that same week. I would wake up in the morning with a tight feeling at the back of my head which I would relieve with Bromo Seltzer. George remonstrated, but I knew I must keep going until after the wedding, so continued with my cure. We exchanged our Christmas presents on Christmas Eve, after the wedding rehearsal. Both families were assembled in the library and when George brought in a present for me everyone gathered around. I was quite excited, as it was a large box wrapped in silver paper and tied with Christmas ribbons. When I opened it I pulled out a huge bottle of Bromo Seltzer, a foot high. This caused a roar of laughter. As I was made the complete butt of the party I determined to get even with him.

By New Year's Eve, George's birthday, I had finished my first scrapbook. I had it bound in brown leather, with "George Catlett Marshall" in gold letters on the cover, and on the first page I pasted a cartoon from the New Yorker—a drawing of a man sitting in a lounge chair with a large-sized book open in his hands. His head was turned toward his wife, who was lying on a chaise longue with her eyes closed and her hands folded across her portly chest. Under the cartoon was printed: "I do love you, George, but I just don't feel like talking military tactics with you." This time the laugh was on George Marshall.

Molly's marriage on Christmas Day in Quarters Number One at Fort Myer was the first wedding, I believe, ever to take place in that house. She came down the stairway on George's arm, followed by her maid-of-honor, Mary Winn. They passed through the drawing-room and were met by Captain Winn and his groomsmen at the altar which had been constructed at the far end of the oval dining-room. The bride's path was flanked on each side by white chrysanthemums and tall standards holding white candles. Her gown was of cream satin with an extremely long train, and her cap and veil were of Rose-point lace. She kept her eyes steadily on Captain Winn and his were on her. She said afterwards that this was pre-arranged to keep her from trembling. After the ceremony they walked out beneath the crossed swords of the groomsmen, while the orchestra played Lohengrin's Wedding March. As soon as the reception was over, they left for Panama and I did not see Molly again until she came home a year and a half later with her baby son. The guests departed, the two families left, George and I were alone.

Chapter III

IN SEPTEMBER 1940 the French newspaper LE SOIR had published an article headlined, "More than Roosevelt, More than Willkie, One Man Holds in his Hands the Destiny of the United States: The Generalissimo Marshall." The first paragraph of this article reads as follows:

> "Next November the world will know which of the two, Mr. Franklin D. Roosevelt or Mr. Wendell Willkie, will be charged with the destiny of the United States of America. But whatever may be the result of the presidential election, there is at this very moment a man who, above party, above political competition, has the heavy responsibility of assuring the security of the forty-eight states. This man, on whom the immediate future of the great American Republic depends, is General George Catlett Marshall, Chief of Staff . . ."

January 20, 1941, marked the Inauguration of Franklin Delano Roosevelt as President of the United States for a third term—the first time in our history. Henry Agard Wallace had been elected Vice-President.

It had been an overwhelming victory for Mr. Roosevelt and a bitter fight for Mr. Wallace. After the inauguration ceremony on the portico of the White House, George had to leave me as he was to lead the parade which followed. I was escorted to the Presidential reviewing stand by one of the White House Aides.

As the dull rumble came up the Avenue, indicating the approach of the parade, the President, quite near-sighted, groped for his glasses. The rumble grew to a deafening roar which swelled in magnitude as units from West Point, Annapolis, CCC, and WPA detachments came in sight. Mr. Roosevelt smiled and waved as they passed by. Then General Marshall, on his bay gelding, "King Story," saluted and passed, after which he dismounted and took his post at the side of the President's stand to review the armored and motorized units, approaching in clouds of blue exhaust. Above the rumble of these mechanized forces could be heard the wild cheers of the immense crowds. Possibly in the thunder of those forces the huge throng could hear the not-so-distant battles that would shape the destiny of America and of the entire world.

ii.

From Christmas 1940 it became apparent to me that my one great objective must be to keep Quarters Number 1 at Fort Myer a place of peace and quiet, a sanctuary for my husband where he could rest and relax and gather strength from the time he entered his home in the evening until he had to face the demands of the next day. There were few callers received and we accepted practically no social invitations. The staff performed their duties quietly and efficiently to all appear-

ances; if there were domestic upheavals, and at times these
were unavoidable, my husband knew nothing about them.
From the time he got up in the morning until we retired
at nine in the evening, as far as the home was concerned
there was to be no confusion, no household irritations.
This, I say, was my objective—whether I reached it or
not is another matter; but it is surprising how soon a
group of people will fall in line if you hold a certain
standard up to them and try to live up to it yourself. We
were a team and our watchword was "General Marshall."

When the telephone rang each day at luncheon
time and word was received that the General had left his
office, it was as though an electric switch had made contact through the house, each member of the staff hurrying to get his part done. When George came in the door
all was serene and luncheon was immediately served to
however many he had brought with him—just as if the
number of guests had been known for weeks. This, of
course, was the result of teamwork. As early in the day
as possible his secretary would let us know the number of
probable guests. Sometir es she would 'phone, "There will
be three," then, later, "No, four," or "Luncheon for two,"
or "General Marshall is detained at the White House."
. . . This, I know, sounds maddening to the average
housekeeper but after you get used to uncertainty it ceases
to be uncertain; you expect it and know exactly what
to do.

iii.

So much for the domestic side of the picture in
1941. As for the official side, it was a case of preparing
this country for war; whether war came or whether war
did not, the country must be prepared to meet whatever

might fall. Yet it was dangerous at this time to use the word war. With the whole of Europe aflame, defense was the strongest word the American people would swallow. If you said war, that was interpreted as meaning you wanted war, you were a war-monger. The pacifists and isolationists were busy and their task was not too difficult as their propaganda was what the people wanted to believe. Like the proverbial ostrich, a majority of Americans, it seems, were sticking their heads in the sand. Berlin was assisting this false sense of security with all the cunning of its great propaganda machine. It reached out from some of the Embassies in Washington to our cities and farms, on and on from coast to coast; and it spread its poison through Central and South America. This was only one of my husband's headaches. It was necessary now that he have the funds and the authority to train and equip the every-expanding Army and to use these funds as quickly and effectively as possible. As he expressed it, "A year ago we had all the time and no money; now we have the money and no time."

A basic requirement was the establishment of shelter, hospitals, and training areas in strategic and favorable training localities throughout the United States. The winter, with its usual bad weather, snow, rain and mud, added greatly to the expense and complications of construction. Also it was highly important to provide recreation and provisions for the spiritual welfare of our citizen soldiers. To accomplish these ends George worked that winter with ever-increasing drive.

In January the Lend-Lease Bill was before the Senate and House. The headlines read, "General Marshall's Evidence Supports Lend-Lease Bill," "General Marshall Sees World Facing Crisis," "Isolationists Protest." George had flown hurriedly back from his inspections of camp sites, hospital and recreational centers, to testify before the House Foreign Affairs Committee and to fight for the passage of this bill. His testimony was in a secret session but the very next morning it appeared in the newspapers. I quote a telegram received from General Pershing that day:

> "Am shocked beyond words that your confidential testimony should have been given to the press. Affectionate regards.   "Pershing."

This secret testimony divulged that Britain had strengthened her Singapore defenses, that the Pacific Fleet was to be at once reinforced by dive-bombers and the latest type of Army and Navy fighter airplanes, and that five hundred American troops had reached Manila. My husband, appearing before the House Military Affairs Committee after this leak, said, "Gentlemen, we are now playing poker with an exposed hand."

iv.

In my scrapbook I find this pencilled note: "General, if you get in a real jam I want to get into the Army. Make me Assistant Military Aide to the President. No physical exam (underscored). How about it? Harry Hopkins." On the outside is written in my husband's handwriting, "A note from H. H. handed me during an interview with the President after Hopkins' return from England. G. C. M." I remember that this note touched my husband deeply for Harry Hopkins was a very ill man.

Also I have treasured another encouraging note, written on paper with the heading, "Major Floyd L. Parks,

2nd Armored Brigade, Ft. Benning, Georgia." To the letter is appended this postscript: "Just thought of something that might interest General Marshall when he needs a little good news. When the newsreel showing General Marshall on his horse, leading the Inaugural Parade, was shown here the audience of about 1,500 soldiers burst into instantaneous and long applause. It was a tribute unequalled by any other, for soldiers don't do such things unless they mean it. I know it would do General Marshall's heart good to know of this feeling among his troops." And so, the sweet was mixed with the bitter.

As soon as George's testimony for Lend-Lease was over and his work with the General Staff well in hand, he would be off again to be with the troops. As his program began to materialize, such headlines as these appear: "General Marshall Chats with his Men at MacDill," "Chief of Staff Visits Air Base," "Marshall Terms Ft. Bragg a Miracle," "Chief of Staff Marshall Toils All His Waking Hours to Put Army in Fighting Trim," "General Marshall Inspects Troops at Tampa." And here is another heartening note—sent to me by Mr. Lowell Mellett, then Director of Reports at the White House, it was written to him by a former head of the United Press, living in Tampa: "My dear Lowell: I merely want to report that General Marshall came and simply wiped up Tampa and all of Southern Florida. I mean that, no fooling. He was everything that they did not think a General was and there isn't a mother or father in this end of the South that wouldn't send her or his youngster to any old war under his leadership." Such letters were indeed encouraging to the Chief of Staff in the midst of many and conflicting cross currents.

v.

While George was away on these inspections, I was in the house alone. It gave me a chance to catch up with my mail and war work. I was on many Boards; sometimes it seemed that life was just one board meeting after another. Fortunately I was seldom called unless something went wrong—a trouble shooter; but while I did not actually do the work, as that would have been an impossibility, I had to attend meetings, appoint the Army committees to work for these organizations, and see that they functioned. This required constant 'phone calls, letters and replacements as the Army personnel in Washington was rapidly changing. I would no sooner get one committee working than its chairman or a member would have to leave, her husband having been ordered elsewhere. My mail, too, was daily growing larger. I had no secretary and for two hours after breakfast I was tied to my desk.

Most of these letters were from mothers of boys who had been inducted. Some were pathetic, many courageous, a few amusing. I recall a letter from a mother who asked that I have her son ordered to Long Island to help her weekends in her restaurant. Another said that if I had any heart I would have a certain Sergeant ordered back to the writer's town, as her daughter had been going with him for four years and they were so in love. The mother said she was certain her daughter would die if I did not help. As the Selective Service grew, so did this type of personal mail. I was interested in these requests, but had no more power than the writers to order things done by the Military forces. I suppose they thought that the quickest way to reach General Marshall was through his wife instead of through the War Department.

Along with these requests came many from souvenir hunters and autograph collectors, people who wanted pieces of my husband's neckties, buttons or insignia from his uniform. One asked for a candlestick for her collection, another a walking cane for his. Endless requests were received for pictures and autographs and envelopes from George's letters. Of course I could send all these requests to his secretary at the War Department, but the letters from the mothers I answered myself. Finally a magazine unwittingly came to my rescue. It published an article which said General Marshall had no intimates—"his only confidante is his wife." The effect of this was to double my mail so it became essential to have a secretary, and from then on to the end of the war most of this load was lifted from my shoulders, though I still had innumerable personal letters to answer.

I was interested in the word "intimates" in the article mentioned, as several articles had given the impression that we were cold and unapproachable. It was quite the reverse. If they meant by "intimates" people who feel free to run into your home at any hour of the day and with whom you discuss your personal and family affairs, they were right—General Marshall has no such intimates. But if they meant intimate friends, they were wrong. He has them from Dan to Beersheba, friends whom he has treasured from childhood, early manhood and on through his Army life, friends who come to him in their deep sorrows and with their joys, friends whom he has not seen for years who take up where they left off in their mutual understanding and companionship. When he admires anyone he is almost extravagant in the giving of his friendship, and that friendship is a deep affection, as unaffected and sincere as the man himself.

vi.

During the inspection trip after his testimony on the Lend-Lease Bill, George was called back to Washington to appear before a Special Defense Committee of the Senate and explain the large amount of money spent, above the original estimates, in construction of cantonments and in training the Army. Taking full responsibility for these expenditures, he testified that if the funds had been available for construction in the summer the expense would not have been nearly so great, the winter conditions having played a large part in the high cost of building these cantonments and training centers. His testimony was long and arduous. It seemed to be a source of amazement to the Senate and House that he testified without notes. As the newspapers put it, the facts were neatly filed away in his brain. Some of the highlights of this testimony were: "The new National Army is over the hump—we now have 1,250,000 men in training and by June 30th that number should be increased to 1,418,000; War Department plans are well advanced for an Army of 2,800,000 in case Congress feels impelled to call for it; we have two coordinated Armored Divisions of 11,000 men each; by June 30th the Army is scheduled to consist of 27 divisions which will include four Armored Divisions, 40 regiments of antiaircraft artillery, 27 regiments of Field Artillery, and 15 regiments of Engineers."

It became increasingly evident to my husband that the Selective Service Act, by which the National Guard, Reserve Officers, and Selective Service men had been inducted into the Army, would have to be extended. The

Act had read, ". . . for twelve months training and service *unless Congress declares that the national security is imperiled,* when such service may then be extended by the President to such time as may be necessary in the interest of national defense."

The key question was whether an emergency existed or did not exist. Again the isolationists and pacifists gathered their forces, and again the Chief of Staff fought back.

There is an interesting sidelight on the development of the situation at this time. The leaders in Congress had informed the President that it would be politically impossible to extend the period of service of the National Guard and the Selective Service men beyond one year. Therefore, it was equally impossible for the Chief of Staff to get a formal proposal submitted by the White House to the Congress recommending the extension.

The battle over this extension had been waged continually since April. It was now June. Drastic action would have to be taken by the War Department, commencing in August, if a year's extension was not authorized; in fact, the newly formed Army would have to be dissolved.

On June 22nd the Germans launched their treacherous attack on Russia and the most destructive, the most catastrophic campaign of all times threatened not only to obliterate Russia, but also the civilization of the entire world, for the Russian Campaign was the Nazis' master stroke for world dominance.

General Marshall desperately faced the fact that his efforts had failed utterly to get the necessary action to protect the American Army he had so painstakingly created. He felt it was essential to play on the team—that it would further divide the Nation if he broke loose in an individual appeal to the American people; yet their security was his responsibility and they should know and fully comprehend that the Nation was never in greater danger—that the virtual demobilization of the Army at this time would invite future disaster.

While horseback riding he recalled that during the previous summer he had declined to prepare the usual annual report of the Chief of Staff, due July 1st. This gave him the idea for which he was so desperately seeking: He would establish the practice of making a Biennial Report and submit it on July 1st. Thus he could employ a dignified procedure in bringing the situation and his recommendations to the attention of the Nation. This proved to be a stroke of sheer genius.

Returning to the War Department he got to work at full speed and prepared his first Biennial Report, covering the period July 1, 1939 to June 30, 1941. With the assistance of his Staff he succeeded in drafting this report in five days and on July 1 he released it to the Press.

The Biennial Report described the build-up of the Army during the past two years, the grave dangers of the situation, and the urgent necessity for extending the term of service of the National Guard and the Selective Service men. Within an hour after its release, the report provoked a storm of discussion and precipitated a White House conference with Congressional leaders. The decision was reached to introduce a bill to accomplish what the Chief of Staff had so urgently recommended; and although a stormy political summer resulted, the act was finally passed—by the narrowest margin.

Two more Biennial Reports followed in due course, recording great historical events and victorious operations.

During the torrid debates of the period above covered, General Marshall testified:

> "I believe that Selective Service provides the only practical and economical method of maintaining the military forces that we inevitably are going to be required to have in the future and I think with all my heart that Selective Service is a necessity to the maintenance of a true democracy."

This had been a long, ruthless and exhausting fight. To serve political purposes seeds of discontent were sown among Army troops in an attempt to persuade them to write letters of protest. Further, the Army High Command was accused of double-dealing and bad faith in not keeping its word—the clause, "unless necessary in the interest of national defense" being wilfully ignored. The great National Army, then only half trained, which had required millions in money and exhaustive planning, seemed doomed. But, fortunately, this calamity had been averted.

TIME magazine of July 28, 1941, published the following article:

> "The President has sent in General George C. Marshall, Army Chief of Staff, to carry the ball. Good soldier Marshall pounded down the field through center, off tackle, around the ends. The watching President couldn't believe his eyes, even the isolationists admitted the logic of fully training the half-trained U. S. Army. By now General Marshall had smashed all the way to the one-yard line. The President took the ball and carried it over for a touchdown."

On August 3rd there appeared on the front page of DAS REICH, a nefarious German propaganda weekly, the following report of the American Chief of Staff written by their Acting Military Attache:

"Berlin.　.　.　.　After Roosevelt's demand that Congress permit the sending of troops outside the Western Hemisphere he had to withdraw a few days ago as he was over-shooting the mark. General Marshall received the assignment to plunge the Senate Military Committee into unrest and then make Congress ripe to proclaim a national state of emergency by carrying out an extension of the terms of service for the National Guard and Reserves. General Marshall did not hesitate to enter the field in full-fledged agitation himself, repeating the old fairy tale that the United States is endangered."

On August 1st George received a letter from Joey Stettinius, eight-year-old son of Edward Stettinius. It was printed in pencil and read:

"O. K. General, now I am ready. I will bring everything I need. Also I will bring my pony. I will be ready to go the first of September."

George paused in his preparations for a most important and secretive trip to write the following order, which he attached to an attractive picture of a little boy like Joey appearing in an advertisement of jam:

"August 1, 1941

"Orders for Joey Stettinius:

"Button up your coat. Put your hat on straight. Wipe the smile off your face. Draw rations of beans instead of jam. After you have done all this I will tell you what next to do.

"G. C. Marshall, Chief of Staff."

After I knew the nature of George's most mysterious mission I marveled that he could have found the time that day to make a small boy happy. He left Fort Myer early in August without mentioning where he was going or with whom. From that very fact I felt sure he was to be with the President. His orderly had packed winter clothes, so I knew he was going north, but that was all I knew. I left for our home at Leesburg, Virginia, and wired for my sister Allene Wilkes to join me there. There had been such secrecy about George's trip that I felt sure I would be bombarded by calls from the Press if I remained at Fort Myer. At breakfast the next morning in the Leesburg house I asked Allene to answer any 'phone calls as I had left word at Fort Myer I was out of the city and had given no address. I hoped there would be none but about 11 o'clock the telephone rang. It was the New York Herald-Tribune asking to speak to General Marshall. My sister said, "General Marshall is not here."

"Is he away?"

"He is not here," my sister repeated.

"Who is speaking?" the reporter inquired.

"Mrs. Marshall's sister."

"Well, do you know where General Marshall is?"

"That is funny," Allene answered. "I just bought a Herald-Tribune to try to find out."

"You win!" said the voice, and hung up.

Such was the veil of secrecy surrounding one of the most world heartening events of the year 1941—the meeting off the coast of Newfoundland between President Roosevelt and the British Prime Minister, Winston Churchill, known as the Atlantic Conference. At this conference aboard the U. S. Flagship Augusta the eight-point program, known as the Atlantic Charter, came into existence and gave new hope to an agonized world.

On his return, George brought me several souvenirs of that historic trip, among them a place card of the President's dinner to the Prime Minister aboard the Augusta the first night—a large card with the British and

American flags crossed and printed under them:

"Sail on, Oh Ship of State!
Sail on, O Union, strong and great!
Humanity with all its fears,
With all the hope of future years,
Is hanging breathless on thy fate!"

This place card was autographed by all who sat at that great dinner. Also there were pictures of the religious ceremony aboard the HMS Prince of Wales, taken from the gun turret, with leaders of the world's greatest democracies standing behind the President and the Prime Minister, and the British crew lining the ship's long white decks.

When the President made his return call on the Prime Minister, he wanted to give something to each of the British crew on the Prince of Wales. When asked what they would like best, the unhesitating answer was oranges and cigarettes. Each man was made happy by a present of oranges and cigarettes from the President of the United States. Five months later that magnificent ship lay at the bottom of the sea off Singapore and most of her crew went down with her.

While the President and the Prime Minister held their conferences, the British and American Chiefs of Staff, Field Marshal Sir John Dill and General Marshall, the Lord Admiral of the Fleet Sir Dudley Pound and Admiral Starke, General Arnold and Air Marshal Portal held theirs. I asked George, who of all the British representatives present impressed him the most. He said, "Sir John Dill, the British Chief of Staff, without question." This was the beginning of a friendship that grew with the hazards of the war and bound my husband and Sir John in a close understanding and comradeship such as seldom comes to men of their age.

vii.

That fall George was busy furthering the plans that had been discussed at the conference. They were as intricate as the works of a watch, and as delicate; and required understanding, vision, and endless patience. When he came home at night he would often be too tired to talk. I would send to the library for a pile of books and place them at the side of his chaise-longue. My husband has always been an incessant reader and I was hard put to keep him supplied. He would go through a pile of books with the avidity of a swarm of locusts devouring a green field.

Some evenings he would bring home the maps for me to see and after dinner we would spread them out on the table and he would go over the Pacific area. The islands in the Pacific looked like the stars in the firmament, seemingly countless. He would say, "There are 5,000 Japanese here, 10,000 here, 20,000 here," and so on and so on. . . . "Africa is only so many miles from the coast of Brazil; if the Germans established themselves in Brazil, the Panama Canal is in danger. The Canal and Hawaii must be protected at any cost, also our life-line to the Philippines must be kept open."

On other evenings it would be the Atlantic and the European situation. "If the British fleet fails, the Atlantic Coast is open. Our Lend-Lease to Britain is imperative. To the north, our outposts, the Aleutians, Alaska, and Iceland, must be fortified. So much for the picture outside of our continent. I have mentioned the internal problems."

When I would go to bed after one of these evenings I would lie awake wondering, "How is it humanly possible, how can it be done?" My nightly prayer was, "Give him time, O Lord, give him time." I was thankful that fall when he had to go off on inspection trips, for they released him from his desk and gave him some respite from incessant planning.

In October, while he was off on one of these trips, I became interested in a fashion show at Fort Myer for the benefit of the Soldiers, Sailors, and Marines Club. It was to be quite a large affair and each ticket bore an invitation for tea, after the show, at the Chief of Staff's house. Two weeks before the date chosen I slipped on a rug on our upstairs porch and, falling against the edge of a table, broke four ribs. Fortunately, my son Clifton had come from New York for the weekend and was with me at the time. I was taken to Walter Reed Hospital, where George found me on his return.

Ilka Chase graciously consented to come down for the day to help put the show over. The Committee continued with all arrangements and two weeks later the affair came off. I had been moved back to Fort Myer the day before, bringing a nurse with me. We directed the tea from my bed. The huge crowd downstairs made the Chief of Staff's house sound like the Union Station.

viii.

I did not seem to get my strength back after this accident and when George had to go off on an inspection trip during the first week in December, I left for a friend's place on the coast of Florida. I stayed for several days, returning to Fort Myer on Saturday the 6th. The next morning, Sunday, we had a late breakfast. I was still not well enough to be up and about, so we had breakfast in my room, George eating on a tray beside my bed. After breakfast he ordered his horse and said he would take his usual Sunday morning ride before going to the office. About the time of his return an urgent telephone call came from the War Department. George bathed hurriedly and left for the Department.

That was the morning of December 7, 1941.

Shortly after one o'clock I heard over the radio of the attack on Pearl Harbor. When my husband had not come back by seven that evening, I got dressed and sat on the porch to await his arrival. When he came in his face was grim and grey. What was in his mind, I do not know; but this I did know: Since June 1938—three and a half years—he had labored relentlessly against impossible odds to arouse and prepare America; yet America was still unprepared. Panama, Alaska, the Hawaiian Islands, Wake, Guam, the Philippines—all our outposts, were woefully unprepared. Now the blow had been struck.

On that ghastly night George said nothing except that he was tired and was going to bed. I sat there trying to think of something I could do or say that might help him. But words are futile at a time like that, so I passed his door and went into my room. I knew he would rather be alone.

ix.

In September I had flown up to Poughkeepsie, New York, where Allen and Madge lived, to see my first grandchild. My father had always said you never know what unalloyed joy is until you have seen your first grandchild. When I saw that tiny bit of humanity, with his shock of golden curls, I knew what he had meant. And when I held him in my arms the world's turmoil seemed to melt away, for here was something eternal. I could stay only that day and night but after leaving the hospital I went with Allen to their home, which they had just bought. It was a quaint old farmhouse near Poughkeepsie and I sat up late that night listening to all their plans for an addition here, a garden there. When I arrived home I was so enthusiastic in my descriptions that George said, "You are going to be a typical grandmother." Now a cable arrived from Panama reading, "James J. Winn, Jr., born 4:30 A. M. Six pounds, 15 ounces. Molly fine." I had a second grandchild! The news brought relief and happiness to us both.

x.

Christmas week Prime Minister Churchill and the British Chiefs of Staff arrived in Washington. George suggested, as they were all away from their homes and Clifton was the only one of our family who could spend the holiday with us, that we ask them all to a family Christmas dinner. The British Ambassador and Lady Halifax, Lord Beaverbrook, Admiral Sir Dudley Pound, Field Marshal Sir John Dill, Air Chief Marshal Sir Charles Portal, Admiral and Mrs. King, George, Clifton and I, were at the table.

Christmas came on a Sunday that year. Saturday morning General Marshall's office called to say Sunday was also Sir John Dill's birthday and asked if I could have a birthday cake for him. My cook's cake would have sunk the Admirals and the entire British Commission. A cake was one thing she could not make. It was eleven o'clock then and how to get a birthday cake made in Washington on Saturday afternoon was a problem. I sent for Sergeant Powder and turned the problem over to him. He had long been George's "trouble shooter" and when a thing had to be done Sergeant Powder got the assignment. He was six feet three, a splendid looking soldier, and he could coax the birds out of a tree or crash any gate. The birthday cake was to be plain white, without decoration. Also I instructed him to get two silk flags, one British and one American. Securing the cake proved easy for Sergeant Powder's persuasive powers, but there were no small British flags to be found in Washington. Finally at a Five and Ten Cent Store he found one in a box that had been pushed far back on the shelf.

Sunday the house was surrounded by Secret Service men and guards, for our guests were all too important to world affairs for us to take any chances. I went to the pantry to see that all was in order. The cake was lovely, decorated with candles in the shape of red-coated soldiers, and holly leaves around the edge. From a cluster of berries in the center the little silk flags floated.

The dinner was most informal. Every few minutes a telephone call would come for someone at the table. He would get up without apologies and come back when the call was finished. Some were still eating the main course while the salad was being served, others salad when the dessert was brought in. Lord Halifax was constantly being called to the 'phone, as a serious diplomatic incident had suddenly developed due to the landing of Free French on the St. Pierre and Miquelon Islands in the mouth of the St. Lawrence River. While at the table, between 'phone calls, he and Lord Beaverbrook were deeply engrossed in a discussion concerning the proper procedure to be followed.

As soon as dinner was over, George toasted Sir John

and the cake was brought in. Sir John was so surprised
and deeply moved that we should have known it was his
birthday and have had a special celebration for him that
he was really quite overcome. He said it was his first
birthday cake since he was a small boy. When he cut the
cake he removed the flags, then looked at them closely.
Printed on the staffs were the words "Made in Japan!"
They were quickly disposed of but the incident gave rise
to a good deal of badinage.

George had wanted the affair to be as relaxing as
possible and this bit of diversion certainly added to the
merriment. They could not have been more at home;
they codded each other no end over early memories and
childhood predicaments. For an hour or two at least the
war was forgotten and they were boys once more in Merrie
Old England.

We did not know it at the time but Sir John Dill
was engaged to marry his second wife, Nancy; and she
having heard of a new American custom had cabled Western Union to deliver a singing telegram, "Happy Birthday to You." Alas! as the Secret Service men would not
allow the messenger boy to come in, this hilarious performance was missing. George was provoked when he
heard the boy had been turned away, for a singing telegram was a novelty at that time and he thought the party
would have been greatly amused.

Chapter IV

M Y 1942 SCRAPBOOK opens with a cartoon which depicts General Marshall tearing down the sign: "Defense
War on Home Front," and pasting up one reading: "Off
to Battlefront." A bucket of paste is marked, "$32,768,-
900 War Appropriations." Under this is written, "This
Should Make It Stick."

The Japanese attack on Pearl Harbor had galva-
nized and welded the Nation. War had been declared by
Germany and Italy. The British Prime Minister and Chiefs
of Staff reached agreements with our President and the
American Chiefs of Staff regarding the global strategy of
our combined conduct of the war and methods for the
command and control of British and American military
resources. Unity of command, on which General Marshall
insisted against all opposition, was attained. From the first
Sir John Dill, a man of broad vision and few prejudices,
had worked with George to attain this goal.

The determining factor in this matter was an un-
scheduled, secret conference held at nine o'clock one morning in Mr. Churchill's bedroom at the White House. Gen-

eral Marshall, was determined to settle this all important question. Together they thrashed out the subject, neither man mincing his words.

Propped up in bed with his work board resting against his knees and his ever-present cigar in his mouth or swung like a baton to emphasize his points, Mr. Churchill finally conceded that "His Majesty's senior service" (the British Navy) might conceivably operate under a system of unity of command.

One of the splendid characteristics of Mr. Churchill is his wholehearted support when he is convinced he is wrong—even though he has fought to the last ditch to maintain his ideas.

The issue of the moment was the necessity of issuing a directive to stem the onrush of the Japanese in the Southwest Pacific. There they were rapidly overwhelming an ill prepared, pitifully equipped collection of American, British, Australian, Indian, Dutch, Indonese and New Zealander troops. A confusion of races, religions, and national interests under various Allied commands, were being violently assaulted by a tidal wave of fanatics of one race, one religion, one allegiance and one common purpose.

ii.

In this year—the darkest, most humiliating and bloodiest in our history—our Army passed from defensive to offensive warfare. Staggering under the blows of the Axis powers we began to strike back. The results of the desperately heroic resistance offered by the Philippine Army and United States forces on Bataan and Corregidor, holding back as they did a sizeable portion of Japan's strength, were incalculable. During the time thus gained, men and materiel were despatched to Australia, New Caledonia, and other Pacific Islands. The bombing of Japan by Colonel Doolittle's men was a heartening event in a generally somber picture.

On the Atlantic side the U-boat warfare was ravaging our shipping from Maine to Florida, and in the Caribbean Allied ships were suffering daily casualties. A cartoon, though amusingly drawn, tells the humiliating story. It depicts a German U-boat in New York Harbor, flying the Swastika. The Captain is looking through his binoculars at the tall buildings of lower Manhattan; on the deck are three German sailors bending so far backward in their efforts to be military that they look like pouter pigeons. Under it is written, "Herr Captain, may we slip ashore tonight and visit Radio City?"

I have quite a collection of these cartoons, all originals sent me by the artists, and they present a rather comprehensive and accurate history of the war through the medium of American humor. This same extravagant sense of humor in our GI's was to astound the world and to carry our soldiers through hardships and nightmares of suffering and fatigue that would have been fatal to the morale of lesser men.

In this connection there is a postcard in my scrapbook that makes me smile whenever I see it—it so pictures the spirit of a partly-trained Army of a democracy and the unconscious lack of discipline of G.I. Joe. Mailed at Union Station, Washington, it is addressed to, "General Marshall, Chief of Staff, War Department," and reads:

"Dear Boss:

"We are just in from Fort Dix, New Jersey, on our way to Fort Bragg, N. C. The service was good but the coffee (?)

was cold. Will Confederate uniforms be issued after we pass
Washington?   Also will Confederate money be honored at
the Post Exchange?

> "Love and kisses,
> "The Boys"

I feel sure that this should pass for humor rather
than disrespect, but what other Chief of Staff of a nation's armies ever received such a message from his men?

A headline at this time reads: "The U. S. Army is
Shaken Down Into Three Top Commands—for Ground,
Air, and Supply."   A Radio Digest asked and answered
the rhetorical question: "Who is George C. Marshall? Our
Chief of Staff. He is the Pershing of this war. The
American Army is a monument to him. Get acquainted
with him now, before they start calling him the genius he
is. Then you can say 'I knew him when.'" A little
later appeared, "U. S. Army Ready for Offensive Says
Marshall."

Among the clippings in my scrapbook is pasted a
printed postcard, which reads:

> "Dear Madam:
> "You are advised that Clifton S. Brown enlisted in the
> Regular Army of the United States this date. Branch, Coast
> Artillery Corps Replacement Center. Station, Antiaircraft
> Unit.
>
> > "(Signed)   R. M. Peak, Recruiting Officer"

It is hard for me to say of which soldier I was the
prouder, the Chief of Staff or Private Brown.

An amusing incident happened when Clifton, in a
new GI uniform, stopped at our quarters on his way to
his training camp.   Sergeant Speaman, the colored orderly
who had been with us for some time, came to the porch
where I was writing and stood, first on one foot, then on

the other.   He seemed greatly perturbed, I looked up and asked, "What is it, Sergeant; did you wish to speak to me?"

"Yes, Ma'm, Mrs. Marshall, what shall I call Mr. Clifton?"

"Why, what you always have—'Mr. Clifton.'"

"But, Mrs. Marshall, he will think I don't know the military."

"Oh!" I answered, remembering the GI uniform. "Well, call him Private Brown."

"Private Brown," he repeated dubiously.

"Yes," I said, "that is what he is, Private Brown."

The Sergeant seemed unable to take this in.   "Yes, Ma'm, but . . ."   He left looking more embarrassed than ever. For an old Regular Army man his world had suddenly turned upside down.

iii.

On Army Day of this dark year I was made happy by Congressional tribute paid to George by John D. Dingell, of Michigan.   Mr. Dingell in addressing the House of Representatives said:

"Mr. Speaker, Army Day quite appropriately affords me the opportunity to pay tribute to General George C. Marshall, one of the greatest military strategists which this nation has ever produced.   Although he has been selected for the highest post within the designation of the Chief Executive, with which goes the responsibility of directing our armed forces throughout the far-flung battle areas the world over, he labors silently and modestly without the fanfare of publicity and as a rule far removed from the plaudits of the people.

"His genius, his labors, and his aggressive though unheralded actions cover and make possible the Army's heroic accomplishments from Bataan to Zamboanga in the Philippines, from Port Darwin to Ceylon, and from Iceland and northern Ireland to Panama and to Dutch Guiana.

"Every move of the Army calculated to bring ultimate victory in North Africa and throughout the Near East has been planned and approved by America's foremost soldier.

"I take this opportunity to appraise the real value of General George C. Marshall, Chief of Staff of the United States Army, and to focus the attention of the people upon this quiet though brilliant and productive soldier. He himself shuns and evades publicity, because he is too modest and wholly occupied with the greatest task which has ever been thrust upon a soldier serving in the same capacity. . . .

"I am certain that the House of Representatives joins with me in applauding the brilliant and historic accomplishments of our Chief of Staff. I want to convey to him my personal congratulations on Army Day."

At this time there were many extravagant articles written. I read these articles soberly but not, I hope, cynically, even though they struck me as a case of "Thank you, Mr. Atkins, when the band begins to play." There were small jealousies too. A certain type of person seems to take delight in telling you unpleasant things. Yet neither the praise nor the criticism seemed to have a great deal of effect on my husband. He reminded me of a horse who, when stung by a fly, merely switches his tail and continues galloping down the middle of the road.

One incident of this kind comes to mind. A group of Congressmen were much perturbed over rumors that were afloat in Washington concerning one of George's most trusted Staff officers who was carrying a tremendous load and doing it magnificently. In fact, he was handling his job with such authority and skill that the rumor-mongers said he had his eye on the job of the Chief of Staff. This rumor was fanned into a flame by those who had fallen afoul of him because of their failure to live up to his high standards of efficiency. The group of Congressmen came to warn George. He listened to what they had to say, then smiled and said, "Thank you, Gentlemen. I have heard these rumors. You do not have to worry about me, if I can't control my own Staff I should not be here."

In many of the articles and interviews I have read about General Marshall the writers speak of his retiring nature and his modesty. Those writers have never seen him when he is aroused. It is like a bolt of lightning out of the blue. His withering vocabulary and the cold steel of his eyes would sear the soul of any man whose failure deserved censure. No, I do not think I would call my husband retiring or overly modest. I think he is well aware of his powers, but I also think this knowledge is tempered by a sense of humility and selflessness such as I have seen in few strong men.

iv.

As the winter advanced there was no time for riding or any other outdoor exercise during the day, so when George came home in his car at twilight I would have my hat on in readiness and we would drive to a secluded spot in Arlington and take a brisk walk home before dinner.

On these daily walks I would talk little, for I was listening to a man steeling himself to carry a burden so tremendous in magnitude and so diverse in its demands that it was difficult to comprehend how one man could carry it alone.

He had the gift of facing things head on; there had never been any side-stepping in his make-up. He had disciplined himself for the past forty years in the Army, far more rigidly than he had disciplined his men. But even this was not sufficient to meet the unimaginable demands of the present.

On these walks, though he was talking in a quietly modulated voice to me, I had the feeling he was really talking to himself. It was as though he lived outside of himself and George Marshall was someone he was constantly appraising, advising and training to meet a situation. He would say, "I cannot afford the luxury of sentiment, mine must be cold logic. Sentiment is for others." This would follow an explanation of some particularly difficult decision he had made. "I get so tired of saying 'No,' it takes it out of me, I am really thankful when I can say 'Yes.' . . . It is not easy to tell men where they have failed. . . . My days seem to be filled with situations and problems where I must do the difficult, the hard thing." This self-discipline was true not only of his character but also of his body. He knew that if his health failed it would be impossible for him to carry through. He watched it as though he were a runner in training for a long race.

He once said, "I cannot allow myself to get angry, that would be fatal—it is too exhausting. My brain must be kept clear. I cannot afford to appear tired, for I recall in the first World War that General Pershing, after a long inspection trip, leaned back in the car to rest as we drove back to his quarters in Chaumont and those who saw him took his attitude for discouragement. From that small incident the rumor spread that things were going very badly." Then George suddenly turned as if just aware of my presence, and with his queer twist of humor said, "Now, as far as you are concerned, of course you do not have to conserve your strength, for you are as strong as an Army mule; you could break a cast-iron fixing." I laughed, for just that afternoon I had tripped over an iron manhole cover and he had caught me before I fell. But in spite of his teasing I knew, as if it had been written before my eyes, that he was forging himself for responsibilities such as few men in our history have carried —the lives of eight million men and the winning of a global war.

v.

Early in April George left on his first flight to London. Harry Hopkins went with him. They had plane trouble and had to lay over in Bermuda, where the Governor General, Lord Knollys, and his wife were most cordial. On Easter morning my husband took his first late sleep and when he finally got up to take a shower, Colonel Wedemeyer, later Chief of Staff to Generalissimo Chiang Kai-shek, came in the room to tell him Lord Knollys had telephoned a request that General Marshall read the Second Lesson in the Easter Service that morning.

Colonel Wedemeyer said he had accepted for the General, and that the Second Lesson was from the 4th to the 8th verse of the First Chapter of Revelations. Also Colonel Wedemeyer had obtained from the chef the only Bible in the hotel and suggested to General Marshall that he read the verses in case there were some difficult names to master. After his bath, George began to read the Scripture, but was interrupted by Harry Hopkins coming in to discuss important matters.

At the Cathedral, crowded with the usual Easter attendance and lovely with the lilies of which Bermuda is so productive, the Governor General on returning to his

pew after reading the First Lesson handed George a slip
of paper, on which was written the Second Lesson. Instead of being from the 4th to the 8th verse only, it was
from the 4th to the 18th. George took his place on the
dais and, glancing at the Bible, was confronted by the
names of the Seven Churches of Asia. Only one of these
had a familiar ring—the Philadelphians. He read the Lesson determinedly despite his uncertainty as to the pro-
nunciation of six of the Churches; but when he came to
the one familiar name he fairly boomed out the word
"Philadelphian."

After the service, a lady enthusiastically expressed
her pride that a fellow countryman had participated in
the services. "I'm from Philadelphia too," she added
coyly. And on the day he arrived in London the Prime
Minister, at No. 10 Downing Street, greeted him with a
twinkle in his eye: "I am told you read the Lesson of the
Easter Service in Bermuda most impressively."

The headlines now read: "General Marshall in
London to Plan Allied Offensive Against Axis," "Marshall
Starts Strategy Talks with British," "General Marshall
Pledges Action in Europe."

While in London George was shown a letter written about 1810 by the Duke of Wellington, at the time
in Spain, to the Secretary of State for War, Lord Bradford. George asked for a copy and had one mailed to each
of his Staff and also to each member of the high command
of our Army with this simple comment: "For our guidance in the present struggle."

The letter reads:

"My Lord,
    "If I attempted to answer the mass of futile correspond-
ence that surrounds me I should be debarred from all serious

business of campaigning. I must remind your Lordship, for the last time, that so long as I retain an independent position I shall see that no officer under my command is debarred, by attending to the futile driveling of mere quill-driving in your Lordship's office, from attending to his first duty which is, and always has been, so to train the private men under his command that they may, without question, beat any force opposed to them in the field.

"I am, My Lord,

"Your Obedient Servant
"Wellington"

From London General Marshall, Harry Hopkins and Averill Harriman (later Ambassador to Russia) flew to Ulster, Ireland. George wished to inspect the first contingent of American troops which had arrived in Europe.

He was much concerned over the serious state of Hopkins' health and asked the Prime Minister if it were possible to arrange for them to be housed in a private home where Harry could get proper food and rest before starting on the tiresome hop back to America. Mr. Churchill said it could easily be arranged and he would attend to the matter. When the party arrived in Ulster, their host met them at the airport and accompanied them to his home, a rather small place, very old and with lovely grounds.

Here in America we knew food rationing existed throughout Great Britain but had no conception of the deprivations it entailed. When dinner was announced, George, Harry Hopkins, and Mr. Harriman were shown into a large dining-room, hung with family portraits and heavy draperies. Under the sideboard were large, brass-bound mahogany buckets for the cooling of wine. Soup was served and then what they thought were hors d'oeuvres—thin slices of liverwurst, slivers of carrots on a few lettuce leaves, accompanied by strips of bread the size of your finger. George helped himself rather liberally, but the others held back somewhat, apparently in anticipation of the entree and main course. Instead a fine bottle of wine was served and then a small dessert.

Hopkins and Harriman suffered the pangs of hunger all that evening. Early the next morning George's orderly brought him a note from Hopkins in his room across the hall. It was written on a radiogram blank in pencil and said, "Mr. Hopkins expresses the hope the Chief of Staff slept well and is in reasonable good humor. He begs to enquire whether the General would be disposed to have some pork and beans for breakfast and porridge (oatmeal to you)."

George's answer, on another pink radiogram blank and written in pencil, said, "The Chief of Staff acknowledges the polite inquiry of Mr. Hopkins but feels compelled to observe that the hour hardly justifies Mr. Hopkins in disturbing the rest of so high a military official. The Chief of Staff suggests that instead of a crude meal of pork and beans, Mr. Hopkins would be better off with a small circle of liverwurst, the ragged edge of a piece of lettuce and the false hope of more to come. I'll be along presently. G. C. M."

vi.

At the time George left for London, I went down to Dodona Manor, our house in Leesburg, Virginia. Although we had bought it two years before, this was my first chance to really live in it. We had run down on Saturday and Sunday afternoons for our recreation and worked on the grounds, but there was much to be done

to get it really into shape. As soon as I had learned that
George was going overseas I had started seeing building
contractors, brick-layers and tree men, getting estimates,
and by the time he left the contracts were all signed. This
was to be my surprise for him when he returned.

After seeing George off at the airport I drove down
to the house and settled there. What an inexpressible feeling it gave me! Our own place, our home! Leesburg is 35
miles from Washington in the foothills of the Blue Ridge
Mountains. A quaint and very old Virginia town, it is
about as unreconstructed a place as you could find, allur-
ingly replete with tradition and history. Our home is the
first house as you enter the town limits and was built in
1786 by George Washington Ball, a nephew of George
Washington. The grounds comprise four acres; the house
is of brick painted white, but now cream color from age,
and its architecture is early Colonial. There is a portico in
front with four fluted columns and a brick floor. Great
oaks and elms tower above the house. They must have
been there since Revolutionary Days. The house itself was
renovated by a former owner but when we bought it they
had not finished the grounds. The out-buildings, including an old carriage-house with dirt floor, were still standing but in such a state of decay that they were held together only by a mat of vines—honeysuckle and Virginia
creeper.

When I arrived the workmen were busy tearing
down these buildings and several thousand old bricks I had
bought from the town of Leesburg were being delivered.
I had made a contract with a Mr. Brown, who did the
forestry work on the places around, to take out the many
dead trees, prune and doctor the oaks and elms, thin out

the shrubs, and replant the lilac that had grown as high as the second story.

There was a sloping field in front of the house and this we plowed and seeded to extend the lawn, while the transplanted lilacs and shrubs soon formed a hedge at the foot of the sloping field. This gave the beautiful old house breathing room—took away the crowded, over-grown look of the place and gave us a lovely vista—the greatest improvement of all. Until then, the mass of plant-ing against the house had given me a smothered feeling. Now, each morning I would get up early and hurry down to the portico to look out on the town below, and each morning I got the same delicious thrill.

While the foresters were doing their work, the brick-layers were putting down the old brick to form walks leading to the garage, vegetable garden and tool-house. The builders had torn down the carriage-house and, using the same brick, erected a two-car garage with a storeroom above which would delight the heart of every housekeeper. Both the garage and tool-house were built on the same lines as the old buildings, even the Virginia creeper having been carefully protected so it could again climb over the bricks it had known for many a year. This made the new buildings look as though they had grown there.

The place was teeming with workmen, and the planning of years and realization of my dreams so ab-sorbed me that from the time George left until his return I did not leave our grounds.

Each day when the radio reports came in with the European situation, the War Department would call me on the telephone and give me the latest news of General Marshall's activities and whereabouts. This was my only contact with the outside world.

vii.

A few days before General Marshall's return the work was nearing completion; there was only one blot on the landscape—a wooden Chic Sale affair that stood in the center of what was to be our orchard. It blocked the view of the vine-covered tool-house at the end of the garden and part of the garden itself. Wherever I looked, in fact, my eye would wander back to this unsightly structure. In vain I pled with the workmen to tear it down; they avoided touching it. That building had been built for all time, sturdy and strong, and they did not relish the job of razing it. I would say, "But what am I going to do about it? It can't stay there." They would cast a casual glance at it, shake their heads and walk away.

The thing grew to be an obsession with me. I would wake up in the night and see Chic Sale staring me in the face. Time was growing short and I made up my mind that George should not be faced with that atrocity. At six o'clock of the morning before George returned I gathered an armful of newspapers and taking a box of kitchen matches walked determinedly through the back yard. Upon reaching the eyesore I opened the door, put a match to the bundle of papers and threw the firebrand into Chic Sale. Walking hurriedly back to the house, I heard a roar and turned around. Vesuvius seemed to have erupted in our garden. The blaze was as high as the trees and was leaping out in all directions.

At this delightful moment the milkman drove in. He ran for the hose and played it on the new tool-house. James, the old colored caretaker, hurried down from his room and played another hose on adjacent trees. We worked feverishly and when the blaze was out I had some badly scorched locust trees and a tool-house with cracked windows. But Chic Sale had vanished. My mind was at ease and my heart was happy.

viii.

When George's plane came in he went directly to the Pentagon Building, but he promised me if he could get off in time we would go to Leesburg, which we did. It was a beautiful spring afternoon in early May. As we drove along the narrow, roller-coaster road, the honey-suckle along the fences filled the air with fragrance, the cows were heading toward the barns for their evening meal, while sheep grazed contentedly on the green slopes of the farmlands.

As we drove through our gates, a brilliant after-glow from the setting sun turned the windows of the house into flames of fire, the trees were silhouetted against the gaudy sky. Having just come from war-torn Europe, George gave a sigh of contentment, and then followed the happiest hours of the past three years.

He stopped the car, got out and walked around, taking in every detail. Finally he turned and said in a husky voice, "This is Home, a real home after forty-one years of wandering."

We sat on the lawn until nine o'clock while he told me the highlights of his trip.

On the drive back to Fort Myer he said, "You know, I do not see how you got that finished."

"It is not finished yet," I said, "the bills have not come in." Then I confessed: "Everything went over the estimates, George. All I ask is, when you look them over be easy on me. Remember your testimony before the

Investigating Committee of the Senate on the construction of camps.   It costs more to do things in a hurry."

"There isn't going to be any investigation of this job," he said laughingly.

ix.

The newspaper headlines now read: "Marshall Back from London Talks," "Roosevelt Backs Marshall in Message to Churchill," "U. S. Planning Vast Offensive," "Congressional Medal Given Famed Flyer at White House," "General Marshall and Doolittle Confer with Military Leaders of Southland."

As soon as his duties in Washington permitted, General Marshall left for an inspection trip and invited Field Marshal Sir John Dill to accompany him.   Concerning that trip I quote Sir John's letter on their return:

"BRITISH JOINT STAFF MISSION
OFFICES OF COMBINED CHIEFS OF STAFF
WASHINGTON

"May 2, 1942
"Dear Marshall:

"I want to thank you most sincerely for allowing me to accompany you on your visit to Fort Benning, Jacksonville and Fort Bragg.

"I cannot tell you how much I enjoyed myself and how deeply I was impressed by all I saw.   You must be very proud to command such a splendid body of officers and men, and it was quite clear to me how greatly everyone loved and respected you.

"The kindness with which I was treated wherever we went has greatly touched me and my heart goes out to the Army of the United States as never before.

"With my warm thanks,

"Yours ever,

"J. C. DILL"

And here is the War Department Bureau of Public Relations release:

"May 2, 1942

"GENERAL MARSHALL AND FIELD MARSHAL DILL END AIR TOUR OF ARMY CAMPS IN SOUTH

"General George C. Marshall, Chief of Staff of the Army, accompanied by Field Marshal Sir John Dill, several members of the British Staff, and Lt. General Lesley J. McNair, Commander of the Army Ground Forces, returned today from a rapid inspection trip made by plane to southern Army camps where they observed our modern Army carrying out its intensive combat training program.

"At Fort Benning, Georgia, where the great Infantry School is located, they saw Army officers and officer-candidates receiving instruction in the tactics and technique of the Infantry and other arms. They witnessed the firing of the 60mm mortar, 81mm mortar, 37mm gun, the Garand rifle, Browning automatic rifle, the running of the bayonet course, the throwing of grenades and the various activities of the Infantry School. They also saw the 2d Armored Division training in the most modern methods of mechanized warfare. At another training camp in the South, 30,000 soldiers passed in review before them and at this training area they inspected two divisions of great fame in the World War—the famous 1st Division and the 36th Division.

"At Fort Bragg, North Carolina, over 60,000 troops were inspected, including the 9th Infantry Division, Negro Engineer Units and other military activities of this large camp, which like Fort Benning and others is really a military city having all the installations necessary for a well-run civilian community."

x.

Saturday, May 31st, we left for West Point where General Marshall was to make the graduation speech. The high point of that speech was his declaration that "American troops are landing in England and will land in France." When he said "France" the whole Corps of Cadets let out a mighty roar. The Chief of Staff ended his address to the cadets with this pronouncement: "We are determined that before the sun sets on this terrible struggle, our flag will be recognized throughout the world as a symbol of freedom on the one hand and of overwhelming power on the other." That West Point speech was published from coast to coast and its import rang around the world.

The commentators said:

"The German High Command will, of course, study closely General Marshall's address for clues as to United Nations' strategy, but they will learn only two things—that the U. S. intends to throw its manpower into the struggle more rapidly and on a greater scale than previous announcements revealed, and that the American Air Forces are mushrooming at an amazing rate."

Also, in the light of later crushing victories on all fronts, it is interesting to recall the German attitude in the spring of 1942:

"The Germans are sneering at the stamina of American and British general officers, particularly belittling the physical resistance and training and intelligence of the average American field commander."

xi.

By June Britain and Russia had signed the 20-year

treaty and President Roosevelt and Molotov had reached an accord. Sir Archibald Wavell, Commander-in-Chief of India, was in Washington, also Lord Mountbatten of the Commandoes. George asked them to dine at our quarters with the Combined Chiefs of Staff. We were particularly interested in seeing Lord Mountbatten for he was one of the war's most glamorous figures. An amusing letter had come into the War Department from a Western woman who wrote that she was much concerned over the Lend-Lease to Britain and wanted to know what we were to get in return. She said she was putting in her bid right then for Lord Mountbatten.

Molly, her husband, Major James Winn, and little Jimmy had just arrived from Panama, and George told me at breakfast that he would like Molly to help me receive the guests and then for us to disappear as there were important secret affairs to be discussed at the dinner table.

When Lord Mountbatten arrived he measured up to the many reports we had received on his appearance and personality. Tall, with dark hair and a handsome face, he had the gracious manners of an English gentleman. He wore a white uniform with gold trappings and gave one the impression of a dare-devil spirit, combined with the courtesy of a Chesterfield.

Molly and I greeted him and during the rest of the cocktail period he was absorbed in a conversation with one of the Chiefs of Staff.

Major Winn, Major McCarthy (afterward Secretary of the General Staff), Molly and I then retired to the upstairs porch where our dinner was served. The next day I received a note from Lord Mountbatten making his apologies, saying that he thought my daughter and I would be at the dinner table and that he would have an opportunity to talk with us then, that he regretted exceedingly discussing military affairs during the short time we were present and hoped for another opportunity of seeing us. When George returned from his next trip to London he brought me two very lovely silver ash trays from Lord Mountbatten with further expressions of his regrets.

xii.

In July this report came from London:

"General Marshall May Soon Be Named Commander of All The United Nations' Military Forces."

The newspapers took it up and, "Marshall for the Job," "Marshall is the Man—Let George Do It," appeared in the headlines. General Marshall at the time was again in London.

Later a cartoon came out showing Admiral King and George sitting on either side of President Roosevelt, the table in front of them littered with numerous papers headed, "U-Boat Sinkings," "Planes for Britain," "Supplies for Russia," "Japs in New Guinea," "Japs in Aleutians," "Reinforcements for Auchinleck," "More Troops to Ireland, China, Panama Canal." The President is saying, "Wouldn't it be wonderful if we could narrow it all down to just a second front?" while on the wall in the corner hangs a blackboard inscribed: "Memoranda of Things to be Done on Home Front: Study nationwide gas rationing, Stop inflation, Tell people about Rubber, Get more steel, Find more manpower, *Find more everything.*"

xiii.

Molly with her husband and little Jimmy left us
shortly for Fire Island there to spend my son-in-law's
leave. In the fall, Major Winn being off on maneuvers, my
daughter came back to us and stayed until after Katherine
Tupper Winn, my namesake, was born in February. With
Kitty Winn there came to me the peace that passes all understanding.   George was away a great deal of the time on
long, hazardous flights across the waters. When I felt I
could not stand the waiting and suspense of the war any
longer, I would go up to the nursery and take my little
grand-daughter in my arms and, against all modern scien-
tific methods, rock her to sleep.   What she meant to me
during that time, I could never put into words. For the
first three months after Kitty's birth, Molly was not at
all well and I had the entire care of this darling baby. In
the spring when Molly joined her husband in Florida, she
said, "I'm taking with me a very spoiled child."

xiv.

In August Queen Wilhelmina of the Netherlands
visited Washington and invitations went out for a command dinner at the Embassy.   This recalled a previous
occasion on which General Marshall had indirect dealings
with the Queen of Holland: On a certain Saturday afternoon at Leesburg he was called out of the top of an apple
tree to answer the telephone.   He loved pruning and had
just climbed high to reach a dead limb he had long wanted
to saw off.   The War Department was calling—a German raider was loose in the Caribbean, threatening the
great oil refineries on the Dutch Islands of Aruba and

Curacao which produced approximately sixty per cent of our petroleum. General Marshall had long feared an attack on these refineries because, obviously, the enemy knew the crippling effect of such an attack. He had sought permission to install coastal guns and locate planes on the islands to protect the refineries against submarine bombardment, but there had been delay after delay, and now a crisis threatened.

He called the President at Hyde Park, told him of the crucial situation and asked him to radio the Queen at once, urging her to agree to the installation of some defenses. Then, laden with saw and ropes, he laboriously climbed back up the apple tree.

No sooner had he reached the top, however, than the telephone rang again. Again he climbed down. This time the President wanted more information. George dictated a radiogram to be sent overseas and came back to the apple tree once more. By now he was getting pretty stiff, as climbing trees at the age of sixty-two is rather strenuous. He was not going to be defeated, however, and crawled up once more. Again no sooner was he settled in the gnarled fork with saw in hand than the 'phone again rang. "General Marshall, War Department calling."

He sat there silently for a moment, then said "Call the car, I am leaving for Washington."

Not until three months later was permission finally secured to install the defenses. Guns were landed on the islands on a certain morning and that evening, before they could be set up, a German submarine opened fire on the refineries. Fortunately, George had sent in planes without waiting for approval and they frightened off the sub. That dead, half sawed off limb hung on the apple tree until the following spring.

XV.

About this time General Marshall became alarmed at the percentage of older men being drafted into the Army. On inspections he had found the hospitals filled with them and the training program greatly hampered. He knew that, however willing, men beyond a certain age had not the resistance or stamina for this lightning warfare. The combat troops must be younger men for the toughest war in history—now the average age of men in the combat divisions was far too high.

On a recent visit to Fort Bragg he had been shocked to find so many "old men" stationed there. He apologized for using that term to describe men of 35 to 40, but as they were not suitable for combat service, they were, therefore, "too old" for the Army. Consequently he went before the Military Affairs Committees of the House and Senate to request our Congress to lower the draft age to 18. A bill to this effect went before the House and Senate, and, naturally, it was a most unpopular bill; there were still many who hid behind the axiomatical line in the song, "I did not raise my boy to be a soldier." And of course, the obstructionists, the demagogues, isolationists and others climbed on the band wagon. An amendment was tacked onto the bill by Senator W. Lee O'Daniels of Texas, better known as "Pass the Biscuits Pappy." The Pappy amendment provided that no boy drafted at 18 or 19 should be sent to fight overseas until he had had one year's training in the United States.

TIME magazine came out with an article headlined, "God Help General Marshall." George argued, "Such a limitation would impose an almost impossible administrative problem on the War Department. There is a marked difference between the training of an individual soldier and the training of a complicated machine, like a division. . . To get back to the training of an individual soldier, the length of his training before he can be fitted into an experienced tactical unit varies according to the type of unit and the duties for which he is trained. For one illustration a man who had been a truck driver in civil life would not need to spend a year in the Army learning how to drive a truck. He would be ready for overseas truck driving after three months or so of basic training. Under the O'Daniel amendment, he would have to stick around another nine months in this country, wasting his time and patience and the taxpayers' money, and holding up the Allied war effort to the extent of one truck driver lacking where most needed. Multiply this example by several hundred thousand, and you get a frightening picture of an Army in a straight-jacket trying to fight a war. This rigidity and partial paralysis would be especially serious in the Air Forces' ground and mechanic services, which can be thoroughly trained in much less than a year's time."

The bill was finally passed after an exhausting fight and days of wearing testimony; and here I find a laconic note written in longhand by the President:

"THE WHITE HOUSE, WASHINGTON

"Dear George:

"You win again.

"F. D. R."

xvi.

During the previous summer Allen, my youngest child, had been putting his house in order, arranging his affairs for his wife and little son, so that he might enlist. He was now in the Army, another Private Brown, but this private was in the Armored Force. My brother had gone back in his old National Guard division at the outbreak of hostilities in Europe; his daughter left in her junior year at college and enlisted in the 2nd WAAC training camp; his son, seventeen, left college to enlist in the Navy. Every member of our family of fighting age was now in the armed services; and all, as soon as eligible, got overseas to a fighting front.

xvii.

George had arranged to take a day off and go down the Potomac to shoot ducks on the opening day of the season. His equipment was laid out in his room and we had retired early as he was to leave at five the next morning. At eleven that night the War Department telephone rang. This 'phone, beside George's bed, was equipped with what is known as a scrambler—a device by which the parties telephoning can hear each other plainly but to anyone tapping the wires or trying to listen in there is merely a confused jumble of sounds. After he finished a long conversation, I got up and went into his room, saying, "I hope that call doesn't interfere with your shooting."

He answered, "Yes, I am afraid it does. I will not be able to go."

"But you must go," I insisted. "You do not realize how tired you are. You must get some relaxation. Why can't you go?"

"This matter is very important," he said. "I can't go."

"Oh! Every little thing is important but you!" And I went out, shutting the door rather firmly.

George was much amused, for that conversation concerned a radio from our diplomatic representative, Mr. Murphy, in Algiers, stating that the French General Giraud had just been notified of the date for our landing in Africa and had demanded a delay of three weeks, asserting that otherwise a great catastrophe would result. The greatest armada in history was then concentrating 600 miles west of Gibraltar, and that was the little thing that I had thought unimportant.

A box for a night football game to be held at the Washington ball park, November 8, had been sent to General Marshall, and I was anxious for him to go, but had no idea that my hopes were balanced on top of a volcano that might erupt at any moment. He merely said that he could not be out of touch with his office, so I asked General and Mrs. Arnold to accompany me.

The ball park was packed with 25,000 eager football fans. The floodlights illumined the field as bright as day; powerful searchlights played on the surrounding country.

As General Arnold came to the box the huge crowd sent up a resounding cheer and the kick-off followed immediately. I kept thinking of George, if only he could have come, for it was a thrilling sight. As the game progressed and the enthusiasm of the spectators grew more tense, there came, in the middle of a play, a voice from the loud-speaker: "Stop the game! Important announcement!" The players stopped in their tracks, astounded; the crowd, already keyed up to a high pitch, became breathlessly silent.

Then came the announcement: "The President of the United States of America announces the successful landing on the African Coast of an American Expeditionary Force.   This is our Second Front."

Like the waves of the ocean, the cheers of the people rose and fell, then rose again in a long-sustained emotional cry.   The football players turned somersaults and handsprings down the center of the field; the crowd simply went wild, for this was the heartening news America, agonized by one defeat after another, had been waiting to hear.   We had struck back.

An American commander had set sail with an armada of 850 war ships and transports and had successfully landed on another continent, seizing 1,500 miles of historic shore.

In eleven months plus one day after Pearl Harbor this military miracle had been performed.

Since Hitler first went into action, one after another of the nations on the Continent of Europe had collapsed; even the British had saved themselves only by the most consummate heroism; Russia was still in a death grip with the enemy; the Japs had smashed us at Pearl Harbor, Wake, and Guam, and finally conquered us on Bataan and Corregidor.   In this, the darkest year of our history, it had seemed that the determination and bold spirit of adventure which had made America great had vanished completely; but now America had struck back in an amazing and imaginative way. It had wrested the offensive from the enemy and started the march toward ultimate victory.

President Roosevelt, in an unprecedented White House Service, led the nation in prayer for Divine strength and guidance on this first wartime Thanksgiving in twenty-five years.   The first hymn sung was, "Onward Christian Soldiers," the second verse of which reads; "At the sign of triumph, Satan's host doth flee; On then, Christian Soldiers, On to Victory."

Chapter V

THE SUCCESSFUL LANDING of the United States Army in Africa released the American people from a state of uncertainty and dread and lifted them into an ecstasy of optimism—to such an extent that my husband was greatly worried. The home front had been keyed up to a state of production that confounded our enemies and he feared a let-down would be the natural reaction to our first success on the Western Front. This would have been fatal.

Often, in those days, you would hear people say, on the street and in public places, "It took the Yanks to do it," "We will have the war won by spring," and so forth. To combat this over-confidence, posters were printed and sent to all production centers. In letters a half-a-foot high the posters informed the workers:

> "In all our operations, whether in Africa, out of England, in Asia, or the Pacific, the supply of the men who are doing the fighting is a vital factor. This is your responsibility and we have not a single minute to lose. We must not fail the men who are doing the fighting.
>
> "G. C. Marshall,
> Chief of Staff."

Also there was much indiscreet talking by family and friends of those in the Service. They did not realize the danger to which they were exposing those whom they would most wish to protect. To curb this loose talk a pamphlet was published, on the cover of which was printed:

"A PERSONAL MESSAGE TO THE MOTHERS, WIVES, FATHERS, BROTHERS, FRIENDS OF SERVICE MEN.

"The success of the war will not be assured until men and women at home realize the full extent of their responsibility for protecting our soldiers on the fighting front.
"General G. C. Marshall, Chief of Staff,

"U. S. Army."
"I ask every American who receives this booklet to read every word of it.
"Admiral Ernest J. King, United States Navy, Commander of the Fleet and Chief of Naval Operations."

The chapter heads were: "Careless Remarks Tell the Enemy Plenty," "You Don't Have to Know a Big Secret to Give a Big Secret Away," "Certain few words will tell you what type of information our enemy is especially anxious to get hold of: Where are our soldiers? Where are our men going? When will that ship sail? How many troop ships, planes, and so forth? What kind of duty are they doing?"

General Marshall's words of caution were: "We Americans have always been used to talking without looking over our shoulders to see who is listening. Learning to stop and think before we talk is going to be quite a job for us. The lives and success of the men in the services are dependent on you to think before you speak."

This pamphlet was given wide circulation throughout the country, but still, in spite of this, there was much indiscreet talking. It was difficult indeed for our peace-loving nation so used to freedom of speech, to guard its tongue.

ii.

On December 31st, 1942, Secretary of War Stimson gave the following statement to the press:

"The Army moves into the New Year confident and sure of its mission, backed by a country that today is the best equipped for war the world has ever seen. The men of our Army, now over five million strong, one million overseas, are being trained with more solicitous care for their health and welfare than those of any Army in history. As the citizen who is head of the department to which the Army belongs, I am proud of the magnificent work which has been done by the Chief of Staff, General George C. Marshall."

This tribute by the Secretary of War came to my husband on his 62nd birthday. I presented him with a set of garden tools.

iii.

The 1st of January found my husband packing once more for a secret conference—the historic Casablanca Conference at which the Prime Minister of England, the President of the United States, the French leaders General Henri H. Giraud and General Charles de Gaulle met in Africa. The occasion presented to the Axis a grim future, for at Casablanca it was decided nothing short of unconditional surrender for Germany, Japan, and Italy would be accepted. This was so bold and visionary that it seemed like wishful thinking. I remember that when I first read those words—Unconditional Surrender—I felt we were hitching our wagon to a star—an invisible star at that.

In George's first letter, written enroute, he enclosed a list of the wives of the various English, Chinese and Latin-American representatives in Washington whom he wished me to entertain while he was away. So I had my hands full arranging these affairs.

In the same letter he mentioned the orderly assigned to him during his stay in Africa came from the first company he had ever commanded in the Philippines. There was little he could tell me, he said, because of the strict censorship.

Dr. Douglas Freeman, author of "Lee's Lieutenants," published an article at this time, entitled: "General Lee and General Marshall." It said, in part:

> "At this stage of the war, two items of General Lee's equipment as a commander that are most important in our leadership were his ability to guess well, and his sound judgment. I believe General George Marshall, Army Chief of Staff, is showing exactly the same thorough, detached judgment General Lee showed. The nation can afford to gamble on the gamble General Marshall is taking because behind the gamble is great intellect, sound judgment, and magnificent character."

I sent this article in my next letter to George, as General Lee was one of the two men he admired most in our history, the other being Benjamin Franklin. General Lee he esteemed for his character and ability as a soldier, Benjamin Franklin for his common sense and understanding of human nature.

Before George left for the Casablanca Conference,

Senator Robert Reynolds of North Carolina, Chairman of the Military Affairs Committee, prepared a bill creating the rank of Field Marshal. The President had approved the bill, but my husband let it be known in no uncertain terms that he did not think the rank was necessary and that he had no intention of sponsoring a measure which would give him higher rank than Washington, Lee, Grant, and Pershing. His sole aspiration was to fill his present rank —a four-star general—in a manner that would make him worthy of such company. "Besides," he added, "Marshal Marshall sounds very silly to me."

A typical headline of that time: "Marshall Balks at Elevation to Field Marshal."

Eric Severeid broadcast:

> "The organization, training, and equipment of this great Force of Freedom, with the fact that it is the healthiest, best clothed, best fed, and best paid army in the world is not the result of chance. It stands as a monumental tribute to the genius, indomitable energy, almost superhuman foresight, and leadership of George Marshall. This soldier needs no Field Marshal's baton to make him great and no additional medal to add to the cluster that now marks his distinguished service. I am sure that his one and only ambition in the end is to have the American people say, in the language of the Lord in the parable of the Talents according to Saint Matthew, 'Well done, thou good and faithful servant.'"

On the cover of one of the magazines appeared a particularly grim picture of General Marshall; under it the cut line: "Army Marshall. No other General ever faced the problem of operations on six fronts. . ."

iv.

The day before my husband's plane arrived from

Africa, his orderly and I had washed "Fleet," George's dog. Fleet was a Dalmatian which at the tender age of three months had been given to George by Edward Stettinius. He was beautiful to look at but had not been blessed with a great deal of sense. Frankly, he was beautiful but dumb. However, he loved his master with a devotion and adoration so complete that George's heart was touched.

Fleet, in fact, was the one stupid thing in which I have ever known him to take delight. He always went with George on his rides and his lack of courage amused my husband greatly. He was as bold as a lion where a squirrel was concerned but when another dog appeared he would rush back to his master's side and howl for protection.

Whenever George was away, Fleet would await his return with a melancholy mien. If the absence were prolonged, Fleet would wander away looking for him, but could never find his way home. The Memorial Bridge is located just below Arlington Cemetery and on occasion Fleet even crossed the bridge in his search for his master and had to be sought throughout Washington. His tag read: "Fleet—General Marshall," followed by our telephone number. Every time he was lost I would be called up, day or night, by the person who had found him. The finder would keep him long enough to have a picture taken with the Marshall dog, and the next morning the papers would show Fleet in the arms of some man or woman, looking as though he had lost his last friend. The caption seldom varied: "Chief of Staff's Dog Found by Mr. or Mrs. So-and-So." No society belle ever appeared in the paper more often than Fleet.

The night before George was expected home, after

Fleet's bath I shut him up in the cellar. But his moans and yelps so disturbed the cook she could not sleep and finally she put him out doors for the night.

At six o'clock on the morning of George's arrival, the telephone rang. Some man in Washington had found General Marshall's dog. The man said he was a watchman for one of the Navy buildings and that he had kept the dog all night. I thanked him for his kindness and said I would send for Fleet and would be glad to reimburse him for his trouble. The man said, "Well, I would like you to write a letter to the Navy Department recommending me for a better job." I explained why that would be impossible—I had never seen him and did not know any of his qualifications. The man was most insistent and claimed he had had a hard time catching Fleet. Every time I said it would be impossible, he would repeat, "Well, I caught your dog, didn't I?" Finally I became annoyed, as the man was growing impertinent. "Very well," I agreed, "I will write you a note." I sent post haste for Fleet and did not fail to give the chauffeur a note, on War Department paper, for the man. The note read:

"To Whom It May Concern in the United States Navy:
"The bearer of this note is a good dog-catcher.
"Katherine T. Marshall (Mrs. George C.)"

We finally had to send Fleet to our Leesburg home to save the family bank account which was steadily being depleted by payments of rewards.

But the end was not yet.

At Leesburg he took to killing the neighbors' chickens. Nothing could stop him, and finally when a colored man presented a bill for so many pounds of chickens which Fleet had done away with in one day, we decided to send him to Front Royal to join the Army.

Here he disgraced the name of Marshall completely and irrevocably. He turned out to be the worst coward in the K-9 Army. The Front Royal Training School kept him only to show other dogs what an army dog should not be. In a newsreel that George and I saw of the K-9 School, Fleet made his appearance as the dunce of the school. We hung our heads in shame. As the old colored woman said, "Mortification set in."

v.

On February 10th, George appeared before the House Military Affairs Committee and testified at great length on the Army's needs for increased manpower. Congressmen were pledged to absolute secrecy on all of the testimony involving military strategy or operations. George was being fought in this measure by what was known as "The Farm Bloc," working at the time to prevent young men from being taken from agriculture to fill the ranks of the armed services. The Farm Bloc had some powerful adherents and it was a bitter, exhausting fight. I recall my husband coming home after testifying without notes for six hours and saying, "I get over one mountain and another rises up and stares me in the face."

A cartoon at this time pictures General Marshall running down a hallway lined with doors, the dust rising behind him, the perspiration pouring down his face. One door is marked "House Appropriations Committee;" others are marked, "Senate Military Affairs Committee," "House Military Affairs Committee," "Senate Agriculture Committee," "House Agriculture Committee. . ." General Marshall is saying, "And I thought they only wanted one second front."

Columnists frequently came to his rescue and at this time it was Walter Lippman:

"A few days ago, after General Marshall had laboriously explained to one committee why the Army wants the army it has decided it needs, another committee concerned with agriculture said it wished to hear General Marshall explain why the army must be as large as he says it must be."

vi.

This endless grilling on the manpower bill, following the Casablanca Conference, with its various and vital discussions concerning the conduct of the war in Europe, made even my husband realize he must have some rest.

We left for Miami Beach early in March. For one week he was to drop out of the picture. He flew from Bolling Field as the Chief of Staff and stepped out of the plane at Miami as a rather tired-looking business man wearing dark glasses. The greatest secrecy was observed and a private car whisked us to a house facing the sea far down Miami Beach.

The first evening Sergeant Aguirre, George's orderly, placed two beach-chairs on the seawall about fifteen feet in front of our cottage where we could sit in the moonlight and drink in the cool salt air. George closed his eyes and lay there without speaking. Presently a Coast Guard appeared and said, "You are not allowed on the beach after seven o'clock. You will have to go inside." George, forgetting he was in civilian clothes, replied, "I think it will be all right," and closed his eyes again. I relaxed in a comfortable position and we lay there contentedly.

I was soon aroused by the tramping of feet. George still had his eyes closed. I saw coming toward us a military formation led by an individual in Naval garb, so huge he looked like a floating balloon. He stopped at George's chair and yelled, "Halt." General Marshall rose to a sitting position and before he could speak, this large character in uniform let loose a tirade so violent that his whole body quivered like a bowl of clabber. He told us in no uncertain terms what he had in mind to do with us. Where did we come from? Didn't we know there was a war on?

George quietly collected our pillows and without saying a word started toward the cottage. The Naval file, evidently desiring to make a great showing before his men and, I suppose, being annoyed by George's silence, followed us repeating the same phrase over and over again: "Don't you know there is a war on?"

When we reached the house, George turned around and in the light from the door he was outlined clearly. "That is enough," he said. "What is the reason for this ridiculous display? Does it take you and a patrol of six men to tell me we are at war?" They recognized the Chief of Staff. The balloon collapsed. George opened the door and walked inside.

The next morning we started walking around to see the sights of Miami Beach. My husband was dressed in civilian clothes, with his fishing hat pulled down over his eyes, but had not put on his dark glasses. A jeep came by. The two soldiers in the front seat turned, looked back, then slamming on the brakes, drew up to the curb. "Aren't you General Marshall?" George answered, "Yes, I am; but you haven't seen me." "Yes, Sir." They saluted. "We haven't seen nothing," and they drove on.

My husband then put on his dark glasses and consented to go into a shop with me. I found some beach shoes I liked and when I paid the clerk he took the bill to the cashier and said something to her in a low voice. The cashier looked in our direction and called the manager. The manager came, strolled by leisurely, and taking a good look at General Marshall greeted him by name in a loud voice. Then Bedlam broke loose. One lady in a red hat, with an ornament in the front that my husband said was an apple corer, was still hanging on our taxi door as it rescued us from the crowd.

After that first day's experience we took our swim early in the morning and our sea air from the balcony of our bedroom. "This looks like it is going to be a fine rest for you," I said to George. "Your Dr. Jekyll and Mr. Hyde disguise is certainly working beautifully!" Before the end of the week we flew back to Washington.

vii.

The rumors now grew more persistent that General Marshall was to be named Commander-in-Chief of the Allied Forces in the next invasion.

Press comments: "It is Believed General Marshall, Chief of Staff, Will Take Over Active Direction of the War in European Theater. . ." "There Are Persistent Rumors that General George Marshall Soon Will Release His Post as Army Chief of Staff to Become Commander-in-Chief of Allied Forces in Europe. . ."

Of course I read these comments and editorials and was determined not to be caught napping. George had said nothing and I asked him no questions, but I bought a second-hand trailer and began moving necessary things to Leesburg surreptitiously.

But when the end of March came, General Marshall was still fighting for his manpower bill and the 78th Congress was still investigating. The Army now had over 5,000,000 men and General Marshall sought authority to increase it to 8,200,000. He was testifying day after day, week after week, before Special Committees. Here are some of the points excerpted from his testimony:

> "Emergency manpower shortage cannot be met overnight. . . The 1944 army must be trained in 1943. . . Total war requires total mobilization of resources. This is not being done. . . Proposed cut in the army requires cut in ground forces, abandonment of strategy. . . Agriculture, I realize, presents the most difficult and critical manpower problem, but the Army is the last, and not the first place to look for a solution . . ."

At the time of the struggle for manpower at home, the Army Commanders overseas were suffering from what General Marshall called "Localitis."

"This malady is not caused by global warfare," he said, "but is made more conspicuous because of it. Each theater is demanding more and more men, more and more materiel."

Some newspapers were espousing the cause of their favorite theaters, demanding why more was not being done. General Marshall explained: "Knowing why more cannot be done, would be quite helpful to the enemy. It behooves us, therefore, to remain calm in the face of these protests. Though undoubtedly sincere, they are aggravated by the pangs of 'localitis.'"

The war at this time seemed to me a great mosaic; each piece must be fitted in carefully. If you built up too generously in one direction, there would not be enough pieces to fill some other place. General Marshall was like an artist who must keep the finished picture always before his mind's eye—his vision must remain clear—his objective the defeat of Germany, Italy, and Japan, in the shortest possible time and with the least possible loss of lives.

viii.

Our lives at this time were cut-and-dried. We were up at 6:30 and in bed by 9:00. My husband recited to me endless facts and figures; and during the long succession of daylight hours I attended to such war duties as fell to my share. When I got surfeited I would drive down to Leesburg and pull weeds. There are always weeds to pull and in this way you can work off a great deal of pent-up feelings. To catch hold of a luscious weed and jerk it until it comes out of the ground, roots and all, gives one a very satisfied feeling of accomplishment. As I looked at the piles of uprooted weeds dying in the sun, where they no longer could suck the life of the seedlings struggling for air, I wished that the evils of the human race could be dealt with as satisfactorily. But man is too complex to obliterate his frailties so easily. And the evil he does lives after him.

That spring we were invited to the White House for a small dinner in honor of Anthony Eden, British Foreign Minister. Sitting between Mr. Eden and Sir John Dill, I was much interested in their discussions of the African campaign. Anthony Eden was not quite so tall as I had pictured him. He had clear-cut, chiseled features and was immaculately dressed.

This dinner was quite a treat for me as I had not

been to any kind of social affair for months; but for George the occasion was not one of unalloyed pleasure. On our way home I asked him why his uniform breast-pocket was bulging, and he pulled out eight place-cards, on the back of each of which was a personal request made by one of the guests. Just as a matter of curiosity he kept a record of the correspondence involved in complying with the requests made at that one dinner. They required thirty-two letters and several radios to clear up the lot. So you can well see why he avoided social functions during those pressing years of the war.

The day after the dinner, George left with Mr. Eden and Sir John for a quick survey of the military preparations in the Southeast. In a day and a half they saw about 250,000 troops in training. Mr. Eden expressed himself as greatly impressed by the training and the magnificent quality of the personnel.

ix.

While General Marshall was away on this trip one of the first seemingly authentic messages from any of our war prisoners in the Philippines came in to the War Department. Picked up on April 5, 1943 by a short-wave radio owned by Bob McConkey of Sioux Falls, South Dakota, the message read:

> "I am well, safe, and happy. Do not worry about me. Will write soon and it may be some time before you get the letter. Please send me monthly, chocolate bars, peanut brittle, hard candy, cheese, hard bread or crackers, soluble coffee, fruit cake, jam. All packed in tin. Take care of yourself for me, the separation from you is the hardest thing of all.

Watch over our children, and regards to our friends. Please write or radio if you can. All my love. Please answer soon. Your loving husband,

(Colonel) Charles L. Steel."

We had known Colonel Steel well at Fort Benning; George had often gone wild turkey shooting with him. This radio message seemed like a voice from the dead. In the fall of 1945, emaciated and ill, he was released from a prisoner of war camp in Manchuria.

x.

In May George left for Africa on six hours notice — 2 a. m. to 8 a. m. He accompanied Prime Minister Churchill who had just finished a good-will visit to this country during which he attended conferences in Washington with the President and the Chiefs of Staff.

George was to represent the U. S. Chiefs of Staff at a meeting in Algiers with the Prime Minister and our Allied Commanders in the Mediterranean — Eisenhower, Montgomery, Cunningham, Tedder and Alexander. Anthony Eden came from London to join them.

While George was away I went to New York to christen the troop ship *General Alexander E. Anderson*. I remained for a few days with my sister. The first night we were caught in a blackout while walking along Fifth Avenue near 39th Street. Sirens began to shriek and in three minutes the entire Avenue was as dark as Egypt's night, all traffic at a standstill. My sister and I, with three strangers, pressed into a doorway of one of the shops.

The Easter before, I had gone to Atlantic City for

a week's rest and there, as along the entire coast, each evening all was in darkness. The long boardwalk presented a dismal sight without its gay crowd and brilliantly lighted piers extending out into the ocean. All shop windows were blacked out and the hotels facing the ocean had black shades drawn over their windows.

New York that night in May looked like a ghost city with huge towering buildings rising skywards like mammoth tombstones; they were indeed sentinels of death, for at the time, with the German submarine warfare at its height, 700,000 tons of shipping had been sunk in a single month. The Atlantic Coast from New England to Florida had become a graveyard of ships.

The siren shrieking in our ears like the wail of banshees, my sister and I stood huddled in that doorway on Fifth Avenue in this the largest and gayest city in the world, similar groups all around us in the same situation. I turned to my sister and said: "This experience tonight brings closer than could possibly have been imagined the almost unbelievable condition into which the world has sunken. What has become of the land of the free and the home of the brave? Look at us, cowering here like thieves and pickpockets while waiting to see what Adolf Hitler and his gangsters choose to do to us."

The will of the Axis powers, however, was not to prevail and this was clearly shown by the Chief of Staff's report to the President on General Marshall's return from North Africa. So heartening was the report that Senator Robert Reynolds asked that it be printed in the Appendix of the Congressional Record. I quote from that Record:

"The new American Army now is proving itself in action on every count. Its infantry, artillery, and armored forces showed themselves superior in Africa to the best the Germans possessed. Its leadership outsmarted Hitler's best generals, its air forces now are crushing through with the truth of the wisdom of the concept of daylight precision-bombing as the key to successful use of the bomber as an offensive weapon. American artillery weapons stood up with the best, American fighter planes, which were much criticized early in the war, ran up a score of better than two to one against the Germans. American bombers all along have been in a class by themselves."

Prime Minister Churchill paid a glowing tribute before the House of Commons on his return from America and the North African conference: "The United States is the most powerful community in the world." He called President Roosevelt "illustrious." "Congress," he said, "is an august assembly," and he referred to General Marshall, who had accompanied him to Algiers, as "a man of singular eminence of mind and character."

xi.

In June of that year George and I received an invitation to the graduation exercises of the 39th Class of the Officer Candidate School, Armored Force, Fort Knox, Kentucky. Among the names of the graduating class was that of Allen T. Brown. Allen was now to graduate as a Second Lieutenant.

He had enjoyed many amusing experiences at Fort Knox where no one suspected his relationship to the Chief of Staff. During his basic training, when he had been made a temporary corporal, his old Army Sergeant had taken quite a fancy to him and asked that they bunk together. This gave Allen more privacy and later hours in which to study. The Sergeant greatly admired George and had a large picture of him pinned on the wall over his bunk.   Allen, whenever he wanted to start the Sergeant fuming, would refer to his "Pin-Up Girl." The Sergeant would then tell tales of his intimate knowledge of the Chief of Staff, and like many old Army men he had a vivid imagination.   Allen said he learned more about his own family than he would care to repeat!

The day he graduated the papers got hold of the facts concerning Corporal Brown's family and when he returned to his bunk the Sergeant was waiting for him. He had blood in his eye as Allen sauntered in.

His first words were, "Brown, I ought to break your neck.   For eight months you have made a fool of me. Suppose I hadn't liked the Chief of Staff, where would I be?"

"Exactly where you are now," Allen said. "What kind of a fellow do you think I am?"

The Sergeant came over and put his arms around Allen's shoulder, "I tell you, Brown, I think you are a great buddy."

xii.

At this time General Henri Giraud came to Washington with an urgent requirement for American equipment to arm 300,000 French soldiers in Africa. Congress had taken a recess and gone home for two of the hottest months ever known in Washington. In the previous three and a half years they had been out of session only 23 days.

The heat was so intense that George felt he would like to get General Giraud out of the city if only for a day, and decided to entertain him at Dodona Manor in Leesburg.   The house there was equipped only in the most meagre fashion — merely for us to spend weekends, so when my husband asked me if it were possible to have General Giraud there as a guest I started making a list of the necessities for an exceedingly simple official dinner—only our family, General Giraud, and his military aide were to be present. Nevertheless, the day before the dinner, July the 11th, a whole truck load of china, silver, linen, rugs and servants had to be transferred from Fort Myer. By evening things were in order.

Admiral Darlan had been assassinated in Africa not so long before this and it was imperative that no mishap in this country should befall the Commander of the French Forces. The morning of the Giraud dinner, Secret Service men arrived, and they reminded me of our garden party at Fort Myer, only instead of one G-man in a torn green sweater there were Secret Service men seemingly peering from every corner and shrub.

When the Giraud car, led by motorcycles, drove in George and I greeted the General on the front portico. A tall, distinguished looking soldier with finely chiseled features, he gave a sigh of real relief when we led him to the generous cool shade of a great oak on the side lawn and gave him an iced drink. He spoke little English so his Aide served as interpreter. We were most interested in his account of his dramatic escapes from a German prison. Twice he had eluded the Germans. I asked him what part his wife had played in these escapes and he answered, "Every part. It would have been impossible without her." For months she had smuggled fine wire concealed in pounds of butter she sent to him. This wire, with twine from packages sent to him—many of them from American friends, ("You make good twine in America," he said)—formed the rope by which he had let himself out of prison. It had taken months of cunning and toil to outwit the Germans. When he was once outside, his wife through the Underground had provided his disguise and passport. He had stayed in Germany for many weeks before he had dared approach the border, but had finally escaped into Switzerland. Everything he possessed had been confiscated by the German forces in France.

General Giraud spoke with deep affection of his family, especially his daughter and her three little children, who were then in Africa.

Just after his return from this trip we heard that his daughter and the three children had been taken as hostages by the retreating Rommel forces and placed in a German concentration camp. Later, my husband had word that the daughter had died there, but nothing was known of the whereabouts of the grandchildren. On his return to Africa the General, himself, escaped assassination by a hair's breadth, being painfully though not fatally wounded.

xiii.

In the August issue of "Vital Speeches" the leading article was a speech George had made June 21st before the Conference of Governors, Columbus, Ohio, in which he had said in part:

> "The pattern for victory is clear. If we had set the stage we could not provide a more sharply defined picture than that offered by the battle of Tunisia. There we had: A perfect example of coordinated leadership for Allied action. An assemblage of overwhelming military power, air, land, and sea. The explosive effect of the skillful application of that power."

Press comment:

"Every citizen should read General Marshall's report on the war made to the Conference of Governors last night. He does not think in political terms, the Chief of Staff gives the military low-down straight and unadulterated. If Americans understand this report, we shall know where we are in the war, what has been accomplished and what remains to be done, and what dangers are ahead."

xiv.

Early in August my youngest son, Allen, was about to leave for Africa as a tank officer replacement in the 1st Armored Division. He and Madge, his wife, arrived from Fire Island where they had spent Allen's leave. My sister had come from New York and Molly, her husband, Major Winn, and the two babies were with us. Clifton had come up from Richmond where he was on duty at Antiaircraft Artillery headquarters.

We had a gay party, that Sunday at Leesburg. As George and I came out on the lawn, the boys were stretched full length on the grass and a lively discussion was going on, Jim, a Regular Army officer, and Clifton being a bit down in the mouth that Allen, the youngest and last in the service, was to be the first to get to the front. As we approached them Allen was saying, "Why shouldn't I go over first? I'm a tanker, and the tanks lead the fight."

Clifton broke in with, "Where would the tanks be without the Antiaircraft?"

Jim came back with, "Who clears the way for the tanks?—the Field Artillery."

Molly and Madge were coming to the support of their respective husbands and there was a babble of voices and much laughter and slapping on the back as each one thought he had gotten the better of the others.

George sat down and listened to the din. He was much amused. Finally they appealed to him, "What do you say?"

George answered, "Of course I am only a lowly foot soldier. I do not belong in such august company as that of the Artillery, Antiaircraft, and Tanks, but I would say—when the fighting is at its fiercest, it is invariably the Infantry that carries the ball over for the touchdown." A roar of laughter greeted this remark and we went in to our Sunday dinner in high spirits.

For that dinner I had provided all of the things Allen liked most. The meal was topped off by a bottle of fine Champagne which had been given to my husband in Africa. Originally it had been taken from the French by the Germans, then captured from the Germans by the British, and finally presented to the Chief of Staff of the American Army. It was of an excellent vintage year and George made a truly wonderful toast for Allen's success.

After dinner we had quite a ceremony. In the field below the house I had dug up an old horseshoe, a rather small one that had probably been on the hoof of some ante-bellum lady's riding mare. We gathered in front of the garage while Allen hung up the horseshoe, and we drank to his health once again. I recall that at first he hung the shoe with the points down. A protest went up—his luck would run out—so it was taken down and while Madge held it in place Allen nailed it with the points up. The next morning he flew off for England on his way to the front.

XV.

In that same month of August General Marshall left for the Quebec Conference. It was another conference between President Roosevelt and the Prime Minister of England, to consider Anglo-American military plans.

Mrs. Churchill and her daughter Mary, who was in the Antiaircraft Artillery, accompanied the Prime Minister on this trip. One evening George, noticing Mary at dinner with several officers, paused to chide her for passing him in the lobby of the hotel without saluting. He had known her in England. After he was seated at his table she tore off a piece of the menu and wrote on the back: "Secret. For General Marshall. Sir: It is incorrect for subalterns to salute even Generals with no hat on," and sent it over to him.

George wrote on it: "Whose hat? G. C. M."

She returned this with: "Both hats, Sir. M."

After the unconditional surrender meeting in Casablanca during the previous January, Anglo-American forces under General Eisenhower had swept the Axis from North Africa and after a 38-day campaign had conquered Sicily. The Quebec meeting was to decide upon the next Allied moves. Anthony Eden was present at this conference and he was personally to carry the Declaration of Quebec to Moscow and lay it before his friend Joseph Stalin.

One of the secret decisions reached at the Quebec Conference was that General Marshall should lead the invasion of Europe as Supreme Commander of the Allied Forces, land, sea, and air. General Eisenhower, after his superb leadership in the Mediterranean theater, was to take over as Chief of Staff in this country.

On the President's return from Quebec he announced the continuation of General Marshall as Chief of Staff, as the routine four-year term had expired on September the 1st and the President wished him to carry on until he left for London to assume his new role. This announcement was greeted by the press as follows:

"General Marshall's four-year term as Chief of Staff of the United States Army expired this week but he is not to turn the post over to another. He is, we are happy to report, to continue on as our top man of the Army for an indefinite period, which is as it should be. General Marshall has done and is doing a magnificent job. . . . He is a great soldier, and we salute him for a grateful people."

Earl Godwin, the Blue Network, said, August 31st:

"President Roosevelt today announced at his press conference that General Marshall's term of office as Chief of Staff is at an end today, but of course extends General Marshall's term of duty. This, I think, is the first time such an extension has occurred in war time for a Chief of Staff. MacArthur was the only other Chief of Staff to be extended at all. . . . Just as this country was fortunate to have . . . George Washington and Mad Anthony Wayne in their military jobs, so is this generation of Americans fortunate to have George C. Marshall as a General of the Army and Chief of Staff right now. Now, there is a general of great military ability who can envision and create a vast military movement and explain it so simply that even the dumbest radio commentator takes it in in a single draught. You know, that is a sign of greatness and power."

Shortly after this broadcast the Quebec decision concerning the Supreme Commander leaked out. The Army and Navy Journal appeared with an editorial to this effect: "Move to Drop Marshall as Chief of Staff." The article flatly stated: "Such action would shock the

Army, the Congress, and the Nation at large." This started a controversy in the press, some newspapers being for, others against the proposed change. One paper said, "Marshall is the man for the job of Generalissimo of the Western Front." Others said: "General Marshall's transfer would damage our National defense. . . ." "President Roosevelt should name General Marshall to head the drive. . . ." "There is no more important field in this war than the one General Marshall now occupies. . . ."

The controversy finally grew to such proportions that Secretary Stimson called a press conference and stated that, "Whatever duties General Marshall may hereafter be called upon to perform by the President, it will be with the sole purpose of placing this supremely able officer where he can render the best service toward the successful conclusion of this war."

The President, in a press conference, stated that the free talk concerning General Marshall was hurting the war effort; and the following correspondence took place between General Pershing and the President at this time:

"September 16, 1943

"My dear Mr. President:

"I am so deeply disturbed by the repeated newspaper reports that General Marshall is to be transferred to a tactical command in England, that I am writing to express my fervent hope that these reports are unfounded.

"We are engaged in a global war of which the end is still far distant, and for the wise strategical guidance of which we need our most accomplished officer as Chief of Staff. I voice the consensus of informed military opinion in saying that officer is General Marshall. To transfer him to a tactical command in a limited area, no matter how seemingly important, is to deprive ourselves of the benefit of his outstanding strategical ability and experience. I know of no one at all comparable to replace him as Chief of Staff.

"I have written this, Mr. President, because of my deep conviction that the suggested transfer of General Marshall would be a fundamental and very grave error in our military policy.

"With sincere regard and high esteem, believe me,
"Faithfully yours,
"John J. Pershing."

"THE WHITE HOUSE
"WASHINGTON
"September 20, 1943

"My dear General:

"You are absolutely right about George Marshall—and yet, I think, you are wrong too! He is, as you say, far and away the most valuable man as Chief of Staff. But, as you know, the operations for which we are considering him are the biggest that we will conduct in this war. And, when the time comes, it will not be a mere limited area proposition, but I think the command will include the whole European theatre—and, in addition to that, the British want to have him sit with their own Joint Staff in all matters that do not pertain to purely British island affairs.

"More than that, I think it is only a fair thing to give George a chance in the field—and because of the nature of the job we shall still have the benefit of his strategical ability.

"The best way I can express it is to tell you that I want George to be the Pershing of the second World War—and he cannot be that if we keep him here. I know you will understand.

"As ever yours,
"Franklin D. Roosevelt

"General John J. Pershing
The General of the Armies of the United States
Walter Reed Hospital
Washington, D. C."

While General Pershing felt strongly this way concerning George, Secretary of War Stimson, on the other hand, was equally determined that General Marshall should lead the invasion and command the armies that he had brought into being. He felt this was only fair and just. The President, I think, was torn between two desires—his wish to keep George in this country as Chief of Staff of the Army and his desire to do the fair thing by giving him command of the European invasion forces.

To add to this hubbub, Senator Johnson of Colorado proposed General Marshall as Democratic candidate for President in 1944. The columnists took this up and wrote:

> "On the basis of personal merits, can you think of a more desirable successor to President Roosevelt? Nobody who has any business with General Marshall comes away less than completely sold on him. Men who you couldn't imagine ever wanting to see a military leader made President, say 'Yes' to this one."

The sponsors of the idea were never quite able to muster the courage to approach my husband directly, but from feelers put out through his close associates, the inspired answer came back, "General Marshall would no more think of lending himself to such a proposition than he would resign his post in the midst of a battle."

This last development was most embarrassing to George and when Senator Johnson later referred to having proposed him as a presidential candidate, adding, "and you never thanked me," my husband answered emphatically, "No, Senator, I certainly did not."

xvi.

General Marshall as the Chief of Staff received an invitation from the Mexican Government to be present at their yearly fiesta celebrating, in September, the anniversary of their independence. The State Department felt that he should accept and he was glad of an opportunity at this time to get out of Washington. We made the trip by plane, after I had received only one day's notice. Never having been either to Mexico or to New Orleans I was delighted with the prospect of a night's stopover in that city and two days in the City of Mexico.

Word had been sent ahead that we would dine at Antoine's in New Orleans. When our party arrived, Antoine greeted us, literally with his arms open. We sat down to a Lucullian feast. When the dessert was brought in, followed by Antoine, his face beaming with pride, it proved to be a mammoth affair tipped by two white doves. On the ribbon caught in their beaks was printed in gold letters, "General and Mrs. Marshall." This caused considerable merriment and Antoine rubbed his hands in delight.

The next morning during our flight to Mexico City my thoughts turned to the coming winter at Leesburg. I had sent the little trailer down many times filled with furniture, covered by a green canvas to conceal its contents. We were all but moved out of Quarters Number One at Myer; and our home in the country was now quite comfortable. Storm windows had been made and the furnaces put in condition, all was ready—but there were no servants.

Old Thomas, the caretaker who had come with the house, was too old to do much work; he was merely a retainer. He was devoted to my husband; also he was deeply religious, so George had brought him a little Bible from Jerusalem, the binding of wood supposedly from the Mount of Olives. The old man would sit for hours under the big oak tree in the side yard, just holding this treasure. He had taken it to church the first Sunday to impress his friends, but after that one day, no one was allowed to touch it.

There was, however, one Biblical admonition to which Thomas did not adhere, namely: "Cleanliness is next to Godliness." He had a little kerosene oil stove to warm his room on cool summer evenings and it was the filthiest stove I have ever seen. It smoked and smelled to high heaven. One weekend while he was away I asked our maid, Anna, to clean it. She painted its rusty sides, shined the nickel, put in a new wick and had it back in his room when he returned. It was a whole day's job.

The next morning Thomas appeared very mournful and frigidly polite. He stood as always with his hat in his hand and greeted me with his customary "Good Morning," for Thomas was a real gentleman; but this morning there was no heart in his greeting. I asked Anna later if he was sick. "No, Mrs. Marshall," she said, "Thomas is angry. He said no one had ever cleaned or touched his stove since he got it, and he wanted it left alone. Folks didn't have no right to fool with his things." I do not think he ever liked me after that, and when I asked him one day to paint the wheelbarrow, he said, "Paint the wheelbarrow, Mrs. Marshall? I never heard of painting a wheelbarrow." I asked, "Wasn't the wheelbarrow painted when we bought it, Thomas?"

"Yes Ma'm, but it stands out in the rain."

"Well, isn't that all the more reason it should be

painted? Oil it and keep it in the tool house after this."
Thomas just shook his head. I said, "Thomas, my great-
grandfather was a very wealthy man; but his sons all died
poor. Do you know why?"

"No, Ma'm."

"They would not paint their wheelbarrows." An in-
credulous look came in the old man's eyes. He seemed
worried and I am sure he thought I had lost my wits.
"Yes Ma'm, Mrs. Marshall, Yes Ma'm. The ladies in the
old days, they had no mind for wheelbarrows. They drove
behind fine horses, Ma'm."

"Well, I guess they are flying now, Thomas," I said.
"At any rate—paint the wheelbarrow."

From that day I lost face with Thomas. The wheelbarrow was painted, but not by him.

So on this trip to Mexico I could not dismiss my
anxiety over our servant problems. In vain I had visited
the employment agencies. When I said, "country," that
ended all hopes of securing anyone. In Leesburg itself,
the younger women had left for ammunition factories and
government jobs in Washington. The older women were
resting on the allotment checks of their fighting men. I
advertised—no results. My sister was coming to stay with
me while George was overseas and Molly and her two
babies were with me for the duration of the war.

As all this was running through my mind, an idea
came to me and I asked George, "If I can get two maids
in Mexico City, would it be all right with you?"

"Certainly," he said, "but how are you going to
get them? You do not speak Spanish and we are to be
there only two days and they will be holidays."

"Well, I can try. It might be possible."

When our plane landed we were met by four delegations, the head of each presenting me with a box of exquisite orchids. I rapidly untied the boxes as they were presented and pinned on the corsages. This seemed to please the donors greatly. When we drove into Mexico City I was literally covered with orchids.

After the strain of our daily life in Washington, finding myself in this gaily bedecked city, with its laughing, carefree crowds, was indeed a wonderful sensation. The whole of Mexico, it seemed to me, had come to the capital to celebrate. Thousands and thousands of men and women in picturesque costumes milled through the streets and squares, the women holding on to the hand of the youngest of their brood while the rest of the family, like little stairsteps, trailed along behind.

The city itself was bedecked with flags and gay bunting; colored paper streamers hung from the windows of the buildings. As we drove to our hotel there were motorcycles with shrieking sirens in front of and behind our car and police riding on the running boards waving the crowd back with imposing gestures of which the Southern races alone are masters. Above the shriek of the sirens rose the roar of the people, glad to do their part to add to the gaiety of the great fiesta.

It was like coming from darkness into bright sunshine. Did people really laugh and play and celebrate like this; was this the same world in which we had lived for the past three years? No one seemed to walk, they were all running or hustling somewhere—where I do not know, nor, I think, did they. Excitement was in the air and everyone was breathing it joyously.

When we arrived at the hotel we were escorted to a suite bedecked with rare flowers, overlooking the city. George had to leave at once for a luncheon with the Presi-

dent and officials. I was to rest and receive their wives
at four o'clock.

When my husband shut the door, I sat down to
rest; but immediately my mind turned again to the maid
question. I had only a few hours as my schedule for the
evening and the next day was full. How should I start?
Did I know anyone who spoke both Spanish and English?
Absolutely no one. And then a thought came to me. I
had noticed two guards standing at either side of our door
as we entered. I opened the door and peeked into the hall.
They were there, armed with guns.

They looked very formidable but I mustered my
courage and asked, "Do either of you speak English?"
They stepped forward and one said, "Yes, Senora, I do."
I said, "Will you come in? I wish to speak with you."
They stepped into the room and I explained what I wanted,
ending with, "Do you know two women who would like
to come to the United States, to live in our home—one as
nurse for my grandchildren, one as our cook? Their
wages will be so-and-so." At the mention of the wages
then paid in the United States, the two guards all but collapsed. They explained that their pay as special policemen
was $15 a month and that they were employed only on
special occasions.

"We know many women who would gladly go,"
one said, "but the time is short and we cannot leave our
post without an order from the Captain."

"Where is your Captain?"

"He guards the front of the hotel, Senora."

I went to the house 'phone and requested that the
Captain of Police be sent to General Marshall's apartment.
He arrived breathless, thinking something fatal had oc-
curred. Behind him came a hotel clerk and the manager.

When I explained that I would like the Captain to give the English-speaking guard two hours off to attend to an important matter for me, he was greatly relieved and said, "Most certainly, Senora, most certainly. With pleasure."

In an hour's time the guard was back, bringing two girls, Anna Godinez and Sarah de Martinez. They were the wives of the two guards. Anna, really a beautiful girl, had gone to school in California; Sarah, timid and quiet, spoke no English. Anna had four children and Sarah had three. They were all smiles, eager for the job; a new world was opening to them. But, I explained, I could not be responsible for breaking up their families. Then all began to talk at once. "Senora, it is our great good fortune. The grandmother, she will take the babies, it is always so in Mexico. Our children can be well fed and educated." They pled that I change my mind.

When George returned late that afternoon, the maids were engaged. I think he was as relieved as I, for he had hated to leave for Europe with our domestic affairs unsettled.

The girls were allowed in the United States for only six months and when they left us they cried bitterly. But those six months had tided us over and given them what they considered a fortune. Each Christmas since then, we have had letters of gratitude from the Godinez and Martinez families.

xvii.

As soon as we returned to Washington, George once more became the hub, and I a small cog indeed, in the war machine. I had been asked by the New York Flower Show to receive for Mrs. Douglas MacArthur, who was then with her husband in Australia, a sweetpea named in her honor, and thus to further the then growing "Gardens for Victory" movement. This movement, known later as "Victory Gardens" grew to such proportions that before the war was over it supplied one-third of the United States with fresh vegetables and lifted a great burden from the overworked farmer.

On most of General Marshall's plane trips he was busily working on his current Biennial Report to the Secretary of War. His second one was released at this time and covered in detail the history of the growth and development of the United States Army from July 1, 1941, up to June 30, 1943. There were hundreds of letters concerning this report sent to the War Department and kept on file there. I happen to have two, which were sent to our home. They read:

"September 8, 1943

"Dear General:

"May I be permitted to say that I think your report to the Secretary of War is one of the greatest documents of this war, one of the greatest documents ever produced in the history of this country.

"Yours very sincerely,
"William Hillman
Asst. to the President
Crowell-Collier Company."

"September 11, 1943

"Dear General:

"I suppose you are overwhelmed with comments upon the excellence of your Report.

"When I read it, I thought it was the best thing of its kind that I had ever read, but I am amazed to see how quickly the country has responded to it.

"I would think it is not too much to say that it is the

finest military document that this country has ever produced.
"Sincerely,
"John J. McCloy
Assistant Secretary of War."

Drew Pearson, of the Washington Merry-Go-Round, said:

"The brass ring and a free ride on the Washington Merry-Go-Round go to General George C. Marshall."

The report was published in full in the daily newspapers. Headline: "Marshall's Masterpiece." An edition was published in England.

Many evenings George had read as much of the report to me as he had written, and had gone over the import of each word. To write in detail an abridged history of a global war would in itself be a difficult job for any man, but to write it while at the same time directing the whole range of raising, equipping, housing, training, and transporting our Army with its air forces, of reorganizing the War Department and Army, of guiding combined staffs and committees, of attending international strategy conferences, and of mapping out campaigns in all the major theaters of war, was, to my mind, a superhuman undertaking. I was proud and happy that the public had received his report with such acclaim.

We had arrived home on Monday from Mexico City. That week George was called again to testify before both the Senate and House Military Affairs Committees and he knew they were loaded with questions for him. I will let a broadcast tell of that session:

"General Marshall's appearance was public. The room was jammed and the spectators were almost sitting in his lap. All the time he testified, General Marshall had to look right into the bright lights of newsreel cameramen, and there were flashbulbs exploding in his face. The General wasn't upset, however. He always looks neat and well-groomed, with his grey hair smoothed down. Although he was in Mexico City just the other day, and will be in Omaha, Nebraska, tomorrow for the American Legion Convention, he seemed physically fit and rested. While he was perfectly calm, I have never heard him speak more forcefully and bluntly than he did today."

As the demands of war grew, so seemed to grow the strength of my husband's body and mind to meet them. Secretary Stimson said, "General Marshall's ability has no ceiling, it expands with the job."

xviii.

At the end of November George left for what became known as the Cairo-Teheran Conference. Teheran was the first conference of the Allied forces attended by Marshal Stalin. In talking it over later with my husband I asked his impression of Stalin. He said, "He is a strong leader, direct and practical."

One incident at the conference rather startled the Americans. After toasting Stalin, they drank to the bravery of the Russian soldier, and in answering the toast Stalin said, "In Russia we do not praise our soldiers for being brave—they dare not be otherwise." This was a novel point of view for the officers of a democratic army.

Although the matter of the Supreme Commander had been decided and all plans made at the Quebec Conference, the President had not made a public announcement. There were many questions of the British-American command still to be worked out. These were delicate and complex and required long sessions of the Combined Chiefs of Staff. The President could not announce that General Marshall would be the Supreme Allied Commander until these vital decisions had been settled for the various other theaters of war. The public did not understand the complex nature of these discussions and President Roosevelt was berated in the press and on the air for his indecision and for the confused state of mind in which the American people found themselves.

We are an impatient people in hours of strain, I fear. We like things done in the so-called American way —started, accomplished, ended successfully. It is the strength and at the same time the weakness of our nation. To consider great questions from all points of view, to take time to make discreet logical decisions as to the best means—for all concerned—to attain our objective, is irritating to the public. We are great on snap judgment; yet woe betide the man in a position of responsibility if his judgment proves wrong. So, the controversy was still going on when General Marshall left for the Cairo conference in December.

Toward the end of this most important conference, Harry Hopkins entered General Marshall's room one night and said he had just come from a talk with the President. The President was greatly worried over affairs at home and had asked him to see George. It concerned the announcement regarding the Supreme Commander which must be made on the President's return. President Roosevelt asked that General Marshall see him the next evening.

On the following evening the President asked George in which position he felt he could be of the greater service to his country—as Chief of Staff or as leader of the invasion. My husband answered that he would not attempt to evaluate his own services; that, he said, was for the Commander-in-Chief, the President, to decide; but before he made his decision, George told him, he would like the President to know that, either way, it would be all right with him. The war, George said, was too big for personal feelings or desires to be considered. The President said, "I feel now that I will not be able to sleep at night with you out of the country."

On the President's return from Cairo he announced that General Dwight D. Eisenhower would lead the invasion of the Allied Forces and General Marshall would continue as Chief of Staff. I quote an editorial of that date, headed, "Marshall and Eisenhower":

"In his new role as Supreme Commander of the Allied land, sea, and air forces to be used to smash Hitler on new fronts in Europe, General Dwight D. Eisenhower has been charged with one of the weightiest and most decisive responsibilities of the war, but he is superbly well-equipped to handle it. Not much more than a year ago, before the invasion of North Africa, he was relatively unknown. Since then he has joined the company of the foremost Captains in history. An American under whose leadership an entire continent has been liberated, the Mediterranean swept virtually clean of the enemy, and Italy invaded. The immense responsibility handed over to him now is in the nature of a reward for the greatness of his achievements during the past year. But more than that, it is the logical placing of an extraordinarily difficult command on the shoulders of a man who has brilliantly demonstrated his unique fitness for such a command. The choice of General Eisenhower seems a happy and wise one for yet another reason—it leaves General Marshall in the key position as Chief of Staff, and although some circles once advocated that he be given the task now given to General Eisenhower, there can be little doubt that the present arrangement is better in every respect. Not least of all be-

cause our Allied global command would have lost one of its
greatest figures if General Marshall had been shifted. His
job, after all, is the most important in the Army for, together with Admiral King, he has been directing, in President Roosevelt's words, 'all our armed might throughout the
world' and it has been up to him to plan the strategy of
determining when and where we shall fight. The magnitude
of this responsibility cannot be exaggerated."

The Teheran Conference was one of diplomatic
rather than military discussion and decision, and the Allied Chiefs of Staff were released a few days before the
conclusion of the conference. The Prime Minister, President Roosevelt, and Marshal Stalin remained for further
sessions on these world affairs.

xix.

Several times that fall George had made plans to
visit General MacArthur's theater of operations. At the
time of Prime Minister Churchill's good-will visit to
America his plans were complete. However, the Prime
Minister had insisted that General Marshall accompany
him to the conference of the military leaders in Algiers
and once more the plans for the Pacific trip were delayed.

Now, after the Cairo-Teheran Conference and
President Roosevelt's decision, George felt it was all the
more imperative for him to inspect the Pacific Theater.
He decided to return to America by way of India, Australia, New Guinea, and the Solomons.

He said no word of his plans to President Roosevelt for fear he would not give his consent, for this was
not only the longest trip of George's career, a 35,000-mile
flight; but also involved the then infrequent flight of 3,400

miles from Ceylon to Australia, with no emergency landing fields—except in Japanese-held Java and the Celebes.

When the Secretary of War heard how the Chief of
Staff was coming home, he was greatly disturbed and
radioed his concern; but General Marshall had already
started on his way.

When George left America in December, my sister
Allene, my daughter Molly and I settled at Leesburg with
the children. We were to keep the home fires burning.

George and I had had little chance to know our
neighbors at Leesburg since we had bought our home there.
They had all called but I had found no opportunity of returning their calls until this December.

We were surrounded by what would have been
known in olden days as "gentlefolk"—people with a heri-
tage of fine tradition. As the war had progressed and the
casualty list lengthened, our neighbors met their losses with
great courage. The mothers grew pale and thinner, perhaps, the fathers more silent, but no word betrayed the
grief and agony in their hearts. They were Virginians,
from the town of Leesburg, and they carried on accordingly.

The devotion to their native soil was well ex-
emplified by an old Negro woman, Aunt Annie, who had
been born and raised on the place of one of the older
families. Aunt Annie was known and greatly beloved by
everyone. She had a niece who had gone to New York
and become quite a well-known figure in Harlem, and this
niece had written asking Aunt Annie to visit her. Finally
the old woman was persuaded to go. When she returned,
a friend of "her people," as she called her mistress' family,
met her on the street and said, "Aunt Annie, I hear you
have been to New York."

"Yes, Ma'm."

"Did you enjoy your trip?"

"Yes, Ma'm, I liked it all right, but it ain't never goin' to amount to nothin'."

"Why," asked the friend, "what is the matter with New York that it isn't ever going to amount to anything?"

Aunt Annie looked over toward the Court House, then up and down the shaded street, and said, "It's too fur from Leesburg!"

xx.

That Christmas my grandson James Winn, or Jimmy as we call him, was old enough to know that Santa Claus was coming. He would call up the chimney constantly and was in a great state of excitement when the tree was brought in, asking endless questions, "When would Santa Claus come?" "How would he get down the chimney?" and imploring anxiously, "Don't let Santa Claus burn up!"

This was to be our first Christmas in our own home and we women had decided to make it a gay one, at least for the babies. Kitty was too young to understand what was going on, but she knew something strange and wonderful was happening and showed wide-eyed interest in all our preparations.

On the front door was hung a lovely wreath that had been sent by our Portland, Oregon friends. Oregon holly is superb. Across the wreath was a set of sleigh-bells tied with a big red bow.

Then, on Christmas Eve a wonderful thing happened—my husband flew in from the Pacific. When there is lead in your heart and it suddenly disappears, joy rushes in with such force that it is almost unbearable. So I felt that Christmas Eve.

Inside the house lights were all blazing and the fires crackling. Now it was to be a real Christmas. We hurried about, fixing the presents in the living-room for the next morning. We had waited until the babies were in bed before starting to trim the tree. Now Anna and Sarah, our Mexican maids, were making a barnyard under the tree, with a lake of looking-glass where miniature ducks floated. A group of sheep, with their lambs, were feeding on the lawn and there were miniature houses in the background. Mexicans love any kind of celebration and Anna and Sarah were as excited as Jimmy. Sergeant Victor Aguirre, George's efficient Filipino orderly, was to be Santa Claus. Victor had a most engaging smile. He belonged to our family and our family belonged to him. He was busy helping the girls, having had an eye for pretty Anna from the day of her arrival. There was much laughter and teasing.

We were so busy with Christmas inside the house that we did not hear what was going on outside until the door was flung open and Molly and her husband walked in. My son-in-law had been given a few days' leave to spend Christmas at home.

This was to have been a Christmas for the children, but we were all children that Christmas morning when Sergeant Aguirre came bounding into the room, with his Santa Claus suit stuffed out to make him as corpulent as Santa himself. He gave each one a Christmas package from the pack on his back. Only little Kitty in her high-chair was not amused. The long white beard and false face were too much for her, and after one look she let out a wail and refused to be comforted.

Jimmy was completely and wholly fascinated; he trailed after Santa Claus, his eyes like saucers and, on his face, an expression of admiration and wonder so complete that it made all of us wish life had not taught us there is no Santa Claus.

Chapter VI

AFTER CHRISTMAS, 1943, had passed, the little trailer with the green canvas cover started moving things back to the Chief of Staff's house at Fort Myer. We closed Dodona Manor for the winter and by the New Year were once more settled in Quarters Number One for the duration of the war. An Army Post is very much like a small town—every move is usually known and thoroughly discussed; but I doubt if anyone at Fort Myer had any idea that the Marshalls had all but moved out that fall.

On George's return trip from the Cairo-Teheran Conference he had visited General MacArthur's Headquarters and conferred with him regarding the campaign plans for the Pacific. His inspection covered a considerable portion of the Southwest Pacific Area, visits to Samoa and Canton Island and Army Headquarters in the Central Pacific. At Oahu Training Center he went over the entire course to see first-hand how American Army men were being trained for battle in Jap-infested jungles. Here, while George was inspecting a kitchen, an Army cook splashed hot water down his back. The cook of course was terribly distressed. He said he became so excited when the Chief of Staff walked in that his hands began to tremble and he let the kettle slip.

Several times I had been on trips with George when he was inspecting troops and it was always a source of amazement to me how, apparently, he could see out of the back of his head. Although he made his inspections at such a pace that other officers found difficulty in keeping up with him, he missed little, very little indeed. I recall at Fort Knox watching him inspecting troops lined up in a formation three deep. I saw him pause, go through the first two lines and stop in front of a soldier in the rear line. He talked to the man for a few minutes; and at luncheon, after the inspection, I asked why he had picked out that particular soldier.

He said, "I caught the man's eye and I knew something was wrong. I wanted to find out what."

"Did you find out?" I asked.

"Yes," he replied. "Everything was wrong. The man ought never to have been drafted. He was over-age, had a large family, and was in no physical condition for active service. He was a good soldier too, wanted to do his part, and I had to question him for some time before I could get at his trouble. The Draft Board made a slip-up on that fellow."

I was deeply interested. "Can he be sent home?"

"My dear," George smiled, "that is what I was saying to his commanding officer just now. By now the man has been ordered home."

General Marshall returned to Washington well pleased with what he had seen in the Pacific Area. Before he left the Pacific he had asked if there were any wounded he could bring home with him, so when his plane landed at the Washington Airport there were a number of wounded soldiers aboard.

ii.

There was no wonder that President Roosevelt was concerned over affairs on the home front when he returned from the Teheran Conference. A cartoon in TIME epitomized the story. It showed four fat men with shirt fronts labeled: "Labor Bloc," "Farm Bloc," "Oil Bloc," "Anti-Higher-Tax Bloc." Their mouths were wide open, singing: "My Country 'Tis of Me." The caption read: "The New National Anthem. One standard of duty for soldiers, another for civilians."

But this cartoon did not present the whole distressing situation. The President had returned after highly important discussions concerning ways and means of bringing Axis satellite nations over to the Allies' side. American power, success in Africa and allied unity could do much toward this end. But all these advantages were lost through selfishness.

My husband did not arrive until about a week after the President's return. When he landed he found the President ill with flu. The Army had taken over the railroads; a steel strike was threatened; and the Axis propaganda had easily exaggerated reports of the situation so that it appeared to their vacillating satellites that a chaotic state of affairs existed in the United States and, consequently, that it was no time for them to abandon the Axis ship. All possibility of an immediate break in the Axis ranks—as a result of our successes in the Mediterranean, the intensified bombing of Germany and the meeting with the Russians—was lost.

At a confidential meeting with about twenty members of the press and radio General Marshall explained the tragedy of the situation and the fatal effect that further strikes would have on the war effort. He described the careful planning in connection with the satellite Balkan States and the utter ruin of those plans. A leak of this off-the-record press conference—apparently engineered through a small Florida paper—created a stir in the press and on the radio and even more harm was done. Result: the satellite nations of Nazi Germany were encouraged to continue the war by this show of our weakness and reported demoralization.

In addition, Mr. William Green, President of AFL, came out with a blast, saying that the utterances concerning strikes attributed to General Marshall were "irrational, uninformed, and inflammatory," and demanding that President Roosevelt investigate the mysterious Marshall incident and reprimand whoever was responsible for it. But this was a little more than a long-suffering public could stand. The newspapers now took the matter up in good earnest and the following editorial appeared on the front page of the Washington Post.

"Accepting Mr. Green's assumption that the 'high source' is General Marshall, let us put ourselves in that military leader's shoes for a moment. He had just returned from the Cairo and Teheran conferences and a trip to every fighting front in the Pacific. He knew the details of every strategic plan. He had visited the cemeteries of American dead, the hospitals filled with American wounded. He returned to take over the burdens of the most hazardous military operation in all history; the coming invasion of Europe. And what did he find?

"He found that in addition to his countless other burdens, the Army he, more than anyone else, had built, also had to battle Mr. William Green and run the railroads in this country. Hundreds of his best officers would have to be used to deal with Mr. Green et al instead of Hitler and Tojo.

"And so—and one can understand it—even he is said to have expressed his indignation and brought the strike situation before the public in its true light."

The threatened steel strike did not occur. I do not think there was a more surprised man in this country than President Roosevelt. At this time he was an ill man, far more seriously so than the country knew, but on January 31, 1944, George received the following letter:

"January 31, 1944
"THE WHITE HOUSE
Washington

"Dear George:

"Ever so many thanks for that mighty nice note of yours. I am nearly over the 'flu' but most certainly I do not want to have it again.

"One thing that I am devoutly thankful for in these days —and that is the very splendid help that I have had from you in all of our common tasks. It has meant a teamwork which has succeeded and will succeed. Take care of yourself.

"As ever yours,
"(Signed)   Franklin D. Roosevelt."

iii.

Our ration boards were having a difficult job at this time. It was the peak of the gas rationing when every gallon possible must go to the fighting front. George put away his official car and used instead a small Chevrolet. He drove himself to and from the War Department, thereby relieving his chauffeur of the necessity of making these trips. He would drive home in the evening, leave the car under the porte-cochere, and drive to work in it in the morning. Then the chauffeur would bring it home and drive me to any official meetings I might have, such as Red Cross, Army Relief, or Walter Reed Hospital. I would make my engagements so as to be back at the Pentagon Building by 12:30. My husband would then dismiss the chauffeur and drive us home to lunch.

In this way we used the least possible gas and after lunch the car was there at the house ready for George to drive himself back to the War Department. It was a black car, not the traditional Army color, and he had some amusing experiences driving back and forth in it. As an instance, here is an interesting little article from a home-town paper of one of the girls he picked up on his way to the Pentagon:

"LOCAL GIRL HAS AUTO RIDE WITH
GENERAL MARSHALL IN WASHINGTON

"... Came a Monday morning at 7 o'clock, rain and drizzle and bleakness. I had missed the bus, along with some other girls when a small car driven by a lone officer pulled up to the curb along the highway and opening the rear door said, 'Hop in.' Which three of us did. There was a huge overcoat neatly folded on the seat which I carefully moved over a little and then we 'settled' ourselves for the short ride.

"I spoke to him and said it was kind of him to stop for us on such a rainy morning and said he, 'That's why I stopped, but usually I think you girls should walk.' I was just on the point of saying (I couldn't see his face as I was directly in back of him) 'Well, Sir, with these long hours we're working, I ride when I can to conserve energy.' But something gleaming to the left of me caught my eye and so I casually glanced toward and noticed four stars on the shoulder of an extra coat. (And I nearly lost my equilibrium). Hastily I motioned to the other two girls and the one next to me gulped as she saw the officer's profile and squealed, 'It's the Great Guy, General Marshall!'

"When we reached the Pentagon we drove not up the usual entrance but to a private one; emerged from the car and went up in a private elevator into his private office and were escorted out by a colored attendant who vouched for us to the waiting guard.

"Needless to say we tread on air the rest of the morning. He is a very tall man with a kind voice and I've never seen such shiny shoes."

After the long conference at Teheran, practically every American member of that conference was ill. The President was whisked out of Washington and spent three weeks getting back his strength at the South Carolina plantation of Mr. Bernard Baruch, his whereabouts being kept secret. George, while not ill, had fought a cold during the entire conference, and his long roundabout trip home had not helped matters. To be greeted on his return by the railroad strike—soldiers and sailors had to be moved ("Don't you know there's a war!")—was about as much as any man could endure.

When the strike situation was cleared, we left once more for a week at Miami Beach, and this time it was no Jekyll and Hyde affair. George wore civilian clothes and we took an apartment in the top of one of the hotels run by the Army. It looked out over the ocean and there was a private beach with a delightful cabana where our luncheon was served each day. What a blessing! The weather was warm and sunny and I could see an improvement in my husband's looks and spirits from the day of our arrival.

Each morning the pouch with his official mail was flown down from the War Department in Washington, and each morning Colonel Frank McCarthy, Secretary of the General Staff, came to George at 11:00 to get instruc-

tions.   In this way, when he returned to Washington his
desk was as clear of papers as when he had left—all business was attended to up to date.

What a delightful week! We would have a swim
before lunch, a nap, and then another swim in the afternoon, or George would go deep-sea fishing. In the evenings we ate at various restaurants and took long walks on
the beach.   There were few shops open.   Miami Beach
had been taken over completely by the Army for the training of our great Air Forces, and practically every hotel was
full of trainees, their headquarters and instructors.   Just
like being on a military reservation, no one paid any attention to the Chief of Staff so long as he was in civilian
clothes. The soldiers might give a side glance or nudge each
other, but they knew he was there to rest and rest he did.

Each morning at six o'clock the men would start
for their day's work. They would fall in outside of their
various hotels and as they marched they would sing. There
were 40,000 trainees and as the voices of one group died
out in the distance, another group would come closer, and
then pass by. Their voices in unison with the tramp of their
marching feet was one of the most inspiring things I had
ever heard. Our apartment was high up and I would always run to the window and watch until the last group
had gone and their voices were lost in the distance. These
men looked so young, so strong, so confident. I think there
has never been anything on earth so inspiring, so near
to heaven, as the courageous spirit of our young civilian
army.

The M. P.'s who had guarded our hotel and run the
elevator to our apartment had been most considerate, so
when we left Miami Beach George asked if any of them
were due for a leave.   Frank McCarthy found two who

were entitled to furloughs but had not enough time to get to their homes in New York and back by train. George flew them in his plane as far as Washington. They were two radiantly happy soldiers.

iv.

While we were at the Beach the following editorial was carried by the Associated Press. It was copied in London and in the South American newspapers.

"CASE OF PERFECT JUDGMENT

"One reason why we are for Roosevelt is the acumen and courage he showed in picking General George C. Marshall as Chief of Staff, and in backing him to the limit in his building and directing of our powerful, streamlined Army.

"General Marshall is the outstanding military figure in the whole world. Behind his modest, self-effacing exterior are military genius, blunt honesty and a sense of democratic values that have won him the confidence and admiration of our Allies as well as of the whole American nation. No Chief of Staff in our history ever had such united support from the public, or from a bi-partisan Congress. Even Candidate Dewey has hastened to proclaim that there will be no change in the Army setup headed by Marshall, in case he is elected President. . . There were at least 34 reasons why the then Brigadier General Marshall should not be appointed to the top army post. They were the 34 generals who outranked him. And we may be sure that the claims of some of these officers were urged strongly upon the President. . .

"But Roosevelt had broken precedents before, and this was no time to be bound by army red tape, or nice considerations of seniority. He was looking for a great leader, and he went down the line until he found him."

My husband called this article fulsome. Maybe so, but nevertheless such a tribute to him warmed my heart.

v.

On my return I left for New York where I had an engagement with the Committee of the 4th War Bond Drive for a 20-minute talk. I was assured that my appearance would be for just that length of time and no more. However, after my talk one of the leaders asked if I would consent to have some pictures taken outside of the building in front of the "Doughnut Wagon." It was explained what a wonderful thing this doughnut company was doing for the Committee, giving doughnuts free to all war bond buyers.

I consented and went downstairs.

It was a bitterly cold March day, with a howling wind blowing, and as I came out of the building I encountered a number of photographers and a still larger crowd of spectators. I was pushed through this crowd and placed against the Doughnut Wagon. First, pictures were taken of me with a war bond in one hand and a doughnut in the other; then I was asked to hand a doughnut to a man, then he was asked to hand one to me; then some bright cameraman said, "Will you take a bite out of the doughnut, looking this way?" Other cameramen called, "We didn't get that, will you take another bite, looking this way." Then a moving-picture man asked if he could take a picture of me eating another doughnut. Just as I had finished one, another moving-picture man came up and I was asked if I would please eat still another doughnut for him.

By this time I was trembling from the cold and

had begun to have a peculiar feeling midway of my anatomy. Also, the crowd was growing huge, as New York loves a free show, and they certainly were getting one. I said, "Now this will be the last doughnut." But I was informed that the president of the doughnut company was on his way down to 14th Street to have his picture taken with me, and, further, he wished to give me a box of doughnuts to take home. I protested that I could not stay as I had another appointment up town. However, just then I noticed considerable excitement on the edge of the crowd and a man pushed through—the president had arrived! Again I posed, this time holding a box of doughnuts—first smiling admiringly at the president, then smiling at a war bond. For one hour I stood in that icy blast.

When George arrived at Quarters Number One, Fort Myer, that evening I was walking the floor in agony. What the icy wind had not done to me, the doughnuts had; and I don't think I ever saw my husband so outraged. He simply raved: "After taking you to Florida for a week to get the sun, you undo all the good accomplished in one hour—standing on 14th Street in New York for one hour, eating doughnuts! What, in Heaven's name, have doughnuts got to do with the War Bond Drive? If you can't say 'No' you ought not to be allowed out alone!" I had to laugh in spite of my pain; but, in fact, it was not a laughing matter. For a month I was confined to my room with the worst case of sinus trouble I have ever had.

A year later I was called to the telephone to answer a long-distance call from Baltimore. It was the Chairman of the War Bond Drive asking if I would do them the honor of having my picture taken standing in front of a doughnut wagon which would give free doughnuts to all war bond buyers. When he used the word "doughnuts" something simply did a flip inside of me; my heart grew cold, and I answered: "I regret exceedingly, but it will not be possible."

vi.

In March 1944, the plans for D-Day were well advanced. In May 1943 when General Jacob L. Devers, who had built up the Armored Force from four to sixteen divisions, was sent to England to command our troops in the European theater, there had been but a single United States division in the United Kingdom. On D-Day, June 6, 1944, the strength of the U. S. Army in that theater was 1,535,000 men. The building up of this force, together with corresponding accumulation of supplies of all kinds, involved a tremendous job of transportation. Joint exercises and maneuvers by the ground, sea, and air forces which were to make the attack were being held along the southern coast of England. It was a full-dress rehearsal.

General Eisenhower, who took command of all Allied forces in this theater in January, 1944, wrote my husband:

"There is no question at all as to the readiness of the troops. They are well trained, fit, and impatient to get the job started and completed. In forecasting future possibilities, it is, of course, necessary that we seek ways and means to bring to bear those factors in which we enjoy a great superiority over the enemy. These are control of the sea, command of the air, including resources in airborne troops and armor. I am trying to visualize an operation in which we would bring in behind the initial beachhead a great strength in armor and seek an opportunity to launch a big armored attack in conjunction with a deep and very heavy penetration by airborne troops."

The air attacks on Germany and occupied France, known as the softening up process, continued with increasing intensity and devastating power. The air war reached a climax at the end of February, 1944, when the Luftwaffe made a determined effort to sweep our day bombers from the skies. The battle raged for a week and resulted in the German fighter force being severely crippled. We had gained complete control of the skies.

Three months before D-Day, Allied air forces gave their attention solely toward preparing the way for the invasion. Through destructive attacks on key bridges and rail centers the invasion coast was effectively isolated. The ability of the enemy to shift reserves to critical areas was severely restricted.

vii.

On March 26th I received the following radio from my son Clifton in Italy: "My love and greetings on Mother's Day." From Allen, a letter was received: "My men and I have been relieved after 28 days at the front. I have permission to visit Clifton. We are only seven miles apart. P. S. Tell the General the only thing worse than K-ration is D-ration. I coughed after eating it the other day and set the whole forest on fire."

George laughed heartily at this. He had always held that it was the soldier's prerogative to grouch. A night or two before this we had dined at the home of a certain Senator of whom George thought very highly. The Senator told us of a complaint he had received from one of his constituents stating that her son was not receiving proper food, the Army Mess was a mess, and she wished an investigation made. George had the case looked into immediately and the investigation showed that this particular boy, during the six weeks since his induction, had gained 15 pounds. George sent the Senator the papers on the case with a note at the bottom, "This mother, not the Army, should have been investigated."

viii.

George now left for Yale University to be with his friend Sir John Dill when the latter received the Howland Memorial Prize for outstanding service to this country.   This greatly pleased my husband.

Also at this time the President left Washington for a rest.   He had hardly settled in his retreat before the rest turned into a political nightmare. The "Marshall for President" rumor broke out once more in the press. David Lawrence came out with an article which bore the headline, "President Roosevelt Should Retire."

It would be difficult to exaggerate how embarrassing this controversy was to my husband. He immediately let his position be known and the New York Herald Tribune came out with the following helpful article.

"The New York Herald Tribune is able to state without a chance of contradiction, that the Army Chief of Staff has views even more positive than those of the late and much-quoted William Tecumseh Sherman, who said: 'If nominated, I will not run.   If elected, I will not serve.'

"If General Marshall were in a position to talk about the topic, which he is not, his friends say he would go General Sherman one better by putting his disavowal as bluntly as this:

"'I'll be in my grave before I'll be in politics.'"

On the President's return George left Washington

on an extended inspection of troops in Texas and on the West Coast. He wired ahead and had a dinner arranged at San Antonio for a number of his old friends—retired Army officers—who had made San Antonio their home. They did not know that he was the host or even of his presence in San Antonio until he entered the room after they had gathered. On his return from this trip, in his mail was the following letter:

"March 17, 1944

"Dear Marshall:

"Your dinner on Sunday night at the St. Anthony was a beautiful gesture of true friendship. It is hardly necessary for me to tell how deeply your thoughtfulness of the old fellows was appreciated. While every man there knew how characteristic of you such an act was, yet we all realized how few men in high position would ever have done anything of the kind. Your thoughtfulness and your confidence will remain with each one of us as long as consciousness is retained.

"Personally, I want to tell you I appreciate, as much as I ever appreciated anything in my life, your special consideration of myself. I want you to know how deeply I feel; I could in no manner properly express myself and so shall let this short letter do what it can along that line.

"I want to add, I was happy to see you apparently standing up so well under the strain. That pleases me above all things—not only for yourself but also for this nation. For upon you, more than upon any man alive, the future of this nation's welfare rests.

"My best always,
(Signed) "H. A. WHITE."

There was also a letter awaiting him from General Montgomery, Commander-in-Chief of the British Army:

"Headquarters 21 Army Group
London, W. 1
3 March, 1944

"My dear General:

"I was delighted to receive your letter of 12th February,
and your kind wishes for the success of the task which faces
us all. With the magnificent co-operation of your grand
American soldiers I am confident of the future.

"Please accept this photograph of myself which I have
just had taken. I should much appreciate one of your
photographs in return!

"Yours very sincerely,
" (Signed) B. L. MONTGOMERY,
"General
Commander-in-Chief."

ix.

Easter Sunday came on April 9th that year and
George had been asked to offer the prayer at the Sunrise
Service in Arlington amphitheater. It was quite a cold
morning and the President was not allowed to attend the
Service in the open air, but Mrs. Roosevelt came and I sat
with her in the President's box.

George has always laughed at a habit I have of tearing my program to bits whenever he is speaking. He is
perfectly calm, but I am panicky. Try as I will I have
never been able to control this nervousness. That Easter
Sunday, 25,000 people had gathered to attend the service
and by the time George had finished his prayer my lap
looked like the bed of an Easter bunny's basket. George's
prayer on that Easter morning—possibly the most critical
in American history—was as follows:

"Almighty God:

"May those who have given their lives in the service of
this nation rest in Thy care.

"May those who are wounded in body find spiritual comfort under Thy guidance in the knowledge that through their services a great cause has been served.

"May those who offer their lives in support of that cause, by land and sea and air, find strength in Thy divine guidance.

"May those of us who serve this nation in its great purpose to secure freedom for all peoples be sustained by Thy blessings.

"Give us strength, O Lord, that we may be pure in heart and in purpose to the end that there may be peace on earth and good will among men.

"May we be mindful this Easter morning 'still stands Thine ancient sacrifice, an humble and a contrite heart.'"

x.

My Easter letter from Allen said:

"Dearest Mum: I had the greatest surprise—a box was delivered to me and when I opened it up I had never seen so many good things to eat and read. I am trying to get a ride to Clifton to give him his share."

His letter ended:

"God did make beautiful things when he made Mothers.
"My love to you,
"Allen."

xi.

On Easter Morning George received the following radio in French from General Giraud, in Algiers, who had just been wounded in an attempted assassination:

"Very much touched by the sentiments of sympathy which you have been good enough to express. My injury is nothing. The only thing that counts is the victorious pursuit of the war in close cooperation with the Allies."

At this time Liberty Magazine came out with an excellent picture of the Secretary of War and General Marshall. Under it was the caption: "General Marshall and Secretary of War Stimson Make Plans to Keep Casualties Low." The article accompanying this picture said, in part:

"There will be no needless loss of life in the American Army in World War II if the orders and plans of our High Command are carried out. No post-war poet will sing a new 'Charge of the Light Brigade,' paying tribute to some sentimentally heroic but foolishly sacrificial exploit. No 'Noble Six Hundred' will charge unprotected from the guns. That is not the theory under which General Marshall and our armed forces work. In fact he has a completely contrary view—that soldiers should live, and avoiding losses to personnel is a most important rule of combat."

LOOK Magazine, also at this time, asked 52 leading correspondents to select Washington's Ten Most Useful Officials. This poll placed General Marshall first and Secretary of State Cordell Hull second, and so on. LOOK stated, "44 correspondents had this military genius, this great grave general first on their list," and in speaking of Secretary Hull LOOK said, "For his Latin and American and Russian victories" (the Secretary had just returned from a most successful diplomatic flight to Russia) "and his outstanding statesmanship, Secretary Hull received the second largest poll."

xii.

I now left for Newark, New York, to attend the Gardens for Victory and Rose Festival given each year by Jackson and Perkins, one of the largest rose growers in the country; and I am terribly proud to say, the All-American Winning Pink Rose of 1944 had been named "Katherine T. Marshall" and I was to receive this exquisite produce of the Jackson and Perkins' nursery and to crown the Rose Queen of the festival.

While I was away George and Sir John Dill took a long-planned drive over the Gettysburg Battlefield. They had quite an amusing day as both were in civilian clothes and their guide was not aware that they were officers. They arrived on the field at the point where the second day's action had taken place, so they started with that, proceeded on to the third day's fight, and then turned to the first day's operations. This confused and irritated the guide, who had learned a certain patter and when interrupted or asked a question became confused and had to start all over again.

After more or less wasting an hour, General Marshall, who knows even the minute details of history, suggested that the guide take a rest while they explored the remainder of the battlefield alone. The guide, much incensed, said, "Certainly, if you men are not interested in military affairs."

After they had done both Gettysburg and Antietam, they drove to Leesburg to spend Sunday at our home. George had told Sir John much about the quaintness of the town and the lovely little Episcopal Church we attended. Each Easter since purchasing Dodona Manor we had driven to Leesburg for our Easter Service. Also George related at some length that on our first Sunday, when the rector walked into the chancel, he proved to be an old VMI friend whom George had not seen since their cadet days.

With this background they entered the Church the next morning, both dressed in civilian clothes; and as they were a few minutes late the service had begun and George had no opportunity of telling Sir John that his old VMI friend had evidently been replaced.

After the service they were greeted at the door of the Church by the new minister and George introduced his friend impressively: "This is Sir John Dill, a Field Marshal of the British Army." The rector extended his hand and said, "How do you do, Mr. Dill," then turning to George asked, "And who might you be?"

On the way home Sir John quoted the lines from "Pinafore":

> "He might have been a Rooshian,
> "A Dutchman or a Proosian,
> "But he is an Englishman."

xiii.

On our return to Fort Myer, General Marshall's morning mail brought a V-Mail note from General Eisenhower. It was the one hundred millionth V-Mail message which had been sent from the United Kingdom. On it was printed:

> "One hundred million times soldiers of the European Theater have used V-Mail to send a message home.
> "Dwight D. Eisenhower."

xiv.

The morning before Decoration Day we received letters from our two sons. They had enjoyed three wonderful days together after the fighting at Cassino and before Allen left with the 1st Armored Division for Anzio Beachhead. Clifton had just returned from the beachhead and they had met in passing and celebrated together. The cry was now, "On to Rome."

Clifton said, "The war looks good from here, both in Germany and Japan." Allen wrote, "I feel sorry for any German in Italy. The horseshoe has held my luck. I shall take it down this Christmas and keep it for the rest of my life." George smiled at his "this Christmas." I had written Allen how proud I was of our boys in Italy, and at the bottom of his letter he said, "Mother, there are no American 'boys' in Italy. They may have been boys when they arrived here, but they are all men now."

When George left for his office that morning there was "a song in my heart." An hour later as I stood at the window in my room, I turned to see my husband in the doorway. He came in, closing the door behind him, and told me Allen was dead. He had given his life that morning in a tank battle on the road to Rome.

A blessed numbness comes to one at a time like this. I could not comprehend George's words. I had only one thought—that I must get to Madge, Allen's wife. I do not recall anything of my flight to New York. I kept repeating Allen is dead, Allen is dead—but no realization of what this meant came to me until later.

We received the following citation from the Italian Government:

"The Royal Government of Italy and the High Command of The Italian Army has awarded to:

2nd Lieutenant Allen Tupper Brown

The Bronze Medal of Military Valor (on the field) for the following reason:

This Combatant of the glorious Fifth Army, heedless of the enemy's violent fire, gave proof of a high sense of duty and of contempt for danger.

In recent violent engagements he sacrificed his young life in fighting for the ideals of civilization and for the liberation of Rome.

(Signed) "Roberto Bencivenga,
"Civil and Military Commander."

Allen was awarded the American Bronze Star, with the following citation:

"For gallantry in action on 29 May 1944 in the Vicinity of _____, Italy, Allen Tupper Brown, 2nd Lieutenant, Company A, _____ Armored Regiment. As Commanding Officer of the 1st tank platoon of his company, Lt. Brown led in an attack of a tank battalion against the enemy. Through more than four hours of battle in the face of heavy enemy artillery and small arms fire, Lt. Brown displayed such aggressive leadership and outstanding courage, continually exposing himself to better direct his platoon as to materially contribute to the success of the action and inspire the men of his command. While attempting to take a German prisoner from a machine gun position he was killed by an enemy sniper from a flank position. Lt. Brown's heroic actions under fire are in keeping with the highest traditions of the Armed Forces. . . .

"V. E. PRICHARD
"Major General, U. S. Army
"Commanding"

XV.

On June 4th, Rome fell to the Allies. The New York Times headline read, "Rome Captured Intact by the 5th Army after Fierce Battle. Nazis move Northward."

But the news of the fall of Rome was quickly succeeded on the front pages of our press by D-Day—June 6th, 1944. Headlines read: "Allies Seize Two Beachheads," "Four Thousand Ships, Eleven Thousand Planes Lead Invasion," "Tanks Smash Inland. Our Losses Light," "Hitler takes Personal Command in France," "Petain Breaks Down and Sobs on Radio," "A Mere Beginning, Says Eisenhower," "Bloody Battle Ahead on Road to Berlin," "Dunkerque to D-Day—Four Long Hard Years."

D-Day in Washington was more a day of prayer than elation. The churches were crowded. There was no celebration such as there had been on the night of the African landing. Our hospitals by now were filled with wounded, Nazi prison camps held innumerable Allied prisoners, many wives had been widowed, parents had lost their sons. The nation on bended knees asked the guidance of a Power mightier than all armies that we might win the victory, be through with this dreadful war, our prisoners released, and loved ones brought back to us.

The day after the invasion my husband left for the front with General Arnold and Admiral King. On his flight over he sent me a penciled letter:

"Thursday 2 P. M. Over Nova Scotia

"I will send this back by some plane from Newfoundland. Trip so far quiet, sunny, and comfortable. I hated to go off and leave you. I do hope you stayed over and saw the doctor and will go to Fire Island. Be careful and get back your strength."

Another letter written Friday noon came from England:

"I have received two letters from you. One written the day I left, the other the next morning before you left for Fire Island. I am greatly relieved and do hope you will get ahead from day to day."

It ended: "Soon you and I can retire and garden together."

I had wanted to go to Fire Island to re-orient myself, but felt impelled to clear up matters I was then working on. I had many committee meetings at the time, yet my main interest concerned the Junior Officers Club, which was having trouble getting a building to meet the growing demands that were being made upon it. For two years we had worked toward establishing in Washington a decent place for young officers to go for entertainment. The enlisted men by this time were well taken care of. There were many clubs and places of recreation for them, but none in Washington for the Junior officers. Philadelphia had two such clubs, New York also had two excellent ones. But Washington, with thousands of young officers of the American and Allied Armies stationed here or passing through, had none. Even the mention of the word "officer" produced an inexplicable reaction. The moment you said "Officer," the public seemed to visualize a person of means who could afford hotels, fine established clubs and expensive places of amusement. The truth of the matter was quite the opposite: a high-ranking enlisted man was far better off financially than a junior officer, all his uniforms—to consider one important item—were supplied by the Government, whereas the officer had to buy his. The noncommissioned officer's pay check equalled that of the youthful officer and the demands made on the enlisted men could not compare with those on a commissioned officer, man or woman.

At this time we had three rooms in a federal-owned building, the rest of the building being used by the draft board. We were anxious to secure the entire building as the War Fund had promised to come to our rescue with the sum we needed to remodel it—on condition that the city would turn it over to Junior Officers, Incorporated, which was to include officers through the grade of Captain of all the armed services, Army, Navy, Marine Corps, and all the women's branches—WACS, WAVES, and SPARS.

I went to see Commissioner Young to ask his aid in securing the whole building, and while I was talking to him, fortunately, the Chief of Police came in. The Chief of Police was much concerned over the growing night-spots that were springing up all over the city—Honky-Tonks, he called them—and the juvenile delinquency problem. The amazing part, he added, was that so many young officers were found in these night-spots. I could not have dictated a more helpful statement.

I waited until he had left, then said to the Commissioner: "I will make a trade with you. We will keep the junior officers out of the so-called Honky-Tonks if you will give us our building for their club. Nearly every young officer would prefer a decent place to go, but when there is none he will not spend his evening in some cheap hotel room or in the hall room of a boarding-house, and I do not blame him."

We got our building and under the splendid leadership of Mrs. Russel L. Maxwell and her committee, the Junior Officers Club, Incorporated, was formally opened by Mrs. Roosevelt. It was the resting and eating place and the recreation center for thousands of men and women in our services and those of our Allies, for the duration of the war. Here they gave their parties and entertained their friends and families, when in town, and here many were married.

Also the club carried itself financially. The loan from the War Fund was repaid. In fact, it was the only completely self-supporting war work, so far as I know, which was carried on by the women of Washington.

As soon as I had seen Commissioner Young I called a meeting of the board at our house in Fort Myer to report our conversation and his agreement. The next morning I left for Fire Island.

xvi.

I took the train to New York, drove to Bayshore, Long Island and boarded the ferry for Ocean Beach. As we crossed the Great South Bay, Captain Robertson, an old summer friend of mine and the boys, left the pilot house, came down and sat beside me. He was a sea-faring man of few words and he spoke none, simply sat there until we docked. This was his tribute to Allen, whom he had known since childhood days.

The boat landed and there was the usual line of small boys along the wharf, each with his wagon to haul the passengers' hand luggage. There are no roads on this part of the island, no automobiles were allowed. My sons had started this small wagon service when they were little boys and it had grown into quite a business for the youngsters.

As I looked over the crowded dock I saw few familiar faces.   Most of the people were refugees dressed in the latest beach regalia, many heavy with jewelry they feared to leave in their cottages. I passed through this crowd and stopped at the Post Office.   Mrs. Pierce, our postmistress for the past twenty years, came to the window.   When she saw me, tears filled her eyes and she said, "Mrs. Marshall, it could not be Allen—our Allen."   I walked toward my house and on the way I passed a small shack. A bent old man came out and walked beside the wagon which held my luggage.   He was one of the natives, a fisherman; and when we reached my steps he insisted on helping the boy carry in my bags.   That done, he turned and gave me his hand.   There were tears running down his face.

I went in the house.   On the mantel of the living-room stood a model ship in full sail, given to the boys by their father many years before. I went to my room and hanging in my closet was a black sweater, from Allen's Woodberry days, with a big block "W" in yellow. I opened my top drawer and a white box lay there. Removing the lid I found the box full of bronze medals such as little boys win at swimming races, and there among the medals was a small gold football marked "Allen Tupper Brown."   A kind of panic seized me and I left the house for the beach.

The ocean was high that day and as I sat watching the huge swells rise and break, then crash into a sea of foam, above the spray two laughing faces appeared. They dove, rose again shaking the water from their hair, one dark, one light, then plunged into the next swell and dis-appeared.   I got up and walked down the beach. Running toward me along the wide stretch of white sand was a figure, with arms bent as if practicing for a race.   It came nearer and nearer—then faded in the sand. I started for the dunes and passed a group of boys playing hand-ball on the beach. In their midst I could see a mop of light hair above a tense, eager brown body, leaning forward waiting for the ball. My knees began to fail me and I climbed slowly up the steps to the dunes. A stiff breeze was blowing. Something seemed to break inside of me. A low cry escaped me. It was caught up by the wind and carried out to sea, "My son, oh, my son—Allen!"

I left Fire Island and went back to Washington, where I wired for my sister. She joined me, as she has always done in my hours of trial, and together we went to Leesburg. There I became ill.

Most opportunely, at this time the War Department sent down a book of letters of sympathy compiled at General Marshall's request, with a note saying he had answered each one personally before leaving. They were touching letters from all over the country. Most of them expressed the same thought—sincere sympathy that General Marshall and I who had given so much to the war effort should now have to make this supreme sacrifice. Yet what sacrifice had we made?—We had lived; I had had my home, my children. I found a letter that brought me comfort. It said, "Your son will always be young and unafraid, he will never have to grow old, he will never know such grief as yours."

As I lay there ill, I thought of my husband who in the midst of his own grief and the strain of the invasion, had gone early and stayed late in his office to answer those hundreds of letters before leaving for the front. I knew he had done this to save me from strain and sorrow and I prayed that I would be given strength to be well by the time of his return.

Then a miracle happened—Clifton walked into my room. He had flown back to Washington as a special courier with a pouch of secret papers for the Air Force. Sitting on my bed he told me of his brother. He had reached the scene a few hours after Allen's death and had been given permission to go to the front. Not wishing to expose a driver to unnecessary danger he had driven himself and had talked to each man in Allen's platoon. He had collected his brother's belongings and attended his funeral on Decoration Day. Gathering some flowers in a near-by field he had placed them on Allen's grave for Madge and me. Only by the lines in his face and the look in his eyes could I tell the agony of that experience. His courage and control gave me strength. By the time George returned I was up once more and ready to carry on.

xvii.

On the 20th of June the following announcement came over the radio from Rome:

> "The fact that General Marshall has made a sudden trip to Italy may or may not be significant. It may have been part of his itinerary when he left Washington. On the other hand, the sudden collapse of German resistance in Italy may have provided an opportunity to hasten the time-table in that area also."

George had gone to the Anzio Cemetery to pay his heavyhearted tribute to Allen. General Devers and his escort had retired while he spent a half-hour alone at the grave. . . .

On his return, General Marshall made the following statement:

> "Our Army feels great pride in the Normandy assault. So must the Navy and our British Allies. The Navy's mission was to transport the troops across the Channel, to land

them properly on the beaches, and to support the landings
with gun and rocket fire.   If the Allied navies had not performed this task brilliantly, the invasion would have failed
before it was well begun.   The combined planning of British
and American staffs, working together as a single team with
excellent knowledge of enemy dispositions, resulted in precise
execution of an operation so complicated that it almost defies
description; its success must be attributed in great measure to
wholehearted Allied cooperation, as well as to the stout hearts
and fearless courage of the men.   The destruction of rail
and road communications by the air forces and their constant strafing of the highways continued to prevent the
enemy from concentrating a superior force against the
beachhead."

xviii.

The Easter before D-Day, Vice-President and Mrs.
Wallace had sent us a little box of his prize seed corn,
prettily done up for a holiday present.   That spring we
had planted it on our hurried trips to Leesburg over the
week-ends.   There was so much to be done in the garden
and grounds, with no gardener to do it, that we decided
I would do what I could on the flowers and George would
devote his time and strength to the vegetables.

Late one Saturday afternoon while George was attending to his planting, I had a caller, a real estate man
who had come to talk over our buying some adjacent
property.   After we had discussed the matter, I said,
"We will go out in the garden and talk to George." When
we approached my husband was lying prone, his head resting on one hand while with the other he dropped the
seed corn into the furrows.   Then he would pull himself
along and drop some more, never getting to his feet.   I
introduced the real estate man and General Marshall

apologized for not rising—he was too tired. They had quite a talk about the planting, during which the man gave George some good advice; then we returned to the house. On leaving my caller said, "Mrs. Marshall, I would like to ask a favor of you. The next time General Marshall comes down, will you give me a ring? I would like so much to have the honor of shaking hands with him." "Why," I said astonished, "you have just been talking to him." "My Lord!" exclaimed the real estate man, "That wasn't General Marshall, was it?"

He gave me no chance to answer, but rushed out to the garden, just as George had gotten to his feet and was trying to straighten up, shook his hand, and was gone without a word.

"What is the matter with that fellow?" George asked as I appeared.

"He just found out that 'you are you'," I said.

The Vice President's corn was a great success. An early dwarf variety, it had all been eaten and enjoyed by July and the stalks left to wither during an exceptionally hot spell. It was then that LIFE magazine sent a photographer to Leesburg to take some pictures of the Chief of Staff at home and found George in overalls wheeling rubbish to a compost pit. The photographer insisted on one view of George standing by the Vice President's almost dead stalks of corn. His pride as a gardener rebelled but the photographer insisted. When this picture appeared in LIFE the entire crop of corn farmers of the Middle West, so it seemed to me, wrote LIFE, the War Department, or direct to George: "Marshall might know his business as Chief of Staff, but he sure knew nothing about corn," "What kind of corn is this pathetic looking stuff?," "He and Vice President Wallace had better come west and

look at a crop of real corn. Would their faces be red?
I'll say they will!" and so forth and so on, until LIFE
had to publish an explanation that this corn was an early
dwarf variety, long since "gone with the wind" and that
General Marshall and the Vice President were both good
farmers in spite of opinions to the contrary.

        This was true too, for we had one of the best
gardens in Leesburg—asparagus, my husband would let
no one cut the first or second year; luscious red raspberries,
the birds got before we did; and endless beets no one would
eat. But, on the other hand, we had lettuce until after
frost, spinach, squash, carrots, beans, eggplant, corn—early
and late—and our tomato crop in August was beautiful to
behold. These tomatoes, also from the Vice President's
seeds, were delicious—we had large red and yellow ones,
pear-shaped pink ones, and tiny little yellow oblong ones.
Our crop was the wonder of our country neighbors and a
source of great pride to my husband. Only the sweet
potatoes and cauliflower failed him, and they had been
put in too late—his military duties had conflicted with
planting requirements.

                            xix.

        Our place at Leesburg was a real source of comfort.
No matter what else failed, the flowers bloomed, the
garden grew, Mother Earth did her part.

        General Arnold, who lived in quarters not far from
ours at Fort Myer, had heard us tell of our gardening at
Leesburg and that no help was to be found; so he asked
to come down some Saturday to get a work-out. This
was like manna from heaven. I had often heard friends
of mine in New York tell how their weekend guests had

helped with their Victory gardening; but personally I could not boast of having any such friends. Everyone who came to Leesburg seemed to come for rest. I worked with the flowers, George with the shrubs, vegetables and heavy planting, and we worked hard, doing many other chores, particularly when a painter or carpenter disappointed us—which was usually the case. So when General Arnold called up and said he would come down for a work-out that Saturday, both George and I were delighted.

As his car drove in, George and I, in army fatigue coveralls, were on ladders painting the trim of the house, George high up, a bucket swung in true painter's style on one of the rounds of his ladder. As he turned to see who had invaded our privacy, a stream of green paint was trickling down his forehead and had about reached his nose. This gave him a most peculiar look. General Arnold's chauffeur, an old Army Sergeant, glanced at George, then turned away in embarrassment. Arnold was immaculate in his summer uniform.

We both greeted him with joy and at once asked eagerly, "Did you bring your work clothes?"

"I most certainly did, and will be down at once," he answered.

While he was upstairs, I said to George, "Put him to work in the rose garden when he comes down." But my husband's mind was on vegetables—he made no reply. I saw him get the long-handled pitchfork out of the tool house.

When General Arnold reappeared in what scarcely looked like work clothes to us—white shirt and white trousers—I disappeared to don a more respectable garb. A little later as I was dressing I looked out of my window over the rose garden, but General Arnold was nowhere in sight. A dreadful thought struck me, and as soon as I could finish dressing I hurried down and asked George what he had done with the General.

"He is getting a good work-out," said George succinctly.

I did not wait for more but knowing only too well where to find him hurried to the back of the garden. There knee-deep in the center of the compost heap was the Commander of the United States Air Forces, painfully, laboriously turning it over and over with the long-handled fork, and only stopping now and then to wipe away the perspiration which was streaming down his face. His white shirt and trousers were now a sight to behold.

This compost heap was the pride of George's heart. Whenever he read of anything that was good material for compost, in it went. By now it comprised about everything known to man.

As I came up General Arnold called: "What has George got in here? The stuff is as heavy as lead. Hardest work that I ever did in my life, but I have it about done."

"George ought to be ashamed of himself!" I said. "Please come out of there."

"Not until I have finished," he answered. And finish he did. He was the best sport I ever saw.

An hour later General Arnold again appeared, immaculate in his uniform, and while we had cool drinks on the lawn, he and George planned three days of real recreation and sport in the High Sierras, fishing for golden trout —before they were to leave for the second Quebec Conference.

XX.

On September 1st, 1944, General Marshall had been Chief of Staff for five years. On September 1st, 1939, Adolph Hitler, boasting about the uniform he would never take off until victory was his, had sent his armored war machine crashing across Poland. When I went to Secretary Woodring's office that morning to see my husband sworn in as Chief of Staff, little did I dream that—considering our pitifully small Army of 174,000 enlisted men —the deathless tale of David and Goliath was again to be reenacted. We were not at war as yet, but even while the "madman of Europe" was on his seemingly irresistible march, there was developing probably unbeknownst to him, thousands of miles away in the United States of America, an army that, together with its Allies, was in five years to expel the Axis from Africa, drive it out of Sicily, Sardinia, Corsica, Elba, and most of Italy; that was to push the vaunted German Army back from the shores of Southern France, freeing Marseilles, Toulon, and expel it from the Valley of the Rhone, freeing Lyons; that was to land on the coast of Normandy, liberate Paris and drive the Germans back across the Seine. By the end of those five years the whole of northern, southern and central France, parts of Belgium and Luxembourg were to be in Allied hands, and the defeated German armies were hurrying to the shelter of the Siegfried Line.

General Eisenhower reported it was his intention to prepare with all speed to destroy the German armies in the West and occupy the German homeland. The people of the United States were awaiting breathlessly the news of new victories, and while they waited, Allied occupation was spreading out over the map of France like an overturned bottle of red ink. This was the situation on the 1st of September, 1944, as my husband prepared to leave for Quebec.

When he returned from this conference, he attended the American Legion Convention in Chicago and his speech there was a solemn warning to this country to keep a never-ending line of supplies moving to the fighting fronts. He said, in part:

> "We are close to victory. The size and fury of the attack must constantly increase. We have a stern duty here at home if our attacks are to surge forward in constantly increasing strength and power during what we all hope are the last hours of the European conflict. The men now dying in the outworks of the west wall are dying as bitterly as those lost on the Norman beaches or at St. Lo. We are close to victory in Europe but the victory in the Pacific is still farther ahead and the cost of both is still to be paid in full."

This speech aroused our people at home to even greater effort. Given publicity across the entire country, it became the subject of editorials even in leading British papers. The question of supplies for both the Pacific and Western fronts became so serious that the shipment of mail—the greatest of all morale factors—had to be suspended for a period. General Marshall was so concerned over this problem that he made a non-stop flight to Paris to inspect the divisions along the front from Belfort Gap near Switzerland to Holland. He boarded the first Air Transport plane flying direct from America to Paris and was met on his arrival at the airport by General Eisenhower, General Bradley, General Smith and many of the staff. I received a radio-telephoto of them shaking hands on George's arrival. A slip accompanying it said:

"This is the first radio photograph transmitted direct from the Continent to the United States." It arrived in Leesburg a little more than an hour after General Marshall had landed at Paris. Washington had received it only a few minutes after his arrival.

xxi.

George asked Mr. Byrnes to accompany him on this trip as he had looked very tired at a Chief of Staff's luncheon a few days before, and George thought a trip to the front would do him good. They had an amusing time outfitting him as a military man on such short notice. I felt great sympathy for Mr. Byrnes. George would always say, "Traveling is nothing. Just throw a few things into a bag. Why worry?" I would say nothing, but thought a lot, as it took his orderly, with my help, a day to pack for his various trips, each article being checked and each bag containing a list of the articles inside, and marked by number according to the order in which they were to be opened. He was so accustomed to saying to an officer, "Leave at once" for some place on the other side of the globe, and receiving a polite, "Yes, Sir," that it seemed a small matter to him. But I often wondered how they managed it, and deep in my heart were great understanding and sympathy for them and, if married, for their wives.

xxii.

With the Allied "blitz" in Europe going at such an astounding speed, General Marshall was turning his mind to thoughts of the United States of the future and the

Army in particular.   He was most concerned with the
future safety of the Nation and with permanent peace for
the Nation once this war had been won.   He publicly advocated a small peace-time professional army with a
trained citizen reserve, flatly stating his belief that a large
standing army has no place among institutions of a modern
democratic state.

I have in my scrapbook page after page of articles
and editorials inspired by the announcement of this plan
of his.   It met with general approval in the press, as indicated by such headlines as: "Marshall Looks Ahead,"
"The Wise Policy," "General Marshall's Wisdom," "Military Training Sentiment Growing," "The Best Military
Plan."

xxiii.

While George was inspecting in France, Molly and
I were closing the Leesburg house and getting settled at
Fort Myer for the winter.   Her husband was at the front
in France; my husband, son and only brother were also
there. Our conversation and thoughts were of little else.
If they were my soldiers at the front, I certainly had one
at home—never, during the entire war, did I hear a complaint from Molly. Devoting herself to the care of her
two babies, she carried her anxiety over her husband with
quiet fortitude, and she carried it alone. Only by the
light under her door late at night, could I tell the strain
which she was under. My children had had a great herit-
age of character left by their father and for the past fourteen years an exceptional example in George Marshall. In
this they were most fortunate.

I was extremely busy with war work at this time
—too many demands for my strength. But I had promised

to speak in Pittsburgh late in October, at the 75th Anniversary celebration of the Pennsylvania College for Women, and I was glad to comply with this request. Many years before, on our way to Chicago, George and I had driven through the glorious mountains of that state in the fall of the year.   And it had been a delightful trip, in spite of the fact that we fought the French and Indian wars up one hill and down another, all the way across Pennsylvania. Even at that time I had become accustomed to this.   I really think I am the 'fightinest' veteran of American Wars in this country, for on our many motor trips I have waged every battle of the Revolution throughout the East, the Civil War from Maryland through Georgia, and have battled the Indians across Ohio, Indiana, and Illinois, as well as in the lava beds of the great Northwest. So the French and Indian Wars through Pennsylvania had been just another campaign added to my military training.

George returned from France just as we finished our move back to Fort Myer; and as his trip had been a long and difficult one, we dreamed of a real vacation. He was to speak before the National Advisory Council of Manufacturers at Hot Springs, Virginia, then to accompany me on the drive to Pittsburgh and while I spoke, he was to visit his sister.   The weather was beautiful and we both longed to be off for the drive through the mountains, arrayed in their colorful fall foliage.

We were to leave on a Wednesday.   Tuesday morning, in order to clear up everything before going, I had three Board meetings. Wednesday morning, about 1 a. m., I awakened with a frightening feeling in my right side— as though I were paralyzed.   I could not move without excruciating pain.   A spoon and glass stood on the table beside me and as I could not reach the bell, I kept rapping on the glass with the spoon.   Finally George's door opened and he asked, "What are you hammering on at this hour of the night?"   In a half-hour the doctor was there, then a nurse.   I had pneumonia.

xxiv.

On the 4th of November Field Marshal Sir John Dill, head of the British Joint Staff Mission in the United States, died of pernicious anemia at Walter Reed Hospital.   His death was a cruel blow to my husband, for not only did it mean the loss of a close friend whom he admired and loved, but also an irreparable loss to the Combined Chiefs of Staff.

General Marshall said at the time: "The fact that the Allied Forces stand poised at the gates of Germany is due in no small measure to the breadth of vision and the selfless devotion of Field Marshal Sir John Dill to our common cause.   I know of no man who has made a greater contribution to complete military co-operation between British and American forces."

Sir John left a request with his wife, Nancy, that he be buried in this country in Arlington Cemetery, as he considered his work here the most important of his life. Lady Dill asked George to read the Lesson at the burial service, conducted at the Cathedral by the Bishop of Washington.

The following letter from Supreme Court Justice Frankfurter may indicate how deep were General Marshall's emotions on this occasion:

"Supreme Court of the U. S.

"Washington, D. C.

"Dear Mrs. Marshall:

"You must let me say that few things that I have heard in my life were as impressive as General Marshall's reading of the Lesson at Sir John Dill's services today. The text that he chose and the manner of its reading in its setting, made that reading for me—as I am sure for all others—an enduring memory.

"Very sincerely,

(Signed) "Felix Frankfurter"

From Nancy Dill, Sir John's wife, the following was received:

"Dear Katherine:

"Thank you so much for your letter, and all the affection and sympathy that you and George have shown me. Jack was devoted to you both, and to have George's trust and friendship meant a great deal to him. He often told me that his last job was the most important of his life, he was happy living in America, and for me—it was just heaven to be with him constantly.

"George has been so kind and thoughtful for me in this difficult time. I was so sorry to know how ill you have been, Katherine. Please take care of yourself.

"With affectionate regards,

"Yours,

"Nancy Dill"

In honor of the services rendered by Sir John, our Senate passed the following Joint Resolution November 25th, a unique action, without precedent:

"JOINT RESOLUTION Recognizing the outstanding service rendered to the United Nations by Field Marshal Sir John Dill.

"Whereas the Congress having been informed of the death
of Field Marshal Sir John Dill, in Washington, District of
Columbia, on November 4, 1944; and

"Whereas the Arlington National Cemetery has been chosen
as the final resting place of this distinguished soldier; and

"Whereas as senior British representative on the Combined
Chiefs of Staff, Field Marshal Sir John Dill, by his wisdom
and devotion to the vital cause of British-American military cooperation, rendered a great service to the United
Nations;

"Now, therefore, be it

"Resolved by the Senate and House of Representatives of
the United States of America in Congress assembled, That the
outstanding service rendered to the United Nations by Field
Marshal Sir John Dill be, and it hereby is, recognized by the
American people and the Congress of the United States."

There was deep grief in our home at Sir John's
death. Even little Katherine Winn treasures to this day
a lamb which plays "Mary Had a Little Lamb," a gift from
Sir John on the occasion of Kitty's first birthday party.
He had sat at the foot of the table, while Kitty, one year
old, had presided from her high chair at the head. Sir
John declared her the most poised and charming hostess
he had ever had.

XXV.

As soon as I was able to travel I left for Pinehurst,
North Carolina, to get my strength back. General Marshall had to inspect at Fort Bragg, North Carolina, where
there were 90,000 troops, and so he accompanied me on
the trip down. My sister joined me at the Carolina Hotel
and remained throughout my stay. The first week was

lovely and we lay out in the warm sun, drinking in health and strength. Then it began to rain and turned gloomy and cold. I wired George I wanted to come home. He wired back, "Please stay. It is raining in Chicago, Boston and Washington much harder and colder than in Pinehurst." I answered, "Yes, but I am not paying $200 a week for it to rain in Boston, Chicago, and Washington."

Before he had time to answer this, the skies cleared and Pinehurst was as delightful as ever—so delightful, in fact, that when I left two weeks later I had taken an option on Liscombe Lodge, the place we later bought for our winter home.

My husband often complained about my desire to buy houses here, there and everywhere. He had several stories on this subject and declared that at every place we had stayed long enough I had begun to look for a home and would come to him all excited about the marvelous place I had found—well within our means! He said it was only due to his Army orders that we were not swamped with houses all across the United States from the Atlantic to the Pacific.

This was more or less true. I was very much like the hen in "The Virginian," I "wanted to set." But it was equally true that George also wanted to set. Ever since he had been of age he had been wandering over the face of the globe; at each halting place he had tried to make a house into a home, always fixing a garden, and then, just as he had begun to feel at home and the things planted had taken root, orders would come to move on and he would start all over again. This had gone on for forty years. Of course it was only what every Army family had to endure, but to us it seemed the most difficult part of Army life. Neither of us liked living in hotels or clubs. George had often said "I prize my privacy more than any one thing I possess." We now had the Leesburg house for late spring, summer and early fall, and Liscombe Lodge at Pinehurst for the remainder of the year. This made us exceedingly happy and we longed hopefully to live in them as soon as the war was won. All our plans were to this end and the making of those plans together was the greatest pleasure of our lives.

xxvi.

The first Saturday after I returned from Pinehurst, December 2nd, George showed me on the maps what had been accomplished during the last three years in the Pacific theater of war. The following Thursday would mark the third anniversary of the day when an astounded and angry America had heard the news of the Japs' sneak attack on Pearl Harbor. Americans, in one voice, had vowed in wrathful indignation not to rest until that dreadful day of treachery had been repaid in full.

Three years had passed. In the first year of war America, recovering from its flare of temper, soberly realized that not only would it be a long, tough war, but that even the possibility of defeat confronted us. The nation went to work. Young men and women volunteered for the armed services. Others went into war work. By the end of the second year the Allied nations had hurled back the offensive thrusts of the enemy and were beating the Axis at its own war game. Supremely encouraging, the possibility of defeat had been eliminated. America was playing on, and the leader of, the winning team. Almost all memories of that frightening first year had been forgotten during the past twelve months. America was heartened by victory on every front.

Distances in the Pacific were almost fantastic. A bomb manufactured in Michigan must travel via Guam almost 6,500 miles before being delivered at Tokyo. The Allies were operating in the Pacific on a battle-front of 6,000 miles. MacArthur was moving up the main chain of island land masses from New Guinea towards the Philippines. Covering his flank and seizing operating bases for ships and planes, a series of attacks had been launched through the Central Pacific to capture key islands in that tremendous waste of water—Saipan, Guam and Peleliu. Finally in October these two advances joined in a surprise assault on the island of Leyte in the center of the Philippine Archipelago, and the liberation of the Philippines was under way. The destruction of Japanese shipping in the China Sea was soon to follow, which would isolate the enemy's troops in Burma, Indonesia, Indo-China and Southern China itself. The day of reckoning was indeed at hand.

In connection with the decision for the landing on Leyte it is interesting to consider the magnitude and complexity of the planning and co-ordination involved. Originally it had been intended to carry out two operations to the south preceding the Leyte coup, but a reconnaissance by Admiral Halsey's forces had convinced him that conditions warranted advancing the schedule by some two months. This would initiate the liberation of the Philippines by the landing at Leyte.

He radioed this recommendation to the Chiefs of Staff while they were in Quebec. It was immediately communicated by them to General MacArthur, who at the time was actually engaged in a landing at Biak. His reply, accepting the proposal and designating October 20th as the date, was delivered to General Marshall during a dinner for the United States Chiefs of Staff given by Canadian officials. With Admiral King and General Arnold, George retired from the table and, after a brief conference, a reply was drafted to General MacArthur and to Admirals Nimitz and Halsey, to go ahead on the basis of October 20th. The three Chiefs of Staff then returned to the table and finished their dinner.

As my husband entered the elevator on his return to the Hotel Frontenac he was handed General Mac-Arthur's reply, acknowledging receipt of the message and stating that he would go ahead with the preparations on the new basis. When one considers the importance of these decisions, the tremendous distances involved and the fact that General MacArthur had received these messages in the midst of a landing operation, the rapidity of this momentous conclusion is surely astounding. Indeed, with our Nation's existence and civilization in the balance, we may thank God for leaders whose knowledge was sure and whose minds grasped and solved great problems with the speed of light.

xxvii.

As our hospitals filled with our wounded, the prisoner of war camps here in the United States filled with German and Italian prisoners. I had seen several of these camps. The Germans, far from beaten in spirit, looked at you with bold sneering glances. Apparently, in spite of their imprisonment, they still considered themselves the Master Race. In each of the camps American papers were distributed telling of Axis defeat after defeat; but many of the PW's would not read this news, and those who did considered it merely propaganda. To cling to the belief that you cannot be defeated after you have been hopelessly defeated is just plain stupidity; but these Nazis seem to have a curious characteristic. They not only had to be captured and lodged in a prison camp far from their homeland, but had to be made to realize they were prisoners after being placed behind barbed wire. Our Army was so scrupulously careful to observe the Geneva Convention's rules that our PW's were able to stage many scenes that would have meant torture and death in either Japan or Germany. However, it was a price we were willing to pay in order to exemplify the civilization in which we believe.

At Sheridan, Illinois, I recall 1,300 Nazi prisoners of war went on a sit-down strike, refusing to work because one of their compatriots had been removed from his position as a group leader. A bread-and-water diet soon brought them to terms. These German PW's were brutally cruel to any fellow-prisoner who strayed from the Nazi fold, and yet fellow-prisoners dared not report these cruelties. Even though 3,000 miles from Germany in an American prison camp guarded by American soldiers, the fear of the Gestapo still obsessed them.

After V-E Day, when we started returning prisoners to their Fatherland, some tried to escape or begged that they might be allowed to remain in America. Many had been used as farm laborers and our people, quick to anger and quick to forget, sent letters to the War Department and to their Congressmen, saying the German war prisoners working on farms should have better and more plentiful food. At that time they were receiving a larger ration of meats than our average citizen.

xxviii.

On December 8th, 1944, the Congress passed, with very slight opposition, a bill to create eight war-time Five-Star Army and Navy commanders. For one reason, this was done to make the top ranking American officers approximate in grade the British Field Marshals with whom they had to deal. These officers were, for the Army, Generals Marshall, Arnold, Eisenhower and MacArthur; for the Navy, Admirals Leahy, King, Nimitz and Halsey.

At this time Secretary of State Hull, who had been in poor health for some years, sent in his resignation to the President. His trip to Moscow in 1943 was, I think, one of the most selfless acts of the war. A great statesman, the Secretary's historic settlements on that trip were a diplomatic triumph. With a deep feeling of personal loss General Marshall wrote to the Secretary upon his retirement. Mr. Hull's answer follows:

"December 9, 1944

"Dear General Marshall:

"Your recent letter about my resignation is one of my most treasured possessions. It means much to me to have this expression of your good opinion of my work during the years that I have been in Washington. As I look back over the past I know that I could never have had a finer and truer associate and friend than yourself. For your never-failing cooperation and assistance I shall remain eternally grateful. I also want you to know of my profound admiration for your distinguished record of service to our country and to the United Nations.

"My confidence and affection shall be with you always.

"With every good wish to you and Mrs. Marshall, in which Mrs. Hull joins me,

"Sincerely,

"Cordell Hull"

xxix.

George was using every opportunity now to place before the public his post-war military training program. Congressman James J. Wadsworth introduced a bill which favored compulsory military training for all able-bodied American young men after the war. Opposed to this bill was a powerful bloc composed of college professors, Churchmen, and some women's organizations. It seemed strange to me that the women—mothers and wives of our soldiers—were the most open-minded when it came to considering both sides of the argument. If they were once convinced that military training was essential to preserve the peace and protect our country, they did not hesitate to change their minds and espouse the cause. But not so the men of the other two blocs. When they took a public stand they seemed to feel that their manhood required them to stick to their guns, no matter what logical reasoning was brought to bear, nor how many of their objections were answered conclusively. Their attitude was very much like that of President Coolidge who, when asked what he thought of sin, said: "I am against it."

xxx.

The end of this terrible war was now in sight—at least on the European Continent—and America was beginning to breathe easily once more. Each day, as reports of our successes in Europe and the Pacific rolled in, life grew more normal. The blackouts and siren warnings had ceased, the rationing of food and other supplies had grown less strict, the tenseness and pinch of war less severe.

Opposition groups tolerated no thought of military training for the future. Their type had been responsible for our unpreparedness for both World War I and World War II; and now they refused to see beyond the near future—peace, overflowing schools and colleges and the horn of plenty.

Into this state of myopic complacency for the future of the United States, a rude note was struck. General von Rundstedt attacked with a force of 24 divisions in France. Eight German Panzer divisions broke through our lines on a 40-mile front and the enemy drove through to a depth of 50 miles. This, the now famous Battle of the Bulge, was our first real set-back since our troops had landed on the coast of Normandy. It proved to be the dying struggle of the great German war machine on the Western Front. By Christmas the weather ceased to favor the enemy and permitted our overwhelming air force to strike back. By the end of January our First and Third Armies had eliminated the bulge and our Seventh Army had frustrated a New Year's attack on our southern flank. The cost to the enemy of this desperate strategy became apparent later.

xxxi.

Christmas of 1944 was quite different from those of 1942 and 1943. In the hearts of the people there was a great longing—intensified by time—for their loved ones overseas; but there was also happiness that the war was obviously near its end. In thousands of homes that Christmas, in spite of the empty places at dinner table—many never to be filled again—there was thankfulness for the successes of our fighting forces and a prayer that our soldiers and sailors would soon be home.

Also in the Chief of Staff's heart there was happiness in the knowledge that his plan for the soldiers' Christmas would be carried through again, as it had the Christmas before. Each soldier was to have his Christmas turkey dinner with all its "trimmings." If he could not bring them home to eat it with "Mom" and the family, he had managed against odds and difficulties such as the average citizen could hardly imagine, to get it to them wherever they might be, for, as he said, "A turkey dinner means home to an American soldier."

In our quarters at Fort Myer, Christmas Eve was spent by George and Molly working until midnight putting up a unique display of soldiers for the children. A wonderful collection of hand-painted lead soldiers from the early Indian Wars up to the present day had been sent to Jimmy Winn by a friend of ours. This friend had spent 30 years, I believe he said, making the collection; so we moved the small library from the sun-porch and here George and Molly built Indian villages and set up stockades for the defense of the American pioneers against attack by the Redskins. There were also British and French soldiers, battlements made of papier-mache painted to look like rocks, Cavalry charges, Infantry marching, in the style of the early days of our country. Present-day warfare was represented with its air fields lit by tiny flood lights, planes, trucks, ambulances, modern barracks with soldiers doing their laundry, sitting outside their tents writing letters, attending to all the various chores that constitute a soldier's everyday life, armies in tents, armies on foot, signal and motor-cycle corps—all these soldiers and their equipment, tents and barracks, beautifully made and colored.

I am sure no other little boy ever had a more fascinating display and I only wished that all might see it. At least, on Christmas Day Jimmy's class at Kindergarten was invited to come in to play with it and have ice-cream and cake. All day the house was full of children from the Post and children of our civilian friends who had come to see the collection. The display really was an amazing sight, with an electric train running across the room packed with soldiers going into camp. I had busied myself the night before with the Christmas tree downstairs, but with such competition upstairs my tree was hardly noticed.

As there would have been only George, Molly and myself for Christmas dinner, I asked the bachelor officers on George's Staff who were away from home to have dinner with us. It was a busy Christmas with children running and calling through the house. The day passed before we knew it, which was just as well, and that evening George and I sat on the sun-porch and read the letters, radios and telegrams which had poured in. We had over 1,000 pieces of mail at the house that Christmas.

I quote one of the letters:

"Supreme Headquarters
"ALLIED EXPEDITIONARY FORCE
"Office of the Supreme Commander
"23 December, 1944

"Dear General Marshall:

"Receipt of your Christmas letter to me was the brightest spot in my existence since we reached the Siegfried Line. Short of a major defeat inflicted upon the enemy, I could not have had a better personal present.

"For my part, I pray that the coming year will see all of your great efforts and plans well on the road to fulfillment and, for the United States, my most fervent hope is that your health and strength will be preserved to carry your great burdens until victory has been achieved.

"With warm personal regards, and with the request that you pay my respects to Mrs. Marshall.

"Sincerely,
"DWIGHT D. EISENHOWER"

On General Marshall's birthday, December 31st, an informal gathering of a few of the Staff was arranged by General Arnold as a surprise affair. The Secretary of War, Colonel Stimson, in a toast paid George the following tribute:

"As a result of my experience during a somewhat long life, I have become accustomed to placing the various holders of public office with whom I came in contact in one or the other of two categories—first, those who are thinking primarily of what they can do for the job which they hold; and second, those who are thinking primarily of what the job can do for them. I think that General Marshall stands at the very top of my list of those whom I would place in the first category, namely those who are always seeking to see what they can do to make effective the work of their office regardless of its effect upon themselves personally. I feel, General Marshall, that you are one of the most selfless public officials whom I have ever known. In spite of your deep feelings and affections you have always been able to consider first the requirements of the job and to disregard all other considerations.

"To you may well be applied the language of the phrase in Proverbs, 'He who controlleth his spirit is better than he who taketh a city.' I feel that it has been a great privilege to have been associated with you and I devoutly hope that you will continue your leadership until the victory is attained."

Chapter VII

AFTER THE MIGHTY accomplishments of 1944, I dislike to start the New Year of 1945 on a somber note, but things were in truth somber. I quote from the last chapter of "The Curtain Rises," the best seller by Quentin Reynolds, the War Correspondent:

> "I've been home for a month now and for the first time in seven months I'm completely bewildered. It was a shock to pick up the papers and read columns of criticism of our war effort. Everything I saw in the war zone led me to believe that our materiel was the best in the world; that a military miracle had been achieved in the rapid training of our troops; that our war effort was being handled with a minimum of red tape, lost effort and inefficiency. . . . Yet, from the papers, one would think that Washington was a mad house inhabited by certified lunatics, crooks or shady politicians. It was disheartening, because when you're first home you're so thrilled with pride at the great job America has done and is doing that you feel like waving a flag."

The alarm was raised that the influence of the mili-

tary was becoming too dominant. War production shortages and resultant tightening of manpower and Selective
Service controls, sweeping orders and recommendations
from War Mobilization Director James F. Byrnes, the
President's own request for reconsideration by Congress
of the National Service legislation issue—all these things
were supposed to prove that the General Staff thinking
was dictating the policy on too many domestic problems.
All-out Liberals viewed this with concern, believing that
in a democracy—even during a war—civilians should be
telling the military what to do.

Of necessity there were many curbs at this time on
civilian rights, but obviously they were essential to the
conduct of an all-out war effort. Orders were issued to
close the racetracks, cancel conventions, draft farm workers, put ceilings on livestock, tighten up rationing of meat,
butter, sugar, and canned goods, cut back civilian goods
production, take over Montgomery Ward and similar
trouble spots, cut down on coal consumption, turn off display advertising lights to save power. Naturally these
were all unpopular curbs. The manpower shortage bill was
being fought in Congress. The solution would have been
the passage of a National Service law a year before. When
the Army had to furlough men to make tires and steel and
help harvest the crops, that certainly indicated that the
men behind the men behind the guns were falling down
on the job. If a little more attention had been paid earlier
to military thinking on manpower and production controls, this manpower crisis might have been averted.

My husband and Admiral King now appeared before Senators and Representatives at a meeting in the
Library of Congress. Legislation was not mentioned by
either, nor was the manpower crisis referred to directly,

but each of them in referring to the high points of shipping and military personnel problems, as well as other shortages, gave Congress the real picture. It was hoped that their frank statements of the war shortages would influence prompt Congressional action.

George was not only pressing for manpower control at the present but, looking far ahead, he was fighting for Universal Military Training for national safety. He appeared before the Association of American Colleges at its annual conference in Atlantic City and made a one-hour "off the record" speech in favor of universal training. It was reported to have been most forceful but he converted only a handful. The final sense of the meeting was that Congress should postpone all action on Universal Military training at this time.

After this speech a cartoon appeared showing a college professor dinging facts into a student's head. Caption: "When a college professor states to a student the facts of the nebular hypothesis, that is education." A second drawing showed General Marshall telling facts to a professor. Caption: "But when our most distinguished military authority states facts of Universal Military Training to a College Professor, that is nonsense (to a professor)."

The Times Herald came out with an editorial which stated:

"SHALL WE MAKE THE SAME MISTAKE TWICE?

"We have much respect for American university and college executives as educators. But when they branch out into such fields as statecraft and international politics, many of them frequently come up with bizarre ideas.

"In this case, they are starting out on the same tack as a

lot of educators, uplifters and serious thinkers took after the last war with regard to universal military training. They utilized the post-war disgust with war and hatred of high taxes to talk us out of adopting universal training. Thereby, they did their bit to help bring on Pearl Harbor."

ii.

On January 20th, 1945, ceremonies were held inaugurating President Roosevelt for his fourth term of office, and Vice President Truman for his first.

The night before the Inauguration, the Inaugural Dinner, given by the Presidential Electors in honor of President Roosevelt and Mr. Truman, was held at the Mayflower Hotel. Mrs. Roosevelt was present but the President, conserving his strength for the next day, did not appear. It was a very beautiful and elaborate affair. Mrs. Roosevelt led the procession with Mr. Doyle, Chairman of the Electoral College; following in the order named, came Vice President and Mrs. Wallace, Senator and Mrs. Truman, Chief Justice and Mrs. Stone, the Speaker of the House and Miss Reyburn, Secretary of State Edward Stettinius and Mrs. Stettinius, and Mrs. Woodrow Wilson. All members of the Supreme Court and Cabinet were present, as well as the military leaders and their wives, and many distinguished guests of official Washington.

The members of the various armed forces, carrying the standards of the 48 States of the Union, and the Guard of Honor carrying the National Colors, the flag of the President and the flag of the Vice President, marched in at the end of the procession. As soon as the flags were in place, the United States Marine Band played the National Anthem. It was a stirring and memorable evening.

The menus were beautifully gotten up in book form, with the coat-of-arms of the United States in heavy gold on the cover, and tied with red, white and blue silk cords. Inside were sepia portraits of the President and Vice President-elect Truman, unbound and suitable for framing.

It was quite late when we arrived home at Fort Myer after this dinner. The next day was Inauguration Day and as George had to go to his office before the religious service, to be held at the White House at 10 a. m., we were up betimes. After this religious service, the Inauguration was to take place at 11:45, followed by a luncheon and then the parade. That evening there was to be another official dinner. In fact that whole week was overcrowded with official affairs.

The Inauguration ceremony was held on the South Portico of the White House, so that the thousands crowded in the White House grounds and the streets beyond could see the President take his Oath of Office for the fourth time. The day was bitterly cold. The President was pale and drawn, his hands trembled constantly, his voice appeared weak. He bore little resemblance to the forceful figure that had stood on that portico four years before, his head thrown back, his voice clear and powerful. It was tragic to see the havoc the past four years had wrought. The handwriting on the wall was unmistakable, despite all denials on the part of those surrounding him.

The most interesting and pleasing part of that ceremony were the grandchildren—from tiny tots to Elliott's oldest son, a boy of ten or eleven. They were grouped on the steps at one side of the portico and were the source of great interest and the subject of much picture-taking,

none of which seemed to perturb them in the least. A
perfectly natural group of cousins, they were engrossed
in their own affairs, their secrets and little differences.

I marveled that luncheon could be served at the
White House to the hordes that were present. However,
it was a very simple affair. A long table was set in the
center of the room, you took a cup of coffee and a plate
with a roll and chicken salad on it. That was the entire luncheon, but it gave the crowd something before
they went out in the wintry blasts once more for the
parade.

At dinner that night Mr. Jessup, the Toastmaster,
began his speech by saying he had had his first luncheon at
the White House that day. He turned to Mrs. Roosevelt
and said, "Mrs. Roosevelt, I wish to ask you seriously how
it is humanly possible to make chicken salad with so much
celery and so little chicken." Mrs. Roosevelt immediately answered, "I do not know, Mr. Jessup. I had a hard
time finding any chicken myself." This brought down
the house.

iii.

The end of January George was to leave for the
Yalta Conference. It had been a cold, damp month in
Washington and the flu was prevalent everywhere. The
whole city seemed to be a huge kennel with everyone barking, barking; the disease affected the throat and, though
not dangerous, was most persistent. Our home was no
different from others—Molly, Jimmy, Kitty and I all
coughed incessantly and the babies looked pale and run
down. We had just bought Liscombe Lodge at Pinehurst, North Carolina, as a winter home, and George insisted that we all go there as soon as he left for the Yalta

Conference.   There was an airfield a few miles from
Pinehurst and from Washington to Pinehurst was only an
hour and a half's flight.   Our plan was that my husband
would join us over week-ends when possible, which plan
proved to be an excellent one after his return.

The sunshine and dry climate of the sandhills of
North Carolina soon put us all back in good condition.

George's first letter after he left for this overseas
conference enclosed a picture of the grounds and gardens
at Valmante near Marseilles, France, where he stayed for
two days to confer with General Eisenhower, enroute to
Malta and Yalta. He also enclosed an invitation for dinner from the Governor of Malta and Lady Schrieber. It
was quite cold at Malta where a stop was made for a Combined Staff conference, and George caught cold, his first
misfortune of this kind on any of his travels.   The old
Crusader building in which he was quartered was indeed
a chilly proposition.

Pictures taken of President Roosevelt aboard ship
in the Malta Harbor showed him looking drawn and ill.

At the historic meeting in the Crimea between
Marshal Stalin, Prime Minister Churchill and our President, with their military advisers, an agreement was
reached for the final push against fast-weakening Germany—the doom of the Nazis. By February 7th they
were discussing a secure peace.

In my husband's first letter from Yalta he sent me
a picture postcard of the castle in which he was billeted,
with a description of his room the window of which he
had marked by a cross. It had been the bedroom of the
beautiful but ill-fated Czarina. A door in the adjacent
boudoir, assigned to Admiral King, led to a stairway which
was alleged to have been used by Rasputin, the Czarina's

evil genius. There he could enter unseen by the members
of the Royal household.

George also told me that Frank McCarthy, the
Secretary of the General Staff, had acquired a fine painting of considerable value—the only really good souvenir
brought back from that trip. It seems that Frank, like
all the rest of the men, had procured some GI woolen
underwear to wear in Russia. He appeared one morning
looking so ill that General Marshall asked, "Are you getting the flu?"

"No, General," he replied, "but I simply can't
stand these itchy woolens. I may freeze, but I am
through with them."

That day Frank saw the painting for sale at a price
far beyond his pocketbook, but woolens were priceless in
Russia then and he had a bright idea.

"How would you like to make a trade?" he asked
the dealer. "I'll give you my woolen underwear for that
painting."

The dealer was delighted but the question of his
commission worried him, for the woolen suit would have
to go to the owner of the painting. He could not divide
it to obtain a commission, so where did he come in? Frank
told him, "I have two pairs and will trade in both." So
in exchange for his uncomfortable woolen underwear he
came home with a really fine work of art.

After the Yalta Conference George visited the
Mediterranean Theater of Operations and made an inspection tour of the Fifth Army front in the Appenines. He
arrived at 15th Army Group Headquarters on a Monday
and reviewed a guard of honor composed of American
white and Negro troops, Brazilians, Canadians, Poles,
Scots, Welsh, Irish, New Zealanders, Italian Army and

Italian Partisan troops, and a female contingent composed of American, British, and Polish servicewomen.

A newspaper account of his visit said:

> "The Chief of Staff arrived at the 5th Army CP Monday night after driving over the famed Giogo Pass to battered Firenzuola.   There he made his first talk.   His straight-forward and unpretentious manner almost knocked the caps off some 300 assembled GIs and officers.   Even his "At Ease" was conversational.   His only on-the-record activity was a haircut."

I had to smile at this last item, for whenever George feels fatigued he gets a haircut.   Certainly Sampson and he have nothing in common in that respect, for wherever George's strength lies it certainly is not in his hair.   The shorter his hair is, the more buoyant is he.

Prime Minister Churchill wrote to Field Marshal Wilson, after the Yalta Conference, while my husband was in the Mediterranean Theater:

> "Pray give General Marshall my warmest congratulations on the magnificent fighting and conduct of the American and Allied armies under General Eisenhower, and say what a joy it must be to him to see how the armies he called into being by his own genius have won immortal renown.   He is the true 'organizer of victory'."

While my husband was helping to make world history I was making our new home gay and livable to receive him on his return.   Liscombe Lodge had been furnished, and very attractively so, when we bought it, but the hangings, which were dull and heavy with fringe, reminded me of a somewhat pretentious funeral parlor. My mother had always said if you put me on a desert island I would immediately begin to "fix it up."   So I started to fix up the Pinehurst place. I had the walls repainted, put up bright chintz hangings, hung up some gay hunting prints Sir John and Nancy Dill had brought us from England, and added to them two lovely Audubon prints from our Leesburg place. By the end of February the grounds were all "policed" and I was anxiously awaiting my husband's arrival.

George stayed in Washington only long enough to settle pressing affairs on the home front and flew down for his first week-end.

The hour his car was expected I began putting lightwood on the fires so as to greet him with a cheery blaze. His plane was late and for an hour and a half I went back and forth sticking the lightwood under first one fire, then another. By the time he did come I was well-nigh exhausted.

It was dark when he finally arrived. Jimmy and Kitty were waiting at the door and there was a brilliant blaze on the hearth when he entered. I remember his pilot, Colonel Munson, came in with him and as the children rushed to greet George, Colonel Munson looked around the room and said, "My, what a welcome!" The place did look lovely.

For the first time in years, that Easter we were absent from the Leesburg Church. We attended services in the Chapel at Fort Bragg, near Pinehurst.

I think the only peaceful moments my husband had after the Yalta Conference were when he could escape to Pinehurst late on Saturday afternoons and sit before the big pinewood fire crackling on our hearth, or on Sundays when he would receive his pouch of official mail, and, lying on the sun-porch on his chaise-longue, would answer it.

The Lodge was small and attractive and the grounds were really beautiful. George would work here surrounded by long-leaf pines and magnolia trees, with a lawn of winter grass as green as emeralds stretching out before him. When he had finished the pouch, we would take walks through the sandhills and he would come back refreshed and hungry. Some kindly Providence must have guided us during those war years in acquiring these homes, Leesburg for summer, with its great oaks and serene settings, only 50 minutes from Washington; and Pinehurst, with its delightful climate and semi-tropical growth, an hour and a half's flight distant. They were a God-send to an over-burdened and tired man, when he could take advantage of them.

iv.

On the 1st of March I went up to New York, where George was to speak at the annual dinner of the Overseas Press Club, at the Waldorf. I particularly liked Elsa Maxwell's account of that speech. In her column the next morning she said:

"General Marshall in his off-the-record address painted a picture of our war with such clarity, candor and sheer drama that the layman could easily visualize the design and pattern of strategy on the Western Front and the difficulties our men face.

"He also announced that war correspondents killed at the front will be given the same decorations as any soldier killed on active duty.

"Never before have I heard a more human and compelling document by any person in the public eye. The speech was extemporaneous—good speeches always are. . . .

"We were not allowed to print General Marshall's speech,

but we can take comfort in knowing that the fortunes of our country have been in such sensitive but wonderful hands."

On April 4th George made another off-the-record talk before the Academy of Political Science in New York, in which he strongly expressed his conviction of the need for universal military training. I have two letters of the many received after this speech, one from the Church and one from the Theater:

"ARCHBISHOP'S HOUSE
452 Madison Avenue
New York
"April 5, 1945

"Dear General Marshall:
"That was a wonderful speech. . . . I wish every American could have heard *it* and heard *you*.

. . . . . .

"F. J. SPELLMAN
"Archbishop of New York"

"MOTION PICTURE PRODUCERS & DISTRIBUTORS
OF AMERICA, INC.
"April 5, 1945

"Dear General Marshall:
"May I join with the countless others in expressing my sincere appreciation of last night's occasion. Your own speech was of such a character, quality and effectiveness as no one else could have made, under no other circumstances, at no other time. My appreciation is very personal and sincere, indeed, and I want to tell you this morning how grateful every citizen of the Republic must be for you.
"With kindest personal regards and best wishes to you always, I am

"Sincerely yours,
"WILL H. HAYS"

"If there is anything, at any time, anywhere that I can do to be of the slightest service, please command me.

"W. H. H."

v.

Both on the European and Pacific fronts, the war was going well for the Allies. But now my husband's part in the conduct of the war was well-nigh played. The Combined Chiefs of Staff had completed, to the last minute detail, the strategy and plans for both the Pacific and European fronts. George felt his greatest service to his country now lay in working out, if humanly possible, ways and means of protecting America from other wars. He felt the only logical answer to the problem was universal military training. If anyone had a better way they did not make it known.

As I have said, certain groups were bitterly opposed to the idea, but they offered no other solution. Their attitude was, of course, that the "Brass Hats" wanted war, that universal training was merely a step toward making us a militant nation, and that it was a danger to the peace of the country. I never could understand their argument. Why should a soldier want war? He certainly knows the horrors of it. Does a fireman want fires? Do the Police want crime? Their whole training and duty is to protect us from these ills. Why then is it not the soldier's idea of duty to protect us from wars? Certainly it is, and has always been, General Marshall's paramount desire.

His answer to the opposition was short and direct: "As history has repeatedly proven, it is not with the brass hats but with the brass heads that the danger to our country lies."

vi.

The end of the war in Germany was in sight, the magnitude of our offensive smothered resistance all along the Western Front. During March nearly 350,000 prisoners were taken.

In the Pacific Theater General MacArthur had kept his word. He had returned to the Philippines. He had liberated Leyte. His troops hit the beaches in Lingayen Gulf January 9th, and by nightfall 68,000 troops were ashore and in control of a 15-mile beachhead. Early in March Corregidor fell, Manila Bay was opened. In less than two months MacArthur had accomplished what the Japanese had needed six to do after Pearl Harbor.

In March General Marshall sent the following message to General MacArthur:

"With the reoccupation of Corregidor and the opening of Manila Bay I tender my congratulations to you on the virtual culmination of a flawless campaign. From this distance it appears that the ground, air, and naval forces joined in a perfectly concerted and devastatingly powerful action which redeemed our pledge to the loyal and long-suffering people of the Philippine Islands.

"I send my heartfelt thanks to the forces which liberated the American prisoners and internees, to the troops who rushed and reoccupied Manila, and to the skillful and gallant band which reconquered Corregidor, and also to Krueger, Kenny, and Kincaid and to all the leaders who pushed this initial campaign through to victorious conclusion.

"I hope that the heavy fighting in the mountains to the North and on the Antipolo-Montalban line can be carried out with a maximum of Japanese casualties and a minimum of our own. I was distressed to learn that Mudge had been wounded and hope not seriously."

General MacArthur replied as follows:

"Deepest thanks from all ranks for your generous message. Nothing pleases us as much as your praise. Mudge was badly wounded by a hand-grenade which injured his kidneys and liver. The doctors give him an even chance. I regard him as my brightest field prospect. He has everything. I shall keep you informed of his progress daily until the crisis is past. You can count upon my conserving every life that I can possibly save in the fighting to come."

On April 6th, Army Day, George speaking before the Military Order of World Wars, said:

"The parades of other days are not possible. The combat troops are overseas paraded against our enemies. It is difficult to realize how vast and how successful our military forces are today. It is almost inconceivable that they should have reached such heights of efficiency and power, when we turn back to the military poverty of four short years ago."

vii.

In this month the San Francisco Conference met in California. Its aim was to set up machinery by which the nations of the world could band together to keep the peace, settle disputes without war and work in unison to promote economic and social progress. Longing and prayers were in everyone's heart that this conference might be successful.

President Roosevelt had gone to his "Little White House" at Warm Springs to get in condition to attend this Conference. On April 12th at one o'clock he was sitting by the fireplace while an artist made sketches of him. Suddenly he said, "I have a terrific headache," and in a few minutes he lost consciousness.

At 3:35, Franklin Delano Roosevelt, 32nd President of the United States, died.

By four-thirty that afternoon George was at the house at Fort Myer and together we went to the White House where we found Mrs. Roosevelt leaving for Warm Springs. My husband offered her his services and deep sympathy.

The White House seemed deserted. We were directed to a hall crowded with newspaper men. My husband was taken into the Cabinet Room close by, where the whole Cabinet and Supreme Court had gathered. I waited in the hallway.

As soon as George left me, a reporter came up and asked if General Marshall was at home when the news of the President's death was received. When I answered, "Yes," he asked, "What was the General's reaction when he heard it?"

I said, "I am sorry, but I cannot answer that. If you wish to know you will have to ask General Marshall." Just then George came out of the Cabinet Room and the reporter moved away.

As we left the building George said, "Everyone in that room appears completely stunned. Mr. Truman came up and spoke to me. I have the arrangements for the funeral to consider so thought it best not to stay any longer."

The President died on a Thursday and on Saturday morning the funeral train arrived in Washington. From the time it had left Warm Springs, Georgia, until it reached Union Station in Washington, at each station it passed during the night there was a Guard of Honor standing at attention and crowds of grief-stricken people waiting in silence as the train pulled slowly through, carrying toward its last resting place the body of the man who had led our Nation for thirteen years out of the depression—the aftermath of World War I—and through the dangers, tragedies, and victories of World War II.

Admiral King, George, and I stood together as the train pulled in. Again the entire Cabinet and members of the Supreme Court were present. Mrs. Roosevelt received us in her car. Beside her were her daughter Anna and her son Elliott. She had been up all night and looked ill, yet she was completely controlled. I could not speak, I just gave her my hand and George and I passed on.

As long as I live I shall never forget that slow, tortuous drive from the station to the White House. The streets were lined on both sides by troops at Present Arms, spaced only a few feet apart. In back of them could be seen the faces of the crowds. At each intersection these crowds extended down the side streets as far as you could see. The straining faces were set and looked like masks of tragedy. Complete silence spread like a pall over the city, broken only by the funeral dirge and the sobs of the people—men as well as women—as the funeral carriage passed.

The service in the White House was beautifully simple, opening with a prayer, and then the President's favorite hymn. It took place at four o'clock in the East Room of the White House where he had greeted so many thousands of his fellow-countrymen. The casket had no flowers; it was covered only by a United States Flag.

After all those invited to the services had been seated, Mrs. Roosevelt came in and everyone arose. After her came Anna Boettiger, her daughter, followed by the

President's four daughters-in-law. Those six women in black presented a tragic picture of war times. Elliott, the only son who had reached Washington in time for the services, was with his mother. Mrs. Roosevelt wore no veil to hide the extreme pallor and lines that told the story of the shock and strain of the past two days. I felt that I was in the presence of courage that was almost holy, such as soldiers see on the battlefield.

My husband did not accompany the funeral train that evening to Hyde Park. He and Admiral King flew up to West Point the following morning and drove over to the Roosevelt home. I remained in Washington.

Mrs. Roosevelt returned to Washington the evening after the funeral and George received the following note from her, evidently written on the train. It was in longhand, in a trembling handwriting that showed she was near the breaking point:

> "THE WHITE HOUSE
> WASHINGTON
>
> "April 15th
>
> "My dear General:
> "I want to tell you tonight how deeply I appreciate your kind thoughtfulness in all the arrangements made. My husband would have been grateful and I know it was all as he would have wished it. He always spoke of his trust in you and of his affection for you.
> "With my gratitude and sincere thanks,
> "Very sincerely yours,
> "ELEANOR ROOSEVELT"

The evening of the day that President Roosevelt died, Vice President Truman was sworn in as President of the United States. During the week after President Roosevelt's fourth term Inaugural Celebrations I had sat

next to Vice President Truman at a dinner and I had
said, "Mr. Vice President, I have had no chance to congratulate you on your election but I should like to do so
now." He thanked me, but said it seemed a pity that he
should be Vice President because he truly did not want it
and that he could point out four men in this room who
wanted it above all else in the world.

I then asked, "Since you have made that statement,
do you mind telling me who the four are?" and he picked
them out for me at the various tables. I then said, "Do
you mind answering another question? Why did you
not want to be Vice President?"

His answer was, "I feel that the war effort is the
most important thing in this country at the present time.
I also feel that I could be of far greater help to your husband in the Senate as Chairman of the Senate Investigating Committee than I can as Vice President. That is my
reason."

"You are very patriotic and loyal to your country," I answered, "for to be elected Vice President of the
United States is certainly a magnificent honor."

viii.

On May 8th, 1945, V-E Day, the German surrender was signed. On that morning George spoke on the
radio to the people of the nation.

The reaction of the people on May 8th was somewhat dimmed by a premature report that the surrender
had been signed, given out at the San Francisco Conference
a few days before. An hour and a half after this bulletin
came out, President Truman blew the report sky high.

The crowds in the streets in Chicago, San Francisco, New York, and other cities broke up; people turned off their radios; but the harm had been done. The edge of the people's enthusiasm had been blunted, and when victory did come there was not the wild tumult of joy that had greeted our invasion of Africa. There were still, of course, immense crowds in the streets and all-night celebrations, but in those crowds were wives, mothers and fathers of men still fighting desperately in the Pacific. There were also many whose husbands and sons victory could never bring back. Grief was deep in the heart of our nation, and so the public reaction was one of great thankfulness, I think, rather than wild abandon.

As to the official reaction—the reaction of the men who had carried the responsibility of leading the Allies to victory—it is depicted so graphically in communications on file at the War Department that I shall leave it to these documents to paint the picture for you:

To General Eisenhower from General Marshall:

"You have completed your mission with the greatest victory in the history of warfare.

"You have commanded with outstanding success the most powerful military force that has ever been assembled.

"You have met and successfully disposed of every conceivable difficulty incident to varied national interests and international political problems of unprecedented complications.

"Through all of this, since the day of your arrival in England three years ago, you have been selfless in your actions, always sound and tolerant in your judgments and altogether admirable in the courage and wisdom of your military decisions.

"You have made history, great history for the good of all mankind and you have stood for all we hope for and admire in an officer of the United States Army. These are my tributes and my personal thanks."

To General Marshall from General Eisenhower:

"With the attainment of what at last appears to be the final and complete surrender of the enemy to ourselves and the Russians, I feel a compulsion to attempt to tell you some things personally which have been very real with me during this war but which I have left unsaid for obvious reasons.

"Since the day I first went to England, indeed since I first reported to you in the War Department, the strongest weapon that I have always had in my hand was a confident feeling that you trusted my judgment, believed in the objectivity of my approach to any problem and were ready to sustain to the full limit of your resources and your tremendous moral support, anything that we found necessary to undertake to accomplish the defeat of the enemy. This has had a tremendous effect on my staffs and my principal subordinate commanders. Their conviction that you had basic faith in this Headquarters and would invariably resist interference from outside sources, has done far more to strengthen my personal position throughout the war than is realized even by those people who have been affected by this circumstance. Your unparalleled place in the respect and affections of all military and political leaders with whom I have been associated, as well as with the mass of American fighting men, is so high and so assured that I deeply regret that you could not have visited here after this Army had attained its full growth and before the break-up necessarily begins. Our Army and people have never been so deeply indebted to any other soldier.

"While I personally may attempt in this way to let you know something of the depth of my gratitude, appreciation and admiration, I will always hope that you may, yourself, gain a sense of the extent these sentiments are shared by hundreds of thousands of Americans and their Allies in this theatre.

"While preparing this, your personal message of commendation was brought to me. It so overwhelms. me that I now consider that anything I can say to be a feeble anticlimax. Nevertheless, because of the sincerity of my feelings, I am sending it as I originally intended. I truly thank you for your message."

To General Ismay from General Marshall:

"After the Prime Minister has read the deluge of congratulations from his own people and the heads of State throughout the world, I shall appreciate your passing to him the following:

'It has been a long and terrible road for you, Sir, since the fall of France. I can bear personal witness to the grandeur of your leadership since the meeting in Newfoundland in 1941. The long succession of conferences which followed, notably that in Washington in December of the same year and in London with Harry Hopkins and me in April of 1942, are clear in my mind as great mileposts in the evidence of your vast contribution to the reestablishment of a civilized peace in Europe.

'I can never forget, there will always be in my mind, the breadth of your vision and your generous attitude in effecting the coordination and final crystallization of our combined plans. Personally I will cherish the friendship and confidence you gave me during the seemingly slow and tortuous progress to the greatest, the most complete victory in modern history.

'G. C. Marshall'."

To General of the Army Marshall from the Prime Minister:

"I have waited to answer your message until the stir was

somewhat less, because I wished to tell you what pride it has been to me to receive such words of friendship and approval from you. We certainly have seen and felt together a great deal of the hard inside working of this terrific war, and there is no one whose good opinion at the end of the struggle I value more than yours.

"It has not fallen to your lot to command the great armies. You have had to create them, organize them, and inspire them. Under your guiding hand the mighty and valiant formations which have swept across France and Germany were brought into being and perfected in an amazingly short space of time. Not only were the fighting troops and their complicated ancillaries created but, to an extent that seems almost incredible to me, the supply of commanders capable of manoeuvring the vast organisms of modern armies and groups of armies and of moving these with unsurpassed celerity were also found wherever they were needed; apart from this and in the sphere of major strategy, you have been the mainspring of that marvelous organization, the combined Chiefs of Staff, whose conduct and relationship will ever be a model for the planning and supervision of Allied and Combined operations.

"There has grown in my breast through all these years of mental exertion a respect and admiration for your character and massive strength which has been a real comfort to your fellow-toilers, of whom I hope it will always be recorded that I was one."

At noon on V-E Day, Secretary of War Stimson sent for my husband to come to his office. When he entered, fourteen generals and high officials were sitting around the Secretary's desk in a semi-circle, in the center of which was a vacant chair. The Secretary asked George to be seated. He then asked all to remain seated during his remarks. He turned to George and said:

"I want to acknowledge my great personal debt to you,

Sir, in common with the whole country. No one who is thinking of himself can rise to true heights. You have never thought of yourself. Seldom can a man put aside such a thing as being the Commanding General of the greatest field army in our history. This decision was made by you for wholly unselfish reasons. But you have made your position as Chief of Staff a greater one. I have never seen a task of such magnitude performed by man.

"It is rare in late life to make new friends; at my age it is a slow process but there is no one for whom I have such deep respect and I think greater affection.

"I have seen a great many soldiers in my lifetime and you, Sir, are the finest soldier I have ever known.

"It is fortunate for this country that we have you in this position because this war cuts deeper into the eternal verities than any other.

"We have reached the milepost at the first half of this war. I may not live to see the end of the war with Japan but I pray that you do."

When George returned home that evening he was strangely silent. He made no mention of what had occurred in the Secretary's Office and I knew nothing of it until the next morning when Colonel Frank McCarthy, Secretary of the General Staff, sent me copies of the files with a memorandum stating, "I have had these copies made for you." He added, "All through this masterful tribute to General Marshall I wished that you could have been present. When it was over I passed General _____. You know he is considered pretty hard-boiled, but the tears were streaming down his face and he caught me by the arm and said, 'McCarthy, I have heard many tributes paid to the living and to the dead, but never such a touching, magnificent one as that paid by the Secretary to General Marshall just now. I am all broken up and I am not ashamed of it'."

This was the first I had heard of the occasion and I knew then why my husband had been so silent the night before. His feelings were too deep for words. His gratitude could not be expressed. He had always considered Mr. Stimson the Grand Old Man of the Administration. He spoke of him with deep affection as his "Rock of Gibraltar" for, he said, "When a thing is right the Secretary stands behind me like a rock. His integrity and character are unassailable. The long list of high offices he has held for his country give magnificent proof of his ability. He is a tower of strength to me." George had repeatedly told me how fortunate not only he but the entire country was to have Mr. Stimson as Secretary of War at this time.

ix.

Just as my husband admired and was extremely fond of Secretary Stimson, so had I a great admiration for Mrs. Stimson. They were a most devoted couple—close companions during all their married life. They had no children. Mrs. Stimson possessed great dignity, a keen sense of humor, and a delightfully determined mind.

When I had returned from Pinehurst after my siege of pneumonia, my sister had put whiskey in an empty hair tonic bottle in case I grew faint on the train. After my arrival at Fort Myer I came in late one afternoon from a long day of war work to be greeted by a message from George, "Be ready by 6:30 to dine with the Stimsons this evening." I was extremely tired, had had my hat on all day, but I hurriedly dressed, grabbed a bottle of hair tonic and rubbed it well in and was feeling more refreshed and ready to go by the time George arrived home.

Before we reached the gate at Fort Myer George turned to me and said, "Someone has been drinking." I was incensed. "What are you talking about?"

"Well," he insisted, "somebody certainly has. This car smells like a whiskey barrel."

I stiffened, too indignant to answer.

By the time we reached Memorial Bridge there was no mistaking the odor, it was overpowering. Then, for the first time, I remembered the whiskey in the hair tonic bottle!

When we got to the Secretary's house, although it was a cold winter night, we walked up and down to let the breeze blow through my hair, until I was all but frozen. The first thing Mrs. Stimson said when she greeted us was, "Mrs. Marshall, sit right here by the fire, you look cold." The heat counteracted the "airing" I had given my hair and presently Mr. Stimson, who was sitting by me, said, "Where are the cocktails, my dear?" Mrs. Stimson answered that they had not yet been served. The Secretary looked at me curiously.

I don't think I ever spent such an evening. I could feel the disapproval of the maids, who had been with the Stimsons for years, whenever they came near enough to serve me. What kind of whiskey that was I do not know, but whatever it was it certainly had great staying powers. My only salvation was that we were the lone guests, otherwise it might have appeared in a Washington column that the Chief of Staff's wife was certainly slipping.

x.

George had started his detailed plans for V-E Day two years before that day arrived. Immediately after V-E Day he caused to be released a 20-minute film in

moving picture houses throughout the country. It was
called: "Two Down and One to Go." The picture, in
Technicolor, revealed the strategy of the global war up
to date. It pointed to the problems in the Pacific fighting and presented the Army's "Point System" for dis-
charging men. He talked in the film, introduced the
commanding generals in the Army Ground Forces and Air
Forces, and these generals also gave their commentaries. In
this way the public received the inside information from
the top men. My husband explained why the war in
Europe had been given priority over the struggle against
the Japs and how the two wars were really one. This and
the complicated point system for service men's discharge
from duty were verbally explained by him. The newspapers said:

> "General Marshall's spoken words are more eloquent than
> any printed text and can leave no doubt in any mind of the
> far-seeing wisdom of the high command, or the impartial
> justice of its present plan for the demobilization of what
> suddenly have become 'surplus' troops.
>
> "In the light of General Marshall's revelations, there can
> be no further doubt that it is one global war we have been
> fighting, not two.
>
> "In simplifying and clarifying these matters for the mil-
> lions of Americans in whose minds they long have been up-
> permost, the War Department has performed a service of
> immeasurable value."

Thus my husband had utilized the moving picture
industry, one of the most powerful and far-reaching
mediums, to put the facts of the war, immediately after
the victory in Europe, before the home front and clear
the minds of the people of many doubts and prepare them
for the remaining task in the Pacific.

During the war he had had many magnificent pictures made for the education and information of the troops, to give them the over-all picture and the reasons for which we fought. A number of top directors, writers and producers were engaged in this excellent work. In particular George was fortunate, I thought, in having Colonel Frank Capra, with his great artistic and technical ability, and truly patriotic selflessness, to carry out his plans. I had often seen these pictures in the private projection room in the Pentagon Building and had always found it amazing how you could receive so much instruction without realizing you were being instructed. They were so beautifully done and delicately handled that they were the most interesting movies of the war for me.

Neither the people at home nor the troops overseas had any idea of the planning and vision that this phase of the global war required. The troops were pleased with many USO shows, they "griped" at others. When "This Is The Army" lifted their morale and entertained them they were enthusiastic. To them it was just a fine show of Irving Berlin's. But I had glimpses backstage, so to speak—the luncheons under the apple tree and on our sunporch at Fort Myer where Mr. Berlin and General Marshall discussed detailed arrangements; the visits of Stokowski regarding musical matters; the struggles to get hundreds of chapels built where our troops could worship in peace and quiet. . . . I am sure that few people knew that the Chief of Staff interested himself in plans to send the entire Ringling Circus to Europe to help our men endure their longing to come home. The lack of shipping was one difficulty he could not overcome.

These and many other things seemed just to hap-

pen; but how did they happen? In fact many of them
were born and nurtured in General Marshall's brain. He
used every possible source to keep the men's morale high
and to win the victory. You may say, "What have turkey dinners at Christmas, cigarettes, candy, and ice cream
in Post Exchanges up near the front line got to do with
dying and fighting?" For answer I can only say, look at
the results.

I do not contend that things were perfect. How
could they be in the midst of such a world upheaval?
Plans could not always be executed, but I do say that if
they were not, it was not for lack of vision, planning, and
endless toil on the part of those—both commanders and
General Staff—who carried the responsibility of World
War II.

xi.

June of that year was taken up with the return of
the Conquering Heroes. Never were there men with so
little of the conquering hero attitude about them. They
accepted the enthusiasm of the great crowds that greeted
them as tributes to the men they commanded, not to themselves personally. They were proud of the U. S. Army
and Navy, modest for their own part and grateful for
their superb victories. General Eisenhower received a
tumultuous reception in New York, such as the city had
never before seen. General Patton was greeted from Boston to Los Angeles with wild acclaim. Generals Bradley
and Spaatz were received in Philadelphia with a great ovation and stirred the City of Brotherly Love as it had never
been stirred before. General Devers was wildly welcomed
in Pittsburgh by thousands of his fellow-Pennsylvanians,
and in Louisville, Kentucky, by those who had known him

when commanding the Armored Force at Fort Knox. General Hodges broke all precedents in Atlanta, Georgia. Chicago turned out to a man to greet General Clark and his companions. In each case, so far as it was possible, the commanders concerned were returned to the states of their birth and after the State had received them in its metropolis, went to their home towns to enjoy the more personal welcome of old friends and relations. Each Commanding General had been instructed to select a certain number of his enlisted men and top commanders, Colonels and junior officers who had distinguished themselves, to accompany him on the trip home.

After these receptions by their country, the high commanders took up their new duties at home or returned to their various war theaters to carry through the unfinished task of enforcing the peace terms and supervising the redeployment. Neither George nor I saw any of these celebrations but we listened to each of them over the radio and read about them in the press. He was as enthusiastic and pleased as a schoolboy at their magnitude, for he had personally worked out each detail. He had brought General Young of the 3rd Division back from Bavaria to organize the receptions and to execute his plans. Key men to carry out the plans were assigned and accommodations reserved. It had all been conceived months before. The wives were to meet their husbands on arrival; the Mayor of each city in question and sometimes the Governor of the State were contacted. This was all started as soon as victory was plainly in sight, for my husband, knowing that the occupation would be a tedious and unglamorous business, was determined that those who had led the valiant fight for the victory over Germany should receive the plaudits of the nation before other interests—especially the war in the Pacific—completely absorbed the attention of the public.

xii.

During the last months of President Roosevelt's illness George had hesitated to bother him with his personal affairs, and his personal affairs could be summed up in one word—retirement. The war in Europe was won, the plans for the final blows at Japan were finished to the most minute detail. The Army and Navy commanders who were to carry out these plans were in the saddle and they were men of unquestionable and remarkable ability. My husband felt that he could write Finis on his part of this page of our history. He wanted to be retired, for he also felt that the one great service he could now do for his country was to concentrate all his efforts on getting before the public the compelling necessity for compulsory military training after the war.

The fact that he was tired also played a part in his wish to retire; mentally and physically he was a very weary man. People constantly said to me, "Your husband looks so well. His responsibilities do not seem to weigh him down. It is remarkable how he holds up." I suppose he did look well to them. There certainly were no outward signs of a physically ill or mentally exhausted person, but on my bureau I had two pictures which I called, "Before and After the War." They told the story far better than words. The first one was taken by the Signal Corps the month George had come to Washington, seven years before. In this photograph his arms are folded; there is a calm expression in his eyes and few lines in his face. His hair is auburn, his figure slight. There is an inscrutable smile on his lips. It is my favorite picture, for it shows a man at peace with himself and with the world. The other picture, taken at the height of the war and considered by his staff the best likeness used by the Bureau of Public Relations, shows a deeply lined face, set jaw, eyes of steel, grey hair, and an expression such as you could hardly believe possible for the face in the first picture. There is only cold, calculated determination and indomitable will in that face. There is no peace. The war years had taken a terrific toll.

In August General Marshall presented a request to President Truman by letter, asking for retirement. Each evening when he came home I would ask anxiously, "Did the President see you today?" And each evening I received the same answer, "No, he is over-burdened with problems on the home front. I do not wish to push the issue." In spite of this we spent evening after evening making our plans; we would go to Leesburg, get the place in order for the winter, close the house and be at Pinehurst for the fall shooting, of which George was very fond. He had been a crack shot in his younger army days and was anxious to get out in the open and practice until he could again have the thrill of bringing down a quail on the wing without fail. Then we would go to the Gulf for January and February and do some fishing, returning for an early spring in Pinehurst and a second spring, as it were, later at Leesburg where we would get our garden going. It was all an alluring ideal. The fact is, it was to be a long-delayed honeymoon, for we had never had one. We had stepped from the altar into Army activities and had been following Army dictates and routine for fifteen years.

Once more we worked over maps in the evenings, but they were not maps of the Pacific or the Mediterranean or the Continent. They were maps of lovely spots in which to rest and relax, maps of automobile routes by which we could enjoy our freedom most. It was great fun planning all this. True our hair was grey, but there was nothing grey in those plans. They were what we had dreamed of for years and they were made with an enthusiasm that surprised even ourselves. I do not think either of us knew there was that much life left in us!

xiii.

I now put an advertisement in the Washington newspapers for a caretaker, who would keep the grass cut and live at the Leesburg house that winter. I had two applicants. The first answer came in the form of a whispered phone call: "I can't talk now but I will call this afternoon." That afternoon he came to the house, a gentle old man. He had been a postman for thirty years, was retired, and lived with two nieces. They were strong-minded spinsters who liked his pension. They watched him closely and would not allow him out alone. He said he wanted to get away from the girls, and kept looking over his shoulder and whispering as if his nieces were behind his chair. Much as I wanted a caretaker, I did not relish the idea of a kidnapping suit so I sent him back home in my car.

The next morning I was on the sun-porch when the Sergeant announced: "There is a man downstairs in a zoot suit to see about being a caretaker."

"In a what?" I asked.

"A zoot suit, Mrs. Marshall. He has on a zoot suit."

When he walked in I was dumbfounded. He

was a small, swarthy man with long hair. His suit of brilliant green was fastened with brass buttons, the coat cut nearly to his knees. The trousers flared below the coat and fitted tightly at his shoe-tops. He had a yellow paper chrysanthemum in his lapel.

Before I could recover myself he took the initiative and explained that he had only one hand, his right one having been cut off in a machine. Taking for granted that the job was his, he told me he would need a car. He had met a girl—"the perfect woman"—who had changed his whole life. He did not say from what, but she and she alone had changed it. He would need a car to drive up to Washington to see this girl quite often. Then, with a sly wink, "You know how it is."

"Do you mean you are a married man?" I asked.

"No, but I have hopes."

By this time I had recovered sufficiently to take over. "I think you are taking a great risk," I said, "after finding the perfect woman, to go to the country and leave her."

"No risk," he answered. "She's smart. She knows a man when she sees one."

Well, so did I. I looked at the Sergeant, who was waiting in the doorway, and he came forward and escorted the zoot suited lover downstairs.

When George came home that evening he asked if I had had any answers to my advertisement. I said, "Yes, two. One grown too old and one who had not grown at all."

xiv.

I sent in my resignation to my war committees— the "Red Cross," "Army Relief," "Soldiers, Sailors and

Marines Club," "Junior Officers, Incorporated," and various others, for I had a colossal job cut out for me at home —the emptying of the now bulging Chief of Staff's house.

We had stored the possessions of all the overseas men in our family, all of Molly's wedding presents and furniture; and there were George's military clothes. To turn him into a civilian from a military man was no small job. I recall that before I married Colonel Marshall a friend in Baltimore said, "Do you know what you are doing? I have just come back from visiting a friend who has married into the Army and she showed me one closet of her husband's winter uniforms, another full of his summer ones, a third of his riding and hunting things, a fourth of his civilian clothes, and when I asked where she kept her things (for the house was not a large one) she led me to the attic. Hanging on the rafters was a pitiful display of all she possessed."

Well, I had managed to keep one closet in my room for my personal belongings but even the floor of that one was piled high with trophies sent back by our men folk. So if in peace time an Army house is chock-a-block with uniforms and equipment, you can well imagine the Chief of Staff's house after four years of war—flying apparel for the Artic and the tropics, bedding rolls, every conceivable kind of uniform for the field and for dress occasions, to say nothing of gifts and souvenirs sent to us during the six years of our occupancy of Quarters Number One.

All the third floor of the house had been turned into a pseudo-museum and art gallery. There were 26 oil paintings, plaques and drawings of General Marshall. There was no question about some of these being works of art. But I recall one had a note on it: "Painted after six lessons." The shoulder on one side had such breadth that the frame covered it, while on the other it was only half across the canvas. Another had the body of a WAC and a head the size of a lion's. I do not know whether these were painted in a delirium or not, but the artists certainly achieved a nightmare.

A replica of a noted fort done in bronze required six men to get it to the storeroom; and there were endless flags and staffs used for official affairs, captured machine guns, a bust of Hitler, swords, guns, sabres from every theatre of the war, sent by men who had gone through purgatory to secure them. There was a canteen with water from Bataan still in it.

I came across a dress-box covered with dust. How it got there I do not know; but when I opened it, there was George's full-dress uniform with the yellow sash that he had refused to wear at our first official reception at the White House. Packed with it was my silver lame dress in which he had said I "glittered."

On the second floor all closets, not filled with clothes, were packed to the ceiling with pamphlets, reports, endless papers, and boxes of books. It seemed to me that every person who had written a war book sent an autographed copy to the Chief of Staff. They form a fine war library. Also George's own pre-war library on the first floor had to be packed.

There were boxes of souvenirs, such as a piece of marble from Hitler's desk, blown to atoms in the bombing, a pig made of iron from the first Kaiser output, a gold miniature boxing glove engraved, "To The Champ," a stuffed owl labeled, "For he was a wise old owl." There was a Chinese sword—a priceless museum piece—from Dr. T. V. Soong with a note which read:

"I learned that tomorrow is your birthday so take the
liberty of sending you an antique bronze sword of the Chin
Dynasty, B.C. 255-207, as an augury that you will lead the
American Army to smite the Japanese hip and thigh!"

Here, too, was my treasured collection of original
cartoons, all signed by the artists and giving an amusing
and most accurate history of the war.   There were autographed pictures of practically every war leader in the
world, except those of the Axis, and even a large box of
German decorations. Many medals were given to women
for having from six children on up to as many as twelve
—for the Fatherland.

If it tires your mind to read this partial list of
what was in the Chief of Staff's house at Fort Myer, think
of what it did to my back to pack these things.   By the
time we did leave the house I was a sorry sight.   If the
German women deserved medals for having children for
the Fatherland, I deserved the Iron Cross for moving
George Catlett Marshall from Quarters Number One.

But I am getting ahead of events—the day of release had not yet come.

xv.

The week after I finished packing I had met in
New York a woman who said, "Mrs. Marshall, what a
fascinating life you must lead.   Just one party after another."   "Well, that depends on what you call parties,"
I answered.

To further illustrate this fascinating life: in the
early spring we had gone into the chicken business.
Neither George nor I were insane enough to seek this venture; but I had been deeply hurt when calling the grocer

and asking in my most pleading voice if he could send us a fresh chicken not cold-storage, to hear him call across the store to the butcher, "Hi, Al! Come over here— Madam Queen is on the 'phone." So when 100 baby chicks arrived from one of my husband's admirers we, in our ignorance, received them with open arms.

We went to work with a will to have fresh chickens of our own. These were not ordinary chicks, but Barred Plymouth Rocks, and a very special Barred Plymouth Rock at that. Instructions came with them. A brooder had to be made (you couldn't buy one) and put in the cellar; mash and chick food were bought; also sawdust for their feet, vitamins for their water, special feeding troughs and drinking cups.

I did not know that chicks had to have vitamins, but these did. The very day they arrived a dear friend had called; and she, like every other grandmother I knew, had her grandchildren living with her. She also did much war work, and as she looked quite tired, I insisted she give up some of the work she was doing for the Army. "No," she said, "it is not the war work. It is the vitamins they are giving the grandchildren. They are killing the grandmothers!"

So if vitamins put pep in children, why not chicks. Anyway, after three weeks of phenomenal success the chicks had grown apace and needed more room. A run had to be built. Still they grew, and an outside coop and larger runways were made by a kind carpenter after his work hours—just because it was for the "Chief of Staff." His bill—$125. By this time we had 98 chickens—and such chickens! Lime and sand now had to be bought along with chicken feed, mash and more vitamins. The coop was too small for such birds, and so of necessity we had chickens fried, broiled and panned, daily to relieve crowded housing conditions.

Still they grew, twenty-four huge hens and three roosters. General Marshall said, "We will save twelve hens for laying next winter and two roosters. Look at them! Did you ever see such hens?" I never had. They were Amazons, and the roosters were magnificent. Our hens had just started laying when we were packing to leave. We left the flock with General Eisenhower.

Raising those chickens and having a vegetable garden gave me a consoling philosophy with which to meet the high cost of living. No matter what the prices in the stores, they seem cheap to me. When they say a chicken is so-and-so and other customers gasp, I wonder how the store can do it. The price of fresh vegetables is a constant source of amazement. Anything a farmer raises to eat is worth whatever the consumer has in his pocketbook, so far as I am concerned. It is cheap at any price.

Adding up the bills for our chicken venture and dividing the sum per chicken was so astounding that I am ashamed to write it. In the first place, you would not believe me and, in the second, you would think the Marshalls were not quite bright. Nevertheless, "Madam Queen" had fresh chickens all summer.

xvi.

Early in July President Truman, Secretary Byrnes, and the military leaders left for the Potsdam Conference in Berlin. This was the first conference where the Chiefs of Staff of the Red Army, the British and the United States Armies met.

My husband did not know how long he would be

away but judged it would be for some weeks. Molly, the children and I were to stay at Leesburg.

The week General Marshall's plane left, Mr. Wallace's seed corn became ripe and I was determined that George should have at least a taste of the fruit of his labor, so I got up early one morning and packed a dozen ears of corn, with the dew still on them, in a small carton together with a half-dozen large tomatoes from our garden. I sent them to the War Department and asked if the package could be put in that day's pouch to Potsdam.

George wrote me that the vegetables arrived as fresh as when picked and that the fresh corn and tomatoes caused a great stir when brought unexpectedly into his mess. They were a treat beyond words, and he was a proud farmer among diplomats and military commanders.

The Prime Minister asked George to dinner the first night of the Conference. They dined together on the terrace of Mr. Churchill's quarters. The only other people present were Mary, his daughter, and Colonel Frank McCarthy, who had their dinner in the house. George wrote: "Frank is unbelievably efficient. In fact he is my right hand." On Frank's return he was appointed Assistant Secretary of State—the youngest, I believe, in our history. George was as proud of him as he would have been of his own son.

Mr. Churchill was soon to leave the Conference to be in England when the results of the election became known. He left confident of success, but it was Mr. Atlee, the new Prime Minister, who returned to represent Great Britain.

I think our entire country was greatly surprised when the news came over the radio that Churchill—the voice in the wilderness before the war, the savior of Great

Britain after Dunkirk—had suffered a devastating defeat.
I say Mr. Churchill, but the defeat was not his—it was
the defeat of his party. He, personally, had received a
vote of confidence, but the Labor Party had the bit in its
teeth and he went down with the Conservatives.

At Potsdam final military agreements were reached
regarding the general conduct of the war in the Pacific.
America was to lead the way with its vast operations,
naval, air and ground; and the unknown (to all but a
select few) atomic bomb was to precipitate in a few weeks
time the surrender of Japan.

On August 8th, three days after the first atomic
bomb was dropped on Hiroshima, the Union of Soviet
Socialist Republics declared war on Japan.

xvii.

George got his haircut at Potsdam, so I knew all
was well, but it was not so well with Joe Abbate who had
been his barber for the past seven years at Fort Myer and
in the Pentagon Building. Joe had even named his son
for my husband, and when a picture appeared in the
press—taken in General Marshall's bathroom at Potsdam
—of another barber in the act of cutting the Chief of
Staff's hair, Joe's nose was completely out of joint. Seven
years' faithful service and then another man's picture in
the newspapers!

My son Clifton had written me saying he was in
the Army of Occupation and might not be home for two
years. Now I received word from him in Bavaria that he
was to be evacuated to a hospital in France. It seems
that an old radium burn on the sole of his foot had flared
up after his long service in Africa, Italy, France and Ger-

many and skin grafting would be necessary.   This worried
me greatly.   My only brother, General Tristram Tupper,
was still with General Devers in Germany after five years'
service; Jim, Molly's husband, was commanding an artillery unit in Germany; George was at Potsdam.   Molly and
I hesitated as to whether we would let George know about
Clifton.   Then his letter was followed by a radiogram
saying that the hospitals in France were being evacuated so
rapidly that they would be unable to take a case requiring
such a long period of convalescence, so Clifton was ordered
to Walter Reed Hospital in Washington.

By the time George returned from Potsdam my
son was about due to arrive home, and when he sighted
the coast of New England from the plane, so he told me,
he felt like jumping out and kissing the ground.

The first thing that happened after his admission
to the hospital was the announcement of his engagement
to Em Bowles Locker of Richmond, Virginia.   He was
given a month's leave before his operation and they were
married the end of August.

George and I went down for the wedding, a lovely
one in St. Stephen's Episcopal Church, followed by a
reception at the Country Club.   Em, a beautiful bride,
had Molly as her maid of honor.   Frank McCarthy was
Clifton's best man.   Mr. Harry DeButts, Vice President
of the Southern Railway, graciously took us down in his
private car so that my husband could return to Washington that evening.   I was happy that the young couple
made the most of that gay party, for it was not until
March of the following year that Clifton was released
from Walter Reed, apparently cured.

xviii.

A few days after we returned from Clifton's wedding a message came from General Wainwright reporting his arrival, together with sixteen officers and enlisted men, in Chungking and his return to control of the United States Army. The message stated that he expected to leave Chungking on the 30th of August for Manila and thereafter proceed to Tokyo with General MacArthur's party, and that all members of his party were in good health. George immediately radioed him as follows:

"August 28, 1945

"Dear Wainwright:

"I was profoundly moved a few moments ago to receive your first message and I have already repeated the substance of it to Mrs. Wainwright. A more detailed response will follow later. Meanwhile I reaffirm the expressions of my last message to you a few hours before the fall of Corregidor in deepest appreciation of all that you did and have done for the honor of the Army."

From Chungking came the following reply:

"August 29, 1945

"Your personal message of August 28th leaves me without words to express adequately the gratitude which I feel for your consideration and sympathetic attitude. Your last message to me at Corregidor was received at 4 o'clock in the morning when the fall of the Island was imminent. The sentiments which you expressed at that time afforded me the greatest consolation during the trying experiences of that day and throughout my long period of captivity. The original copy of that message has been in my personal possession since it came to my hands and it will always be one of my most cherished possessions. I look forward to the day when I can thank you in person for your many kindnesses and I thank God that our country possessed a soldier of such distinction to lead her armies through the difficulties which beset an unprepared nation to final and glorious victory. I leave here morning of August 30th to join MacArthur in Manila to accompany him to Tokyo to witness the formal surrender. My highest personal and official regards to you.

"Wainwright"

When General Wainwright arrived in Washington, George and I drove to the National Airport to greet him. Great throngs lined the roads all the way. Mrs. Wainwright was nervously waiting for his plane to come in. George stood with her as it landed, but when the tall emaciated General came down the steps George fell back and Mrs. Wainwright and her husband embraced for the first time after all those long weary years of suffering and anxiety. It was a most touching reunion. When they started for the War Department George sat back with Mrs. Wainwright in an open car, while General Wainwright remained standing to receive the plaudits of the people.

I followed with an Aide in a closed car directly behind theirs. I suppose the people were so eager to see General Wainwright that they failed to see his wife in the same car. This created a most embarrassing situation, for they evidently mistook me for Mrs. Wainwright. I could hear on all sides: "There she is! There is Mrs. Wainwright!" and great applause greeted my car.

I said to the Aide, "I do not know what to do. If I do not smile and acknowledge their greeting they will think Mrs. Wainwright is a very strange wife." So I decided it was best to receive Mrs. Wainwright's ovation for her. All down that long drive I was the radiantly happy wife of our most famous war prisoner, smiling,

bowing, returning the waves of the people. I truly never
felt such an imposter nor so humble inside, but I did my
best for her.

xix.

Even after Potsdam, President Truman made no
mention of General Marshall's retirement. Matters at the
War Department were growing embarrassing. Post-war
problems and appointments were constantly coming up,
and George felt that his successor should make his own
appointments and formulate his own policies. It was
neither fair to him nor to the incoming Chief of Staff to
have these important affairs and many changes initiated
by George, later to be carried out by his successor. General
Eisenhower had long been decided upon by the President
as the new Chief of Staff and George felt he should be
brought home immediately to take over. This was quite
possible, as some months before, George had released his
Deputy Chief of Staff, General McNarney, to go to
Italy. He was available to relieve General Eisenhower in
Germany.

Also, after General Eisenhower's superb leadership
to victory in Europe, my husband felt it was fatal to leave
him longer in Germany where post-war bickerings, which
were bound to develop, would inevitably damage his international prestige as the leader of the Allied Armies.

General Marshall finally decided to take the matter
up again with President Truman. The President had been
opposed to releasing him until victory was won in the
Pacific. So now the atomic bomb not only ended the
war with Japan but also, incidentally, released my husband from his burdens as Chief of Staff. The President

consented to his release from active duty as soon as General Eisenhower could be brought back from Germany, but not to George's retirement from the Army at this time.

At least this would give George a breathing spell in which to carry out our personal plans, and I cannot tell you how much joy President Truman's decision, when it was finally made, brought to our home. A great load seemed to roll off my husband's shoulders. At breakfast he was carefree, the heavy lines between his eyes began to disappear, he laughed once more.

With a feeling of abandon hard to express we watched the trucks laden with our earthly possessions leave Fort Myer for Leesburg.

George would go to his office early, to do his day's work, tying up many loose ends; while I would follow the trucks to see that our belongings were put in their proper place. Then he would come down in the late afternoon and we would drive up the next morning together.

I have never been so fond of the fall of the year as I am of spring. I do not like to see things fade and die, but this fall was not the end, but the beginning—of a new life for us. The leaves were turning, the countryside was a blaze of glory. The maples vied with the sumac in brilliance of color, the great oaks and elms on our place were still in leaf, their huge limbs spreading out as if to protect us from all harm. If the evenings were growing too short for our fancy, the sunsets compensated us by their arresting glory. The whole sky over the Blue Ridge would be on fire as the sun went down. The beauty all around us brought us happiness and contentment that passed all understanding.

XX.

George was busy now with the demobilization of the Army. An editorial of September 21st stated:

> "Whether General Marshall is having a harder time demobilizing the huge wartime Army than he did in getting it together in the first place is an open question. But in both tremendous tasks he has shown the same vision, the same frankness, and the same deeply human qualities.
>
> "No man living or dead was more responsible for Allied victory than our modest Chief of Staff. And no man hates militarism and loves peace more than this soldier's soldier. George Marshall is a great American."

My husband had gone before the 79th Congress in its first session, September 20th, and made a long statement on the demobilization. His remarks were put into a pamphlet by the Senate and distributed widely. There are many pages in my scrapbook given to articles and editorials based on this speech.

In short, the war was truly over and not only the Army was demobilizing, but Secretary Stimson had resigned. The team was breaking up. Earl Godwin in a broadcast said:

> "That Grand Old Man, Henry L. Stimson, the Secretary of War, held his final press conference today before retiring on Friday which will be his 78th birthday. Never has an American citizen labored so long and so well for his country's good."

The War Department gave a great farewell reception at Dumbarton Oaks and made elaborate plans to honor Colonel and Mrs. Stimson. Under Secretary of

War Robert P. Patterson was appointed by President Truman as Mr. Stimson's successor.

At Quarters Number One the team was also disintegrating. Sergeant Victor Aguirre had received his discharge and left for his home on the West Coast, to be received by his neighbors as "the home town boy who made good"; Sergeant Powder, who had become in effect George's non-commissioned A. D. C., was retiring and busy buying a trailer and making plans with his wife for a tour of the country; Sergeant Dumcke, who usually drove me, left to become General Eisenhower's chauffeur; Sergeant Farr also was assigned to General Eisenhower; Henry, the gardener, long since entitled to Civil Service retirement, was to stay on attending to the grounds for the new Chief of Staff. Only the colored orderly, Sergeant Speaman, was left with us, and he at that time was in the hospital with high blood-pressure. All had done their part and given the best they had in the service of the Chief of Staff.

George and I now moved from the house so that the workmen could come in, and during our last few days at Fort Myer had an apartment at the Officers' Club. Here we could have meals and George could continue his work until General Eisenhower arrived in Washington to take over.

xxi.

It was at this time that General Marshall's third and final Biennial Report was published. It was released by the War Department on October 9th. The publisher who brought out the commercial edition reported an initial sale of some hundred thousand copies. For seven weeks the report was rated second on The New York

TOGETHER

Times' list of best sellers and for twelve weeks continued well up on that list.

There were hundreds of copies sent to George to be autographed—many came from fathers who wished them for Christmas presents for their small sons, saying it was an historical document of such import that they would be proud to own it when grown. George laughed at this and said he would be the most unpopular man in the country at Christmas time, for he knew how he would have felt if his father had given him a military report for his Christmas present when he was a small boy.

My husband had assigned all royalties, tendered by the publishers of the commercial edition, to The Army Emergency Relief.

I will not try to give the headlines in the newspapers, magazines, and foreign publications on this his last contribution before his retirement. It is enough to say that in the midst of World War II he had written, in his three Biennial Reports, an accurate outline of the history of that war from the United States Army point of view—this for future generations of Americans. I think he had earned what, many years before, one of the columnists had said he would most prize—the verdict of "Well done, thou good and faithful servant." The war for him was ended. The time for his retirement had come.

Secretary of War Patterson sent the following letter:

"November 24, 1945

"Dear General:

"Your retirement, though I had ample warning of it, came about so abruptly that it is hard for me to adjust myself. It is hard for me to imagine the Army without you at the head of it.

"You are the great figure of the war. Your ability as a soldier is plain enough in the results achieved. Your steadfastness in all situations has been a tower of strength. But above all that, the simplicity of your devotion to the country's cause has been the inspiration of millions of men who have followed you. You may rest assured that nothing can change the regard that your countrymen have for you.

"As for the Army, it will continue to be a great Army in spiritual strength, and its traditions will be stronger by reason of your having served in it.

"With affectionate regards, I am,

"Sincerely yours,

"ROBERT P. PATTERSON

"Secretary of War."

General Harding sent me the following Epilog to his poem that had greeted me on my arrival at Fort Benning fifteen years before:

"EPILOG (1946)

"Your versatile husband has had little time
To dance and to shoot and to ride,
So the life you have shared has taken a course
Quite other than that I implied.

Now only he knows just how much you have helped
Him to carry the load that he bore;
But you've been on the team and you rate a full share
Of the credit for winning the war."

xxii.

In the closing pages of George's Report he paid his final tribute to our Army and made a powerful plea to the Nation to hold the peace through preparedness—so if unscrupulous bandit nations again arose we could face

them with strength rather than weakness. He felt that
only by this means could we hope to abolish war. Our
Army casualties in all theaters, from December 7, 1941
until the end of the war, had totaled 943,241, including
201,367 killed, 570,793 wounded, 114,205 prisoners, 56,-
876 missing. If weakness, if lack of preparedness had
brought upon us this staggering sacrifice, even with the
nation straining every resource to ward off the blow, how
could people still argue against military training for our
young men. Compared with such casualties, what indeed is one year out of their lives devoted to learning the
essentials of protecting themselves and their country from
such another catastrophe as this?

It seems to me that if this had been our first war
and we had been caught napping for the first time, there
might be some excuse for such wishful thinking as the lack
of need for military training; but when history has repeated itself over and over again—for in our short history we have been engaged in six major wars and have
tried unpreparedness after each conflict—then why is not
military preparedness our only possible means of maintaining the peace for which our Nation, the mothers and
fathers, the Church and the educators are clamoring? This
is a question that you may be able to answer better than I,
but to me—who for years have had real cause to dread wars
—there is neither rhyme nor reason in our past attitude,
only a blind determination not to face facts. And my great
fear now is that the blind determination on the part of a
few may cause the agonies of war—of death and destruction—for the many.

xxiii.

General Marshall accepted an invitation to speak
on October 29th before the New York Herald Tribune
Forum in order to get his universal military training
plan before the public. The reaction to this speech was
encouraging, which was amazing for on the program
just before George spoke, Paul Robeson read a poem that
made the training and equipping of armies appear to be
futile. Robeson delivered the verses with all the power of
his magnificent ability. I do not recall the exquisite phras-
ing of the poem, it was a long one and beautifully delivered. It eloquently advocated peace, but the sense of it, as
I recall, was to the effect that we would not outlive another
war, that the valor of fighting men would be unemployed
and would be replaced by coils of wire and push buttons,
that courage would not again be the sacred trust of armies,
that such things as armies, drilling, encampments, em-
barkations, were things of the past—museum pieces—to
be placed beside pikes and arrows. This was a perplexing
introduction for General Marshall's blunt, logical speech
in support of universal military training.

xxiv.

The day we left Fort Myer for good, we sent down
an orderly to see that all was in readiness at Leesburg; then
dismissed the chauffeur and drove down together, alone.

For once we were selfish and picked up no hitch-
hikers. It was my husband's custom to give a lift to
anyone who signaled him. Often this had proved amusing. As he always wore civilian clothes and usually drove

himself, people expressed themselves freely and so he
gained both knowledge and pleasure by listening to their
opinions and reactions to affairs in general. Once, a few
weeks before, we had picked up a soldier. It was at the
time the point system had been put into effect for discharge from the service. This soldier told us of his three
years' service overseas and his many battles; and George
remarked that he could be discharged immediately.

The soldier answered, "Not a chance."

"But you are bound to have enough points,"
George said.

"Points!" the soldier answered, "that stuff is all
hooey. You have got to have a wife and children."

"What do you mean, 'all hooey'?" my husband
asked. "The War Department has announced that if you
have as much service as you have had, and fought the
battles that you have fought, you can get your discharge."

"That's what you think. But it doesn't work that
way. I have to have a wife and children or it's no go."

"A wife and children," George repeated. "Now
let's see. You have 72 points for overseas service, you
have so many for your battle engagements, why you must
have 96 points and you only have to have 85 to be released. A wife and children have nothing to do with
your case."

"You are talking stuff you read," the soldier replied. "That's what the Brass Hats tell you, that's War
Department hooey. I tell you I have to have a wife and
children."

This was too much for the Chief of Staff and he
said, "Well, I'll tell you. I am General Marshall and you
will be out of the Army tomorrow. What is your name
and outfit?" The man sat speechless for a moment and

then he said, "General, I was overseas with the 106th Division and was caught in the Battle of the Bulge and taken prisoner a few months after our arrival in Europe. I have just come home as a released prisoner. I thank you, Sir, I'll be getting out here."

On another day we had stopped for gas on our way down to Leesburg. We had gotten our gas and were about to start up when a car from Fort Meade drove up and parked squarely in front of us. Two privates jumped out. They were in great feather for each had his girl along. They cocked their caps on the sides of their heads and leaned on the door of their car making wisecracks to the girls inside. They must have been extremely witty, for everything they said was greeted with peals of laughter. The subject was whether they would have Coca-Cola or Seven-Up.

We waited at least five minutes while this badinage continued. Finally, although we were enjoying their gay spirits, George had to leave. He leaned out and asked, "Will you please move your car so I can get clear?"

The soldiers gave him one glance and then turned back to the girls and continued their discussion. When good and ready, the matter was decided—two "cokes" and two Seven-Ups, half-and-half was the last brilliant witticism that sent the girls into a complete state of convulsions. As they passed our car to go into the station, leaving their car where it was, one of the boys stopped, leaned in our car and said, "Keep your shirt on, Buddie, just keep your shirt on."

When we got home about fifteen minutes later, I explained our delay to Molly, who asked, "What did 'Colonel' do?" I said, "He kept his shirt on."

XXV.

But on this particular afternoon we needed no outsiders to amuse us on our way down to our home. We were full of our own thoughts and plans. There is a gas station just before you get to the entrance of our place and as we passed it a juke box was blaring out an old and to me, very familiar tune. It had been popular after the first World War and my children used to play it night and day at Fire Island and dance to it until the cottage floor rocked—"Hallelujah! Hallelujah!" . . . I could not remember the words but I began to hum the refrain— "Hallelujah! Hallelujah!"—as we entered our gate. George looked at me and smiled.

When we got out we stood for a few minutes on the portico. The sun was shining through the trees, the surroundings were beautifully peaceful. It all seemed a good omen. We entered the house and I started up the front stairs to go to my room for a little rest before dinner. Halfway up I heard the telephone ring. George went back to answer it.

When I came down an hour later he was lying on the chaise-longue, the radio was broadcasting the 3 o'clock news. As I stood in the doorway I heard this announcement: "Mr. Hurley resigns. President Truman has appointed General of the Army George C. Marshall as his Special Ambassadorial Envoy to China. He will leave immediately."

I stood rooted to the floor. My husband got up and came over to me. He said, "That 'phone call as we came in was from the President. I could not bear to tell you until you had had your rest."

A FINAL WORD

April, 1947

WHEN my husband's plane left for China, I drove with him to the airport. I sat in the car for I could not face the crowd that had gathered to see him off. He assured me that it would be only for a few months, and as he said goodbye, he asked that I do something for him while he was away. I think he asked it to keep me from being lonely. "Will you look over, and get into scrapbooks, all the papers you have kept these past years?"

I watched his baggage loaded, the steps drawn up into the plane, the door closed, and the engines warmed up; then the great bird of flight slid down the runway, lifted, and took off. I could see it until it was only a tiny speck in the sky, headed for the west coast.

From the airport I drove to Dodona Manor, packed all my papers, closed the house, and left for Pinehurst, North Carolina. The first three weeks of his absence were taken up with reading and sorting the mass of material into years, then into months, put into large envelopes and marked. After I had done this, in reading the Congressional Records, the editorials, the newspaper and radio reports, and many letters, I had my first perspective of the past years. I had been so close to it from day to day, and such colossal events had piled one upon another, that I was like a man who had swallowed more than he could digest. Now

I had a clear picture of our years together; and I decided, from this picture that while I had a clear vision of George Marshall as a soldier and as an organizer, I did not get, from my material, George Marshall as a man. Early one morning, about two A.M., the thought came—I will surprise him on his return, this is something I shall try to do for future records; and so I wrote the book *Together*.

After three months, when I was on the last chapters, a radio came in for me from China. It read, "Will you have injections for typhoid, smallpox, cholera and typhus immediately?" I knew that this meant my husband was coming home; also that he would have to go back to China, and I would go with him. I wrote under great pressure to finish the book.

I had put in 1,000 spring bulbs at Pinehurst to greet him on his return. They were just coming into bloom; but they bloomed and faded, and my husband never saw them.

Within a few weeks we were on our way to Chungking, the capitol of China. Chungking is far into the interior, a purely Chinese city originally of about 80,000 inhabitants. When we arrived it was a seething mass of humanity of several hundred thousand. It had been the most bombed city in China and, while many had been evacuated, living conditions were still deplorable. Two weeks after my arrival, the capitol was moved to Nanking, an hour's flight from Shanghai. There we settled in the former German Ambassador's home, which had been left intact during the rape of Nanking. As the heat of the summer came on, I went up into the mountains to Kuling, for July and August.

Each Friday, late, George would come up for conferences with the Generalissimo, who had made it a summer capitol. Kuling was reached by an hour-and-a-half's flight, a trip across the Yangtse by ex-Japanese gunboat, a drive of forty minutes to the foot of the mountain, then a three-hour carry, of six miles, in sedan chair up stone steps cut into the side of the mountain, each chair being carried on the shoulders of six chair-bearers, or coolies, to the mountain peaks. It was a lovely spot and I was most fortunate to spend my summer there. On Friday, when my husband was expected, I would go a quarter of the way down the mountain and wait on a plateau. From this point I could watch the chair-bearers as they wound around the mountain, in and out of the deep gorges, like some medieval procession, bringing up George and his staff. The chair-bearers in their royal-blue coolie dress and the fringed, white tops of the chairs gleaming in the sunlight made a picture I shall never forget. Each Monday morning my husband would go down that long trek back to Nanking and hold conferences with Chou En-lai, the negotiator for the Communists, and with leaders of the minority parties. Then again at the week's end he would come to Kuling to negotiate with the Generalissimo.

For over a year my husband worked to bring the warring factions into some kind of an agreement. Several times it seemed accomplished. Then one side, the Nationalists, or the other side, the Communists, would make demands that killed all hopes of a compromise. It was a cruel year for him, both mentally and physically.

In the fall of 1946, as winter came on, I had to leave Nanking for a warmer climate, because of a severe sinus infection. I flew to Guam, took a Naval transport for eight days, and arrived in Honolulu. I waited there for George to pick me up when he could come home.

After six weeks of waiting I received word that civil war had broken out in China, our troops were being evacuated, General Marshall's headquarters broken up, and that I was to expect him shortly. For over twelve months he had stood as a breakwater against the seething tides of civil war.

Before his arrival the Honolulu papers announced, "President Truman appoints General Marshall Secretary of State." My husband received the public announcement of his appointment from the pilot of his plane when he was over Okinawa on his flight home by way of Honolulu.

We arrived in Washington on January 21st and on that day General Marshall took the oath of office as Secretary of State. Six weeks later, after studying the intricate problems of world affairs, he left for the Moscow conference and I for Pinehurst, again to await his return.

It is spring, the bulbs have bloomed and gone. The dogwood, wisteria, camelias, and azaleas make Pinehurst a fairyland of beauty. I have just received word that my husband is returning from Moscow. I had the garden at Dodona Manor planted so that bare earth would not greet him on his arrival. The honeysuckle, lilacs, bridal wreath, will soon be in bloom. I am in hopes that we can go down on week-ends from Washington and see spring come to Virginia.

I would like to say to you, my readers, that I have learned that there is no sorrow, disappointment, nor circumstance, that can break you unless you allow it to do so. Each person is an entity unto themselves. Events may bend, or change, but they cannot destroy you. Happiness is not a thing to be snatched at, here and there, in a restless search. It is imbedded deep within each one of us. Seek— for it diligently—and you shall find.

Appendix I

George catlett marshall was born at Uniontown, Pennsylvania, December 31, 1880, son of George Catlett and Laura (Bradford) Marshall. He is a descendant of the Reverend William Marshall, an uncle of Chief Justice John Marshall. His father was an operator of coal and coke industries in southwest Pennsylvania. General Marshall received his education at the Virginia Military Institute, where he was First Captain of the Corps of Cadets, an all-Southern football tackle, and a graduate of the class of 1901.

Accepting a commission as Second Lieutenant of Infantry in the U. S. Army in February 1902, he joined the 30th Infantry in the Philippine Islands and served there until November 1903, when he returned to the United States with his regiment for station in Oklahoma. He was senior honor graduate of the Infantry-Cavalry School at Fort Leavenworth, Kansas, in 1907, and on March 7 of that year he was promoted to First Lieutenant. He was graduated at the Army Staff College, also at Fort Leavenworth, in 1908, and remained there two years longer as an instructor.

In 1911-12 he was Inspector-Instructor of the Massachusetts National Guard, after which he served with the 4th Infantry in Arkansas and Texas until the summer of 1913. The next three years were spent in the Philippines, the last year as Aide-de-Camp to General Hunter Liggett. He was Chief of Staff of the Field Force organized for the defense of Corregidor and the Bataan Peninsula, and served with it in a landing at Batangas and Lucena representing a Japanese invasion, which was opposed by another field force.

Returning to the United States in May 1916, and being promoted to Captain on July 1, 1916, he served as Aide-de-Camp to General James Franklin Bell at San Francisco. He was executive officer of a Civilian Training Camp at Fort Douglas, Utah. Later he served with General Bell at Governors Island, New York. In July 1917, he was detailed on the General Staff and sailed for France with the first convoy of the First Division.

During the following twelve months he participated in the operation of the First Division, East of Lunneville in the fall of 1917, and in 1918 in the St. Mihiel front from January to March, and Picardy and Cantiguy from March to July.

He was then assigned to General Headquarters at Chaumont and given the task of drafting the plans for the St. Mihiel offensive. In August he was attached to the First Army and continued work on the St. Mihiel operation. As that battle got underway, he was given the task of transferring some 500,000 troops and 2,700 guns to the Argonne front in preparation for that battle. In October 1918, he was formally released from assignment to General Headquarters and appointed Chief of Operations of the First Army then in the midst of the Meuse-Argonne Battle. In November he was made Chief of Staff of the Eighth Army Corps and continued in that capacity until the spring of 1919 when he was recalled to General Headquarters for work in connection with the proposed advance of our army further into Germany. While overseas he was promoted to major (temporary) in August 1917, to lieutenant colonel (temporary) in 1918, and to colonel (temporary) in August 1918.

In May 1919 he became Aide-de-Camp to General John J. Pershing with whom he returned to the United States in September 1919, and with whom he served until the summer of 1924. Meanwhile he reverted to his permanent rank of Captain in June 1920; was promoted to Major in July of that year, and to Lieutenant Colonel in 1923. During 1924-27 he served with the 15th U. S. Infantry at Tientsin, China. Later he was an instructor at the Army War College, 1927; Assistant Commandant of the Infantry School, Fort Benning, Georgia, 1927-32; Commander of the 8th Infantry at Fort Screven, Georgia; and later Fort Moultrie, South Carolina, 1932-33; and Senior Instructor of the Illinois National Guard, 1933-36. In

August 1936 he commanded the Red forces in the 2nd Army maneuvers in Michigan.

Having been promoted to Colonel in 1933, he became a Brigadier General in 1936, and assumed command of the 5th Infantry Brigade at Vancouver Barracks, Washington. In August 1937 he commanded the Red forces in the 4th Army maneuvers at American Lake, Washington. In July 1938 he was ordered to Washington, D. C., as Assistant Chief of Staff, War Plans Division, General Staff. Three months later he became Deputy Chief of Staff, and in May and June 1939 he served as Chief of the Military Mission to Brazil, making the voyage on the cruiser U. S. S. Nashville. In July 1939 he was detailed as Acting Chief of Staff of the Army, and in September 1939 he was appointed Chief of Staff of the Army, with the rank of General. On December 17, 1944, he was promoted to the newly created five-star rank of General of the Army.

As Chief of Staff, General Marshall was the professional head of the nation's military establishment and commander of the field forces. In this capacity, with the Secretary of War and the President as his superiors, General Marshall had charge of the mobilization, organization, equipping, and training of the nation's military forces, which grew under his command from a scattered combat force in Continental United States of some 1,064 planes and 174,000 troops, to a total in May 1945 of eight and a quarter million men and an air force of over 69,000 planes (of all types). The officer corps on active duty was similarly increased from 13,000 officers in July 1939, to 764,000 in September 1945. During this rapid development of the Army, General Marshall was charged with the development of higher commanders and staffs, and with the occupation of numerous overseas bases.

General Marshall's initial efforts to build up the Army were hampered by the failure of the public to realize the seriousness of the situation which was rapidly developing with respect to the security of the United States. It was not until May 1940, when the German Army overran France and destroyed the bulk of the heavy equipment of the British Army at Dunkirk, that he was able to make any material advances with his plans.

In the summer of 1940 General Marshall urged the establishment of Selective Service and the federalization of the National Guard for a year of training. Congressional action was taken on these matters in the early fall. This involved an increase in the strength of the Army to approximately one-and-one-half million men. To provide training facilities for this force, a huge construction program was carried out during the winter of 1940-41.

July 1, 1941, General Marshall urged the extension of service of selectees and the National Guard and that restrictions limiting use of the National Guard and selectees to the western hemisphere be removed. He stated that in his opinion a grave national emergency then existed and that governmental action should be taken accordingly. After prolonged discussion, Congress provided, by a majority of one vote in the House, for retention of the National Guard and selectees for an additional period of 18 months, but it declined to remove the geographical restrictions on the use of troops.

During the autumn of 1941, the Army engaged in the largest peacetime maneuvers in the history of the nation, involving approximately one million men in the field.

These maneuvers, conducted on the most realistic basis possible, indicated the great progress which had been made in the training of the Army higher commanders, staffs, supply services, and troops during the year which preceded them.

By Executive Order in March 1942, the Chief of Staff was made directly respsonible to the President as Commander in Chief in matters of strategy, tactics, and operation.

By virtue of his office as Chief of Staff, he was a member of the Joint Chiefs of Staff and of the Combined Chiefs of Staff. He accompanied President Roosevelt on his trip to confer with Prime Minister Churchill of Great Britain at sea in August 1941. It was at this conference that the Atlantic Charter was formulated.

In December 1941, and January 1942, he took part in the conferences held between the President, Mr. Churchill and the British Chiefs of Staff. It was during these later conferences that the principles of unity of command in the Far East were established. This step which required four years for consummation during the World War I was accomplished in the first months of the United States participation in World War II.

Later he participated in every conference held between the President, Mr. Churchill, and later Generalissimo Stalin and Generalissimo Chiang Kai Shek. These included the meetings at Casablanca, Quebec, Cairo-Teheran and Yalta. Following the death of President Roosevelt and the defeat of Germany, he accompanied President Truman when the latter met with Mr. Churchill and Mr. Attlee and Generalissimo Stalin at Potsdam.

Extensive service in China and the Philippines, and several visits to Japan have given General Marshall an intimate knowledge of conditions in the Far East.

For his services in the first World War, General Marshall was awarded the Distinguished Service Medal, and the Silver Star. He wears four stars on his Victory Medal Ribbon (World War I) and is eligible for but does not wear, by his own wish, all three theater ribbons without stars of World War II. His other service medals and ribbons include the Philippine Campaign Medal, German Occupation (World War I) and National Defense Ribbon (World War II). He has also received the following foreign decorations:

Croix de Guerre with Palm (France); Legion of Honor, Grand Croix (France); Order of St. Maurice and St. Lazarus (Officer) (Italy); La Solidaridad (Panama); Order of the Crown of Italy; Silver Medal for Bravery (Montenegro); Merito Militar (Grand Cross) (Brazil); Star of Abdon Calderon (Ecuador); Gran Oficial del Sol Del Peru; Grand Cross of Ouissam Alaouite Cherifien (Morocco); Military Order of Merit, 1st Class (Cuba); Order del Merito (Chile); Order of Suvarov, First Degree (USSR); Knight Grand Cross, Order of the Bath (Military Div.) (Great Britain).

He holds the following honorary degrees:

D.Sc., Washington and Jefferson College, 1939; D.M. Sc., Pennsylvania Military College, 1940; LL.D., William and Mary College, 1941; LL.D., Trinity College, 1941; D.M., Sc., Norwich University, 1942; LL.D., Columbia University, 1947; LL.D., Princeton University, 1947.

General Marshall is a member of the Episcopal Church. He was married (1) at Lexington, Virginia, February 11, 1902, to Elizabeth Carter Coles, daughter of Walter Coles, a doctor of Virginia birth, and resident in St. Louis, Missouri, (died 1927); (2) in Baltimore, Maryland, October

15, 1930, to Katherine Boyce (Tupper) Brown, daughter of the Rev. Henry Allen Tupper, of New York, and widow of Clifton S. Brown, of Baltimore, Maryland.

He was relieved as Chief of Staff, at his own request, on November 20, 1945, and was succeeded by General of The Army Dwight D. Eisenhower. On November 26, 1945, General Marshall was awarded an Oak Leaf Cluster to his Distinguished Service Medal, an award which was presented to him by the President of the United States, Harry S. Truman. The citation is as follows:

"In a war unparalleled in magnitude and in horror, millions of Americans gave their country outstanding service. General of the Army George C. Marshall gave it victory.

"By a favor of Providence, General Marshall became Chief of Staff of the United States Army on the day that Germany attacked Poland. His was the vision that brought into being the greatest military force in history. Because he was able to make the Allies understand the true potentiality of American greatness in personnel and material, he was able to exercise greater influence than any other man on the strategy of victory.

"It was he who first recognized that victory in a global war would depend on this Nation's capacity to ring the earth with far-flung supply lines, to arm every willing Ally and to overcome the aggressor nations with superior fire power. He was the first to see the technological cunning and consequent greater danger of the Nazi enemy. He was the master proponent of a ground assault across the English Channel into the plains of Western Europe directed by a single Supreme Allied Commander. He insisted on maintaining unremitting pressure against the Japanese, thereby preventing them from becoming entrenched in their stolen empire and enabling our timely advances across the Pacific. He obtained from Congress the stupendous sums that made possible the atomic bomb, well knowing that failure would be his full responsibility.

"Statesman and Soldier, he had courage, fortitude, and vision, and best of all a rare self-effacement. He has been a tower of strength as counsellor of two Commanders in Chief. His standards of character, conduct and efficiency inspired the entire Army, the Nation and the world. To him, as much as to any individual, the United States owes its future. He takes his place at the head of the great commanders of history."

The day after receiving the above decoration, General Marshall was appointed by President Truman as Special Representative of the President to China with the personal rank of Ambassador. General Marshall arrived in China on December 20, 1945. He returned to the United States on March 15, 1946, to confer with the President and left again on April 12th for China where he remained until January 8, 1947.

EDITOR'S NOTE: Mrs. Marshall accompanied General Marshall on his second trip to China, April 12, 1946, and remained in China for seven months.

General Marshall's appointment as Secretary of State was announced by Mr. Truman on January 7, 1947, and the appointment was unanimously confirmed by the Senate on January 8th. He arrived in Washington on January 21, 1947, and was sworn in as Secretary of State on that date. On March 5, 1947, Secretary of State Marshall left the United States for the Council of Foreign Ministers to be held at Moscow, March 10, 1947.

More revealing even than citations, commendations and decorations are the innumerable letters received by General Marshall from American fathers and mothers and from service men and women. There are filing cases filled with these treasured messages. Each of which has been answered. They not only reveal the character of George Marshall, but also the character of the American people. As an example:

General George C. Marshall, Chief of Staff U. S. Army,
War Department, Washington, D. C.

My dear General Marshall:

When I met you last Saturday February 20th in Arlington Cemetery and you so kindly helped me to reach the Unknown Soldier's grave, I certainly had no idea who you were. Then the man you asked to drive me there told me, "Lady, that man is only the head of the whole U. S. Army—General Marshall." When I got home I looked up a picture of you, and he was right. I cannot express my feelings how I felt.

I was in Washington on a visit to my son Cpl. Philip Furman, 76th Division, Medical Detachment who is now stationed at Walter Reed Hospital and when I told him I had met you— he was thrilled. I guess it makes a boy proud to know that he is a part of an Army of which the very top man is considerate enough and democratic enough to help a plain citizen and I know it makes him even prouder because that plain citizen was his mother. I assure you it made me prouder than ever to have a son in that Army.

I hope you will excuse me for writing you because I know you are a very busy man, but I had to tell you how much I appreciated the help you gave me and to thank you very much.

Sincerely,

(Signed) (Mrs.) Blanche Furman
1327 Plimpton Ave., Bronx, N. Y.

Album of Official and Semi-Official Photographs

GEORGE C. MARSHALL

Autumn 1945. Victory had been attained on all fronts. "... *Millions of Americans gave their country outstanding service. General of the Army George C. Marshall gave it victory...*" (From citation for oak leaf cluster of D. S. M. presented by President Truman)

After a Sunday stroll, General and Mrs. Marshall relax in the living room of Liscombe Lodge, their home at Pinehurst, N. C.

An inspection tour of the grounds.
Press Assn. Inc.

THE MARSHALLS AT HOME

A family gathering on the lawn at Dodona Manor, shown above. Jimmy Winn proudly shows the General his football, as man to man, while his mother, grandmother, and little sister Kitty show feminine interest. *Life Photo*

MARSHALL
the sportsman

Whenever he can find the time, the General finds relaxation in outdoor activity. At the left, an early morning canter at Fort Myer, Virginia, with the ever-faithful Fleet not far behind.

Shoving off for a few hours' fun.

General and Mrs. Marshall take a walk and, as usual, Fleet goes along.

Resting and arriving

The General takes his grandson, Jimmy Winn, and the small son of an
Army sergeant to the circus.

Playing Chinese checkers on Madame Chiang's lawn.

INFORMAL MOMENTS

Refreshments in Honolulu.

CHIEF OF STAFF

General Marshall takes his oath as Chief of Staff.

Admiral King, Admiral Leahy, and General Marshall.

Meeting at Casablanca, January 1943.

Aboard the *U. S. S. Augusta*, "Somewhere in the Atlantic."

Cairo-Teheran Conference, December 1943. American officers at a meeting of the combined Chiefs of Staff.

British and American combined Chiefs of Staff with President Roosevelt and Prime Minister Churchill.

General Marshall and General Arnold arriving at residence of Prime Minister in the conference area in Berlin, Germany.

General Marshall, accompanied by Col. Frank McCarthy, visits Salisbury Plain with the Prime Minister and high ranking British officers.

As U. S. Ambassador to China, General Marshall stopped off in Tokyo to visit briefly with General MacArthur.

Chinese Ambassador to the U. S., Dr. Wei Tao-Ming, says goodbye as he boards a plane for China.

General Marshall receives the award of an Oak Leaf Cluster to the Distinguished Service Cross from President Truman

MARSHALL
Secretary of State

General and Mrs. Marshall arriving at Union Station in Washington for the ceremony at the White House at which the General was sworn in as Secretary of State.

The General is sworn in as Secretary of State by Chief Justice Fred M. Vinson while President Truman looks on.

At the Big Four Foreign Ministers' Conference in Moscow. Left to right, Ernest Bevin, General Marshall, Viacheslav M. Molotov, and Georges Bidault.

British Ambassador Lord Inverchapel bids goodbye to Secretary Marshall as he leaves for Moscow.

Secretary of State Marshall and Soviet Foreign Minister Molotov in amiable conversation.

A general view of the opening meeting of the Big Four Foreign Ministers' Conference in the all-white room of the Soviet Aviation Industry Building.

President Truman greets Secretary Marshall as he arrives from the Moscow Conference.

General Marshall in 1939 and General Marshall in 1945.

As Secretary of State, General Marshall moves into the new offices of the State Department.